Yesterday's Sarasota

VOLUMES IN THE HISTORIC CITIES SERIES:

Yesterday's Clearwater by Hampton Dunn

Yesterday's Key West by Stan Windhorn and Wright Langley

Yesterday's Miami by Nixon Smiley

Yesterday's St. Petersburg by Hampton Dunn

Yesterday's Sarasota by Del Marth

Yesterday's Tampa by Hampton Dunn

DEL MARTH

Yesterday's SARASOTA

INCLUDING SARASOTA COUNTY

Published in Cooperation with the
SARASOTA COUNTY HISTORICAL COMMISSION

E. A. Seemann Publishing, Inc.
Miami, Florida

Library of Congress Catalog Card No. 73-80594
ISBN 0-912458-26-7

Manufactured in the United States of America

Contents

Foreword

LATE IN THE AFTERNOON of February 12, 1973, this writer sat down with board members of the Sarasota County Historical Commission to discuss a common goal—to publish, and thereby preserve, the picture history of Sarasota and Sarasota County.

More than 120 years had passed since the first homesteader notched together a cedar log cabin near Yellow Bluffs, yet we all felt an urgency about the book. The reasons were everywhere. A newspaper only a few days earlier reported another of the dwindling number of pioneers had died; his recollections of the early days now were gone. Photographs of preceding decades became harder to find; they, too, were aging, often into an irretrievable condition of brittle yellow. And out in the streets, landmarks continued to topple as the land itself was being upended and rearranged for tall buildings.

A cooperative effort was decided upon. The Sarasota County Historical Commission over the years had sought out and accumulated an extensive picture file. They would be made available for the book. Meanwhile, this writer began a six-month, areawide search for photographs. At our pleading, descendants of pioneers rummaged through garages, closets and bottom drawers to find forgotten family albums. Heirs to the negative files of the area's first commercial photographers were contacted. Several of the rarest pictures were found in an attic, in New England. In the end, thousands of photographs were seen, studied and sorted.

At that stage, the task was half completed. With the assistance of Mrs. Doris Davis, county historian, and her staff, Marion M. Almy and Charlotte

Norton, and the cooperation and advice of Historical Commission Chairman Richard Glendinning and Vice Chairman John B. Browning, research began on identifying and dating the collection.

The reader is fortunate so many of his neighbors have an interest in the history of our area. They often interrupted their work or rearranged their plans to help us locate and identify pictures. To all of them, this writer, and the Sarasota County Historical Commission, say thank you.

We especially express our appreciation to Mrs. Bonnie Robarts, Mrs. Pauline Edwards Vanderipe, Mrs. Frances Edwards Matthias, Mrs. R. B. Wyatt, Frank Raeburn, Mrs. Loring Raoul, Gilbert Parker, Helen Watkins, Martin O'Neill, H. M. Wimmer and Mrs. Paul Waner. Their contributions to this volume, in rare pictures and enthusiasm, made it a still better book.

It is the hope of the Sarasota County Historical Commission that this pictorial history will rekindle and perpetuate the preservation of our area's history, and that the reader will make use of the Commission's archives as well as contribute to them.

DEL MARTH

Sarasota, Florida
October, 1973

Yesterday's Sarasota

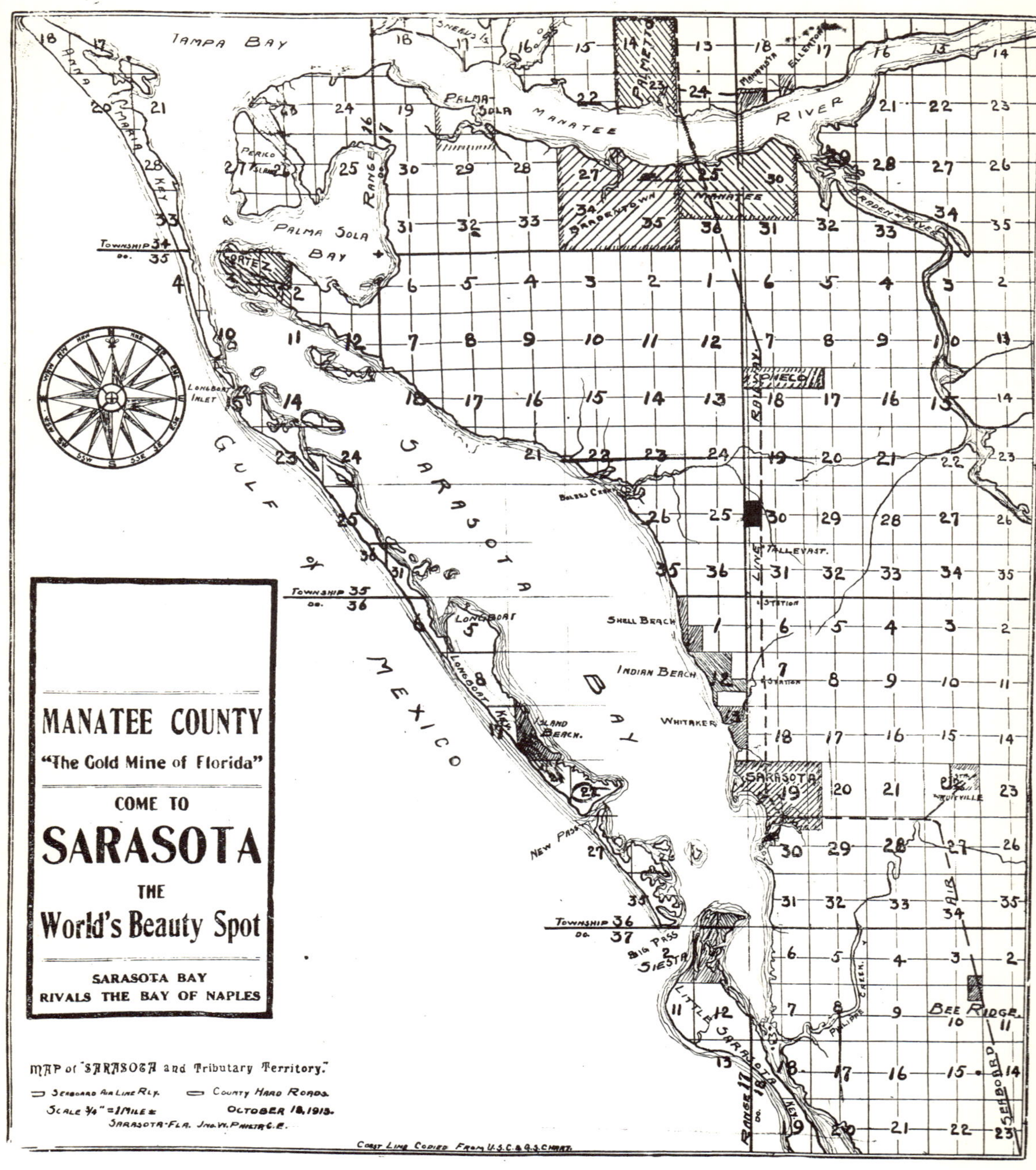

"COME TO SARASOTA, THE WORLD'S BEAUTY SPOT" was the title on this map, prepared in October 1913. Sub-titles stated: "Sarasota Bay Rivals The Bay Of Naples" and "The Gold Mine Of Florida."

Yesterday's Sarasota

FEW REGIONS OF FLORIDA, or the world for that matter, are endowed with such a beauty and magnetism that they entice and envelop nearly all who see them. Sarasota, the historian learns, is one of those rare places.

Long before the New World was discovered, the Indian discovered Sarasota. And the wanderlust of generations of Timucuans and Caloosas and Seminoles forever dissolved on the shores of Sarasota Bay. Yet the Indian of the fifteenth century, like the white man of the twentieth century, could not help boasting of his homeland. Word of a sub-tropical paradise along the west coast of Florida, known then only as an "island named Bimini," was taken back to Europe by Columbus and his men, starting a promenade up and down the west coast by explorers and gold-seekers, marauders and soldiers.

The explorers conquered people, but not the land. In fact, the land became the invaders' greatest adversary and Hernando de Soto, most famous of the Spanish gold-seekers on the west coast, perished in his search for riches that other men, of greater vision, saw all about them.

One of these was young Bill Whitaker.

Only fourteen years old but eager to see the world, William H. Whitaker set out from his Savannah home in 1835 to nowhere in particular. That meant

THE HOME OF BILL WHITAKER, the area's earliest settler, built about 1857 at where 12th Street and U. S. 41 is today, stood until destroyed by fire in 1926. His earlier home at Yellow Bluffs had been burned by marauding Seminoles.

Key West and St. Marks and Tallahassee, then four years soldiering in the Seminole War. When he was twenty-one, he was ready to settle down. Convincing his half-brother, a Tallahassee lawyer named Hamlin Snell, that Snell needed a vacation, the two bought a sloop and sailed south in search of a homesite for Whitaker. High yellow bluffs along the mainland in Sarasota Bay caught their eye, and they lowered sail to drift into a palm-lined bayou nearby. Young Whitaker believed he had found the perfect spot. Dropping anchor, they explored the dense vegetation, marveled at the view over the Bay and the protecting islands toward the horizon, and looked no further. It was 1842; the Sarasota area had its first settler.

The deed to his homestead on Whitaker Bayou covered 145 acres and was granted by the U. S. Government in 1851. Added to the adjoining 49 acres which he bought a year later at the going price of $1.25 an acre, the Whitaker homestead spread for more than a mile along the Bay northward from the present Payne Terminal. At the time, Whitaker's land was designated as being in Hillsborough County. After Florida became a territory in 1823, Congress sliced the area into counties, putting the Sarasota land first in Mosquito County and then, in 1834, splitting Mosquito County by making the western portion Hillsborough County. It wasn't until 1856 that Hillsborough was chopped up to create Manatee County, which Sarasota remained a part of until 1921.

Whitaker worked hard at selling dried salt mullet and roe to Cuban traders, as well as raising a herd of cows bought in Dade City, but he still found time to go courting. The daughter of Col. William Wyatt, a Manatee plantation owner, enchanted him. In 1851, in Manatee, he married Mary Jane Wyatt. The first of their ten children, Nancy, became the first white child born in what is now Sarasota County.

It took the Civil War to part Whitaker from his land. Pillaging expeditions by Union soldiers became so frequent that eventually his livestock and gardens were depleted and he moved his family north to Manatee, not to return to his homestead until the conflict ended.

Less accessible to the Yankees was the land around Upper Myakka Lake, a fact known to Jesse Knight, a Georgian cattleman. After moving to Florida in 1852 with his family of fifteen, Knight bedded down his children and cattle near Tampa at a place known as Knight's Station. He was satisfied to stay there until the war erupted, but then feared his herd would be run off

COVE NEAR WHITAKER BAYOU, near which the Confederacy's Secretary of State Judah P. Benjamin boarded a 16-foot sailboat and fled from the Yankees who were searching for him. Benjamin disguised himself as a farmer during his escape from Georgia, hid out several days in Tampa, then at the Gamble Mansion in Ellenton (near Bradenton), before arranging to buy a boat to get him out of the country. The boat was purchased in Clearwater and brought down to a cove near Bill Whitaker's home at Whitaker Bayou. Whitaker helped provision the boat, while Benjamin made his way to the mooring from Gamble Mansion. After dinner with the Whitakers, the Confederate leader stole aboard and sailed off to Nassau, later to London.

and slaughtered by Union soldiers as was happening along other waterfront areas. As the plains around Myakka were remote, Knight sent his herd and son-in-law, Shadrick "Shade" Hancock, into this hinterland. The cattle flourished so well at Myakka that the Knights moved there after the war. More settlers and cattlemen drifted in, making Myakka one of the oldest settlements in the county.

Although satisfied with his expanding cattle ranch, Knight did not relish living away from the coast. Instead, he explored the waterfront and found a spring-laden site called "Horse and Chaise." In 1868 he chose it as his new home, moving his cattle and family 100 miles to the spot. The caravan took a month to make the trip, but within a year Knight was on his way to owning a cattle empire. His property stretched 10 miles across and 30 miles deep. A rich grazing ground, it eventually fenced 20,000 head.

Within months, the Knights had neighbors; some were friends from Knight's Station, others came aboard a steamer in flight from northern carpetbaggers in southern states. "Horse and Chaise," named so because of the growth of timber on a promontory facing the open Gulf that looked like a horse and chaise to seamen, now is known as Nokomis. Adjacent Dona Bay got its name from the only sailing vessel in the area at that time, Knight's sloop "Dona."

The Knights were too busy building to notice that a few miles north of them a family named Webb had put up a log cabin on Little Sarasota Bay and was nursing back to health the mother of the family, a victim of asthma. John Webb gave up a profitable drug store and dairy farm in Utica, New York, to come to the Sarasota area. Mrs. Webb's physician advised her to seek a warmer climate, and her husband recalled a Federal soldier telling him about a year-round paradise on Sarasota Bay. In 1867, by schooner and sloop, the Webbs searched half a year for the exact site so captivatingly described to them by the soldier as "a little bay somewhere south along the coast, marked by a high Indian mound." Bill Whitaker helped them find it–it was Osprey, so named by Webb after he built his house.

The ensuing ten years were significant. More than one hundred families moved into the Sarasota region, to grow vegetables, to plant groves, to graze cattle, to fish the waters.

Isaac Redd, once Bill Whitaker's hired hand, returned from the Confederate Army to settle the Bee Ridge area, so named because of the large number of bees there. Another ex-soldier, John L. Edwards, opened a "fish ranch" on the bayfront just north of Indian Beach. From Brooklyn came the Jesse Bennetts who, seeking a long life for their tubercular son, settled in the McClellan Park area. The first settler in Fruitville, Charles L.

Reaves, used his own funds to build a school and a road into the community.

Among many settlers to choose the land between Hudson Bayou and Phillippi Creek was Charles Abbe, who in two years became the largest landowner there with nearly four hundred acres. After opening a general store, he petitioned the government for a post office. The request was approved in 1878, and the Sarasota region now had a postmark—the community named Sara Sota. Abbe, of course, was named postmaster.

Life was primitive then, but it also was bountiful. The woods and swamps served up turkeys, deer, squirrels, opossum, coons, ducks, quail, egrets, ibis, and razorback hogs. Many a pioneer shot the meal for his family in the nearest thicket.

Descriptions of fishing at the time by oldtimers sound like tall tales: mullet were so thick in the bay, one school entered the bay in the morning, moved northward all day, and still was in sight at dusk—and rowing across the bay toward the islands always provided a couple meals as fish jumped into the boat during the trip.

Cooking the catch or the game was something else. Open hearths during the winter months proved adequate, but the hot summer forced the housewife to use crudely built scaffold stoves in the backyard.

As suspected, mosquitos made the outdoors unbearable during the rainy months, and nearly all settlers suffered from "chills and fever," namely, malaria. Sand fleas thrived—one could take up a handful of sand, and half of it would jump away. During the night, bugs would so crowd the windows that at daybreak it was impossible to see out.

Roads did not exist, nor did bridges. Clothing was handmade, if you could get to the nearest drygoods store in Manatee for cloth. Reading lamps were improvised by burning oil squeezed from fish heads.

Nevertheless, families were friendly, secure and trusting—until 1883.

That year, nearly every acre in the Sarasota area passed into the hands of land speculators. Settlers who had moved into the region under the Homestead Act of 1862, under which the government turned over 160 acres of federal land to a settler provided he built a home and tilled the soil for five years, suddenly learned they did not own their homestead. Politicians in Florida found a way in 1881 to circumvent the Homestead Act. They did it by pointing out an earlier Federal law gave the state all swamp and overflow lands in Florida. The politicians succeeded in designating 22,000,000 acres as "swamp land," then turned around and sold this new-found acreage to land speculators. Nearly 700,000 acres of the "swamp land" was in Manatee County, meaning the Sarasota area.

It was an immediate disaster for many pioneers, being deprived of their

THE BUILDING WASN'T MUCH but the playground was vast at the Newman Smith home, where children living in the Indian Beach area went to school in 1882. In this dwelling A. B. Edwards, considered "Mr. Sarasota," first went to school.

land. It was also a disaster for the Sarasota region, because the influx of colonizers abruptly ceased.

And it led to formation of the Sara Sota Vigilance Committee.

Anger and resentment pervaded the community of Sara Sota, where a group of 20 men gathered to plan retaliation against the land speculators trying to force them off the land. They called themselves the Vigilance Committee.

In 1884, they "got even." Harrison "Rip" Riley was shotgunned off his horse along a trail between Bee Ridge and Sara Sota. Next, the postmaster, Charles Abbe, was fatally shot while gathering kelp.

Within days, the sheriff and 26 possemen had all 20 Vigilance Committee members in the county jail at Pine Level. After three trials, seven had been convicted of first degree murder and sentenced to life. Several years later all had been released.

Testimony never clearly established the reasons for Riley and Abbe being killed, but years later, the niece of one of the men, explained that the Vigilance Committee suspected both victims of cooperating with the land grabbers by providing exact boundary line descriptions of homesteads to the land agents.

Tax roll records of 1888 reveal that the approximately 700,000 acres of Manatee County turned over to land speculators by the state ended up in the hands of eight companies, three of them Florida railroad firms. Among the other five was the Florida Mortgage & Investment Co., a British concern, which ultimately founded the town of Sarasota.

In Scotland, the 1880s were lean years. Great Britain was warring on several fronts, channeling men and taxes from its empire at the expense of its countrymen, including the Scots. News of a rich and idyllic life elsewhere was most welcomed, and it came in an Edinburgh newspaper in August 1885. A story told about the Florida Mortgage & Investment Co. seeking colonists for a "wonderful new town of Sarasota, on Sarasota Bay, in the richest and most beautiful section of the entire state of Florida." The town is small, but very modern, and a man does not have to work hard for a living, it stated.

The story sounded convincing. A cursory check revealed that the president of the company was no less than Sir John Gillespie, a large estate owner near Edinburgh, and that two of the directors were the Archbishop of Canterbury and the Lord Dean of Guild of Edinburgh. A group of Scots, therefore, began plans to move to Sarasota.

As promised by the company, the colonists were given title to a 40-acre estate and a town lot in exchange for 100 pounds sterling before departure. Having sold their businesses and personal possessions, 23 families totaling 68 people met in Glasgow for the steamship ocean crossing. They called themselves the Ormiston Colony, after the home of Sir John Gillespie.

One month later, aboard a small steamer chartered at Cedar Key, the colonists crept into Sarasota Bay. Crowding the rail, they scanned the

ESCAPING FROM A SEVERE DEPRESSION in Scotland for "the wonderful new town of Sarasota, on Sarasota Bay, in the richest and most beautiful section of the entire state of Florida," sixty-eight colonists from Scotland and England sailed in 1885 aboard the steamer "Furnessia" from Glasgow to New York. Thirty-three days later they stood alongside their luggage in the wilderness of trees and palmetto thickets known as "Sarasota." The town's broad avenues and 40-acre estates, they learned, were merely on a piece of paper–a town plat. A few days later it snowed. Three months after the colonists landed, they straggled back north or to the land they left, hungry and penniless.

OLDEST STANDING HOME in Sarasota today shrinks back a safe distance from the traffic at Wood Street and the Tamiami Trail. In 1884, however, when it was built by Alfred Bidwell, the house was notoriously prominent as the meeting place of the Sara Sota Vigilance Committee. It was at the house warming party on Christmas Day, in fact, that the committee of about 18 pioneers planned the murder of two fellow settlers for being in cahoots with land grabbers in the area. After three trials, four men were sentenced to life in prison. Charges against Bidwell were dropped, but bad memories of his new house prompted him to vacate it. Luke Wood (*left*) finally bought it as a 30-year wedding anniversary present for his wife, who thought it the most desirable place in Florida. Their daughter, Ethel (*right*), lived in the house as late as the 1960s after it was remodeled. It is now a landmark owned by the Sarasota County Historical Commission.

shoreline looking for their new city. There was no sign of it. Alex Browning, one of the young passengers, later wrote of that day, December 28, 1885:

"There was much discontent; we were in a wild country without houses to live in, tired and hungry. Families grouped around their mothers while their fathers were trying to find out where they were going to live. The company store was the only building in sight; a dirt road could be seen leading through the pine and palmetto shrub. The shoreline along the bay to the south was stopped by Hudson Bayou, with Cedar Point (now Golden Gate Point) and a swamp to the north. By the kindness of natives, some of the colonists were located in their homes. Everybody was busy gathering their luggage and getting things separated. Ours contained a tent which we pitched in a clearing under the pines. The colonists were separated from one another, not knowing where the different families were located—strangers in a strange land."

Except for a salubrious New Year's Day celebration arranged by the Americans, the colonists never shook off their disappointment and discontent. Sarasota had been grossly misrepresented to them. It was nothing more than an idea on a piece of paper. The allotment of the "40-acre estates" merely increased their unhappiness. Each colonist was asked to draw a slip of paper out of a box on which a farm number was given. The number specified the land he would have to take, no matter where.

In nearly every case, the "estate" was back in the woods some six to eight miles. Few colonists could find their 40 acres, let alone get to it. At that point, only the balmy winter weather seemed worth coming for, but on January 9, 1886, that, too, turned against the colonists. It snowed.

Freezing, without money, owning only a farm plot that was not accessible, the colonists began pulling out. Three months after leaving Scotland, they were on their way back. Only the Browning family and a few individuals remained.

But the Florida Mortgage & Investment Co. kept planning, determined to develop what it still believed was one of Florida's most beautiful areas. It instructed its local manager, A. C. Acton, to start building the town. He put up a wharf, now the site of the city pier. At Five Points he constructed a two-story rooming house, complete with a dining room and 20 beds. It was named Sarasota House. Main Street was cleared from the wharf to the rooming house, and an artesian well drilled at Five Points. Acton built himself a house, at Link and Morrill Streets. One of the remaining colonists, Dr. Thomas Wallace, put a one-and-a-half story house on the north side of Main near Palm Avenue. Stocking a room with drugs, another with cots for patients, Dr. Wallace soon was operating a clinic.

It was still 1886, and only months after the colonists pulled out, when two of Whitaker's sons opened a general store across from the clinic. Three weeks

PERSEVERING FAMILY was the John Browning clan of Paisley, Scotland. They were the only Scots among the sixty-eight colonists back in 1885 that decided not to return to their native land but to overcome the unexpected adversity they found in Sarasota. An expert craftsman and lumber mill owner in Scotland, Browning began work in Sarasota helping erect buildings for the Florida Mortgage & Investment Co.

A SUNDAY AFTERNOON GET-TOGETHER of early settlers—the Whitakers, the Brownings and friends—was recorded in this 1886 photograph. It was taken on Cedar Point, now known as Golden Gate Pointe. Because of the clothing fashion then, not much of the body was exposed to the swarms of mosquitos thriving in this "paradise" of woods and water, but the head-to-toe garments often were so uncomfortable that folks carried fans with them (*at left*). Wild deer, turkey, and quail were everywhere, and the men seldom ventured into uncleared areas without their rifles.

later a third Whitaker offspring, Hamlin, set up a meat market at Main and Palm, butchering a steer once a week, half of which he made sure of selling within two days before it spoiled; the other half he kept in Manatee, where there was an ice plant. A hustling young man, Hamlin next built a livery stable at Main and Palm. By the Fall of 1886, Sarasota had the semblance of a "business district."

The "boom," if it could be called that, was only beginning. More impetus was added by the arrival of John Hamilton Gillespie, son of Sir Gillespie, the part owner of Florida Mortgage & Investment Co. Only 34 years old, educated at Oxford, a member of the Queen's bodyguard in Scotland, and just married, Gillespie was assigned by his father to take charge of the Sarasota project.

He registered at the Sarasota House, pensioned off local manager Acton, and quickly concluded Sarasota's "boom" was artificial, that as soon as the construction workers finished their jobs on the few stores and offices on Main Street they would leave and the "boom" would collapse.

He was determined to lay a firm foundation for future growth. Gillespie brought in laborers to open up streets. He then turned his attention to building a hotel "for people of wealth and influence . . . the finest hotel on the entire west coast."

Lumber was shipped in by schooner from Cedar Key and Appalachicola. More carpenters were hired. They began building a three story, 30-room hotel, complete with large lobby and dining room, on the waterfront at Main and Gulf Stream. Gillespie called it the De Soto.

Meanwhile, a wooden sidewalk was being laid all the way from Five Points to the wharf. And three more buildings went up along the "thoroughfare"—a home for John Iverson and his bride (later to be used as the town's first newspaper office), and two large two-story houses—one for the widowed Susanna Bartholomew and her children, the other for rent as a town meeting place, dance hall, and church. At Sixth and Central, up went a two-story office building for the British land company.

Had the colonists from Scotland arrived one year later, they would have easily spotted the town of Sarasota from the rail of their ship. Equally impressive would have been the bustle of people, almost an overcrowding. When word was sent out by Gillespie in late 1886 that good jobs were available in the fastest growing town in Florida—Sarasota—the influx of workmen filled the Sarasota House two to six persons in a room. The late arrivals pitched tents and nailed together shacks along the waterfront. Others bunked in schooners anchored offshore. Wages were well worth the inconveniences—$2 a day for craftsmen, $1.25 for common laborers.

LEFT WITHOUT A HUSBAND AND FATHER, Susanna Bartholomew and her three children appear mournful and alone in this 1886 photo shortly after William Bartholomew was fatally injured. The Kansas City attorney, who settled his family on 120 acres in the Fruitville area in 1881, fell from a tree while hunting egrets and broke his back. The bereaved family stayed on the land long enough to acquire the homestead claim, then moved into Sarasota. Fruitville did not earn a fertile reputation in early years; it was called, instead, the "sorriest ground you ever saw" for crops.

The village children were in school, of course, in a small one-room frame building built and paid for by Gillespie on the south side of Main Street about one hundred feet east of Pineapple.

Such a prosperous village needed a post office. The business folks did not like trudging a mile and a half to the community of Sara Sota to pick up mail. To them, it was "out in the sticks." Sara Sota settlers protested the move, but the village to its north now had "influence" and the post office was moved in 1887 to Whitaker's general store on Main.

What the village didn't need, nor knew anything about, was a golf course. But it got one—two greens and a long fairway, the first in Florida and perhaps the country.

A duffer from the old country, Gillespie loved the game and missed it so that he cleared out the woods near the present Federal Building to put in a practice course. A settler recalled seeing Gillespie chop away at the little ball one day and asked what he was doing. Gillespie explained the game to him, then admonished the settler for being so uninformed: "Man, you're missing half your life."

If so, the young man and fellow villagers made up for it the night of February 25, 1887. That night Gillespie's De Soto Hotel opened with a grand ball. It was the first social event in the Sarasota area, and the biggest celebration ever held south of Manatee. It may also have been the longest party then on record, for two days later some of the young men in the village still were not sober. More than two hundred attended. The guest list, still preserved, records folks from Myakka, Fruitville, Perico Island, Bradentown, Manatee, Palmasola, and Fogartyville.

To many of the folks from Bradentown, the hotel opening was to be followed by another celebration, this time the naming of their town as the new county seat of Manatee County.

In April 1887, Manatee County was cut in two, creating De Soto County. For years, the village of Manatee had been the county seat, but in 1886 the county commissioners voted to build a new courthouse at Pine Level, a community 40 miles inland and now nearly extinct.

With the split of Manatee County, Pine Level became a part of De Soto, and a new county seat was needed. Seeking the designation were Sarasota, Bradentown, Manatee, and Palmetto. Citizens of Sarasota offered to build a new county courthouse and jail and to make the county a present of them. The gesture did not win over a majority of voters. Instead, Bradentown was chosen. Looked upon as a poor country relative by the village of Manatee, Bradentown had received strong support in the Sarasota area once Sarasota

MAIN STREET IN 1887 dead-ended at the Sarasota House, the first hotel in the Sarasota Bay region. Built a year earlier, it remained a hotel until razed in 1924 for a bank building. The Palmer National Bank & Trust Co. now is on the site. At lower left (Palm and Main) is the Whitaker and Smith's Livery, Feed and Sale Stable, occupying the site of the present-day Hotel Sarasota. The first drug store, the next building, belonged to Dr. Thomas Wallace; in one room were cots for patients he was treating. Third building from the corner was John Iverson's gift to his new bride, and which later housed the *Sarasota Times*, the town's first newspaper. The next two identical buildings, nearest Five Points, were erected by Alfred Grable, a Lakeland builder who wanted to get in on the "boom" occurring in the 1880s. Widowed Mrs. Susanna Bartholomew moved into one, and the other was used for town meetings, church services, and dancing. Across the street, the Charles Whitaker store served a dual role—as general store and as post office. Residents felt the old post office south of Hudson Bayou was too far out in the country, so they successfully petitioned that Whitaker be named postmaster and his store the post office. Adding still another modern touch to the bustling street was a newly built wooden sidewalk.

was eliminated. The reason traced back to the Vigilance Committee days. Settlers here recalled the posse that rounded up the Committee members came out of Manatee.

With the hotel opening past and Sarasota pushed aside in its bid for the county seat, the village sunk into the doldrums. Gillespie's concern about an "artificial boom" in 1886-87 was real, and he could not head off a recession.

Weeds began growing in the streets. Without work, carpenters and laborers moved out, leaving the Sarasota House deserted. The Florida Mortgage & Investment Co. advertised land in Sarasota for $10 an acre. There were no takers. New settlers were not moving in, because no land was available to them other than from the land speculators. Worse still, the steamers from Tampa stopped calling at the wharf for fish and passengers; there was not enough business out of Sarasota and, besides, a channel north through Sarasota Bay still had not been dredged, and the small vessels were forced into the open Gulf waters.

What would have helped, Gillespie knew, was a railroad. Nearly 350,000 acres in Manatee County sold to land speculators by the state went to Florida railroad companies, yet none put a track into Sarasota.

To get Sarasota off dead center, Gillespie decided to build his own railroad. He had the track down and the first run under way in 1892. The best description of the railroad was given by the people who rode it. They called it the "Slow and Wobbly."

The train consisted of two flat cars and a second-hand wood-burning engine. One of the flat cars was the "day coach," a set of boards on wheels with uncovered plank seats. The other, more luxurious, provided a canvas canopy over the plank seats to shield passengers from sun and rain. No schedule was followed, for several good reasons: the engineer and conductor would not leave until they got enough of a load to make the trip worthwhile, and they did not want to face criticism of not being on time because the engine often broke down, and on more than one occasion actually fell off the tilted tracks.

After two years of spasmodic trips between Bradentown and Sarasota, the "Slow and Wobbly" was retired, the engine and flat cars left to rust on a siding.

Meanwhile, another failure was confronting Gillespie. He and the couple managing the De Soto Hotel for him, Alfred and Annie Jones, took to feuding. Finally, the Joneses gave up their lease and, backed by several wealthy guests, acquired property near Indian Beach and built their own fancy hotel. The Joneses called it a private club; no matter, it ruined business

THE TOWN DOCK at the foot of Lower Main Street in 1888 featured the Vincent Brothers restaurant (left) for those townsfolk and guests of the newly-built De Soto Hotel (right) who loved fried oysters. But business wasn't too good this year, for the "boom" of 1886-87 had just ended. The Sarasota House (at top of street) was nearly deserted; the craftsmen and laborers who during the past two years were busy building houses and the De Soto Hotel at pay scales of $1.25 to $2 a day, began leaving town, and the Florida Mortgage & Investment Co. could not get people to buy land at $10 an acre.

GOLF AND SARASOTA grew up together because of Col. J. Hamilton Gillespie (*above*), the man who in some circles is credited with building the first golf course in the country. Out on Main Street he cleared a woods and laid out two greens and a long fairway. That was in May 1886. By 1905 his obsession with golf, the game he brought from Scotland, blossomed into a complete nine-hole course on a 110-acre tract, plus a clubhouse. He died while playing the course in 1923.

THE FINEST ON FLORIDA'S WEST COAST was what Col. J. Hamilton Gillespie had in mind when he built the De Soto Hotel at the foot of Main Street in 1887. Opened with a grand ball attended by two hundred, the De Soto contained 30 rooms, a large lobby and a dining room—a place for "those of wealth and influence," according to Gillespie. The Orange Blossom Club Apartments now stand on the site.

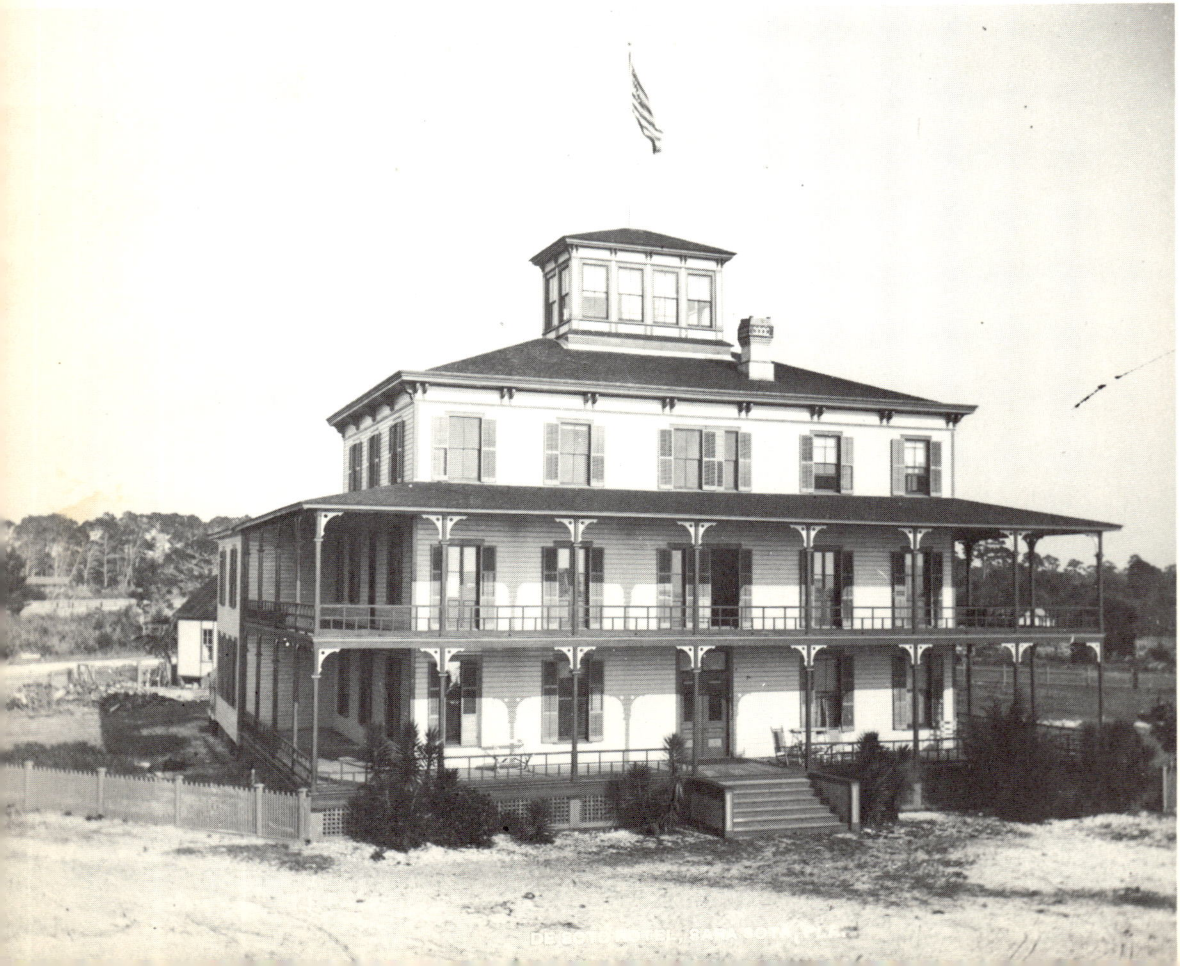

at Gillespie's De Soto Hotel. With the De Soto's best guests now keeping up with the Joneses, the De Soto Hotel closed.

It was enough to send Gillespie packing. And that is exactly what he did, in the early 1890s, taking up residence briefly in Bradentown and then going back to Scotland for a visit.

Gillespie's married life began to disintegrate as the fortunes of Sarasota slumped, so that when he returned to Sarasota shortly after 1900, he came alone. Records do not reveal whether he divorced his wife in Scotland or whether she died.

His absence had little effect on the growth and economy of Sarasota; the village remained lethargic. Even the coldest winter in the state's history, in 1894-95, nearly a statewide disaster, failed to have a severe effect either way on the area. Temperatures fell to 17 degrees above zero, killing the vegetable crop and ruining the season's citrus, but the loss proved only temporary. The vegetables were gone, true, but the frosts south of the Manatee River section were not damaging enough to kill the citrus trees. The next season they bore a normal crop.

The record-setting winter left only the fishing industry untouched. It was no surprise, then, that Sarasota in 1895 was referred to as a "fishing village."

Years later, officials tried to squelch that description of their town, but for the moment it was no disgrace. Fishing was the only economic stimulus in Sarasota and it eventually released the town from a levitating condition.

THE FIRST MRS. J. HAMILTON GILLESPIE. Accounts discredit her as a disagreeable woman who drank too much, and it was common knowledge she and the Colonel had a stormy relationship. The couple moved to the Bradenton area in the 1890s, then took a trip back to Scotland. Gillespie returned to Sarasota, without his wife, rumor having it she had died or he had divorced her. In 1905, the Colonel married a local woman of "culture and dignity," Miss Blanche McDaniel.

Credit must go to the U. S. Government. It sent a dredge into Sarasota Bay to cut a channel across the shoals of Palma Sola Pass, and another southeast of the Longboat Inlet. Now shallow draft steamers from Tampa could safely and profitably include fishing wharfs at Sarasota in their ports of call. And this they did, three times a week, transporting not only fish but goods and passengers.

The return of the steamers at that time was considered by some to be more significant to the town and the back country than the attempted colonization by the Scots or the completion of the De Soto Hotel. Sarasotans felt back in the mainstream. With dependable connections to commercial centers, fruit and produce now could be sold in Tampa markets. Shopping at large and varied stores became practical.

Slowly, but steadily, the pace in Sarasota increased. No one was getting rich, but life was more stimulating, more diverse. In 1898, it lurched forward still further. The Spanish-American War broke out, and nearly forty thousand troops were stationed at the embarkation port of Tampa. Demand for fish soared to unprecedented heights; so did the prices. Sarasota fishermen never saw so much money.

An equal prosperity hit the cattlemen on the plains at Myakka, and at Knight's empire near Venice. By the thousands cattle were driven to slaughter houses in Tampa to feed the soldiers; when the war ended, thousands more were sold at fancy prices to Cuba, where the fighting had depleted the country's stock.

If another "boom" was about to start, the village of Sarasota certainly did not look ready for it. Cattle roamed around the streets, hogs wandered over to the watering trough at Main and Palm to rollick in the overflow, the "business district" had no street lights, the wooden sidewalk was warped and decaying, and if one wished to leave town, it had to be by boat—there was no hard-surfaced road or railroad in any direction.

Nevertheless, folks were optimistic. And not just Sarasotans. Out-of-towners sensed a restless rustle in Sarasota and wanted to participate in what everyone felt was the resurgence of an area destined to become a major city.

With an area population of only 600, it had a long way to go. But the upswing began with the announced sale of the then-closed De Soto Hotel to a group of Tampans. They renovated and refurnished it, boasting prior to its opening in June that "the hotel is fitted with modern improvements, including baggage elevator, bath room on every floor, an observatory enclosed with glass on top . . . and several bath houses on the Gulf Beaches where surf bathing is enjoyed."

SCHOOL WAS TAUGHT wherever the children were, and in this case it was in a backyard on a bench and taught by Mr. Brush. In the community of Sara Sota in the Hudson Bayou area, it was a fishing shack. And to the north, in the Indian Beach area, classes were held in the home of pioneer Newman Smith. The town got its first school about 1887 by furnishing a 16 x 25-foot building on the south side of Main east of Pineapple with benches and desks. Cousins of Hoosier poet James Whitcomb Riley—Anna and Sue Whitcomb—took on the teaching chores without pay.

The De Soto rejuvenation compelled a renovation job at the Sarasota House at Five Points. From that job, workmen moved across the street to help a newcomer, J. B. Turner, convert the meeting house he rented into a general merchandising store. A half block away, near Palm Avenue, a newspaper publisher hung out a shingle. It announced the area was soon to have its own newspaper—the *Sarasota Times*. C. V. S. Wilson, a Bradentown publisher, was confident Sarasota eventually would be bigger than Bradentown as he moved his press.

His first issue, a four-page tabloid, gave him additional confidence; it carried ample advertising, a healthy sign. But as a hedge against his newspaper gamble, he inserted a small ad in the early issues pointing out to readers he sold "the best quality and latest design" wallpaper, at his newspaper office, for three cents a roll.

Wilson also sold real estate on the side, announcing that he had five bayfront lots for sale at rock bottom prices: "These all together will be a splendid site for a summer and winter hotel, having 400 feet frontage on Sarasota Bay and being 170 feet deep, giving a view of Sarasota for six miles north and three miles west to the Gulf of Mexico. The land is scrub oak hammock, the best soil for growing oranges and pineapples, and is now covered with dense native growth. Price for whole 400 by 170 feet, $1,000. Or can be divided into lots of 80 by 170 feet for $200 each, cash." The lots were a quarter-mile south of Main Street.

The same year, 1899, a phone rang in Sarasota. Two of them, in fact. One was installed at the post office, then at Main and Pineapple, the other in Harry Higel's real estate office on the wharf. The other end of the line was in Bradentown. Dr. J. C. Pelot placed the first call into Sarasota, phoning the *Sarasota Times* editor. He congratulated everybody upon "the union by wire between Sarasota and the river town."

Further marvels awaited the village of Sarasota in the century ahead. Many would result from the visit of a dour-faced man who, a few days before the year 1900 was rung in, dismounted from a horse and buggy in front of the De Soto Hotel. With him was his wife, the two enjoying a delayed honeymoon.

Standing on the hotel front porch, Mr. and Mrs. Ralph Caples stared at the view across the bay. And like all that had come before them—the Indians, young Bill Whitaker, the Webbs, the homesteaders—they recalled having never seen "anything more beautiful."

It was a sight, and a land, that Ralph Caples felt others should experience and enjoy. He told a few special friends—and Sarasota was on its way to becoming one of the country's most famous and cultural cities.

Facing page: GULF STREAM AVENUE south of Main Street in 1886 reveals the fact that the Sarasota Bay area was mainly a fishing village in the nineteenth century. The fishing industry actually dissipated after the boom of 1886-87, for steamer skippers never liked the trip from Tampa out into the open Gulf down to Sarasota. In addition, Tampa just had a railroad brought into its town linking it with other parts of the country so that city, with its new ice packing houses, became the hub of the fishing industry.

Sarasota before 1900

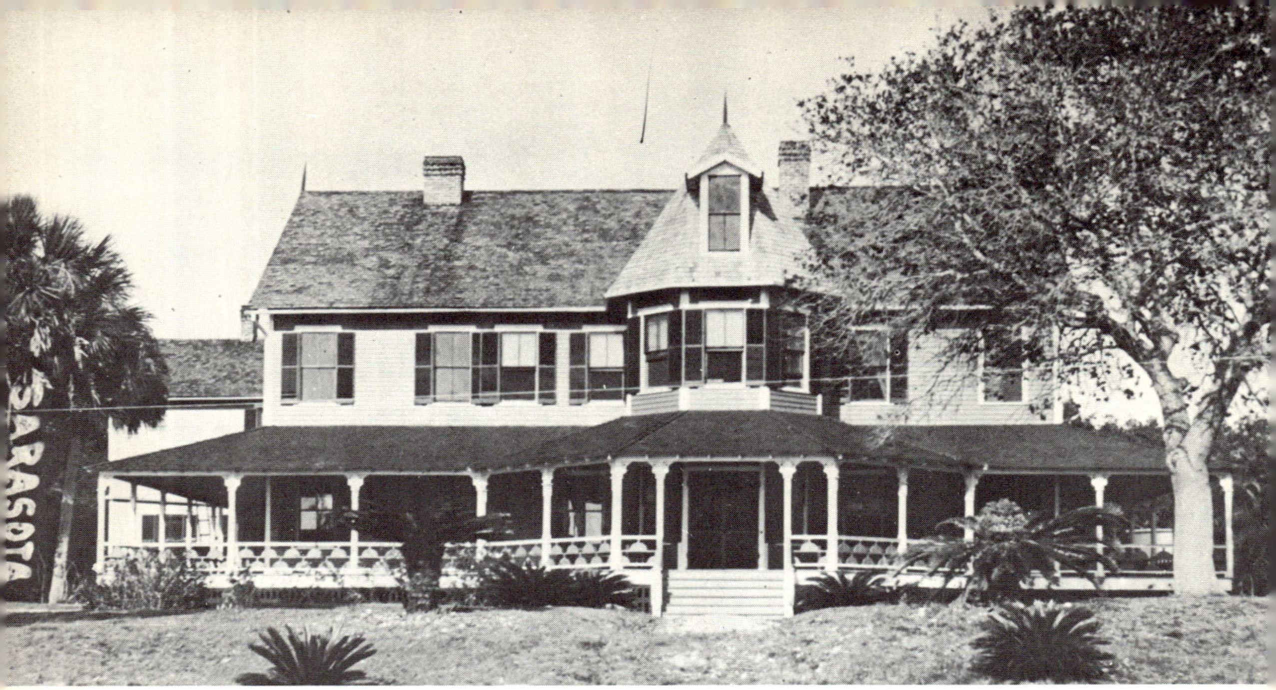

THE BEAUTIFUL TARPON CLUB, built in 1891, is believed to be the result of personal problems between the J. Hamilton Gillespies and the Alfred Joneses. Gillespie, owner of the De Soto Hotel, leased the hotel to Alfred and Annie Jones of Cedar Key, but it is reported Gillespie's first wife proved so unpleasant the Joneses gave up their lease and, with backing of wealthy Chicago and New York sportsmen, built the Tarpon Club. It was designed by Alex Browning, the area's first architect, for a site near 27th Street and the Bay on the old Whitaker estate. Years later it was converted into the Palms Hotel. Its history ended with a fire in 1927.

LOOKING NORTH TOWARD FIVE POINTS from Palm and Main in 1898. The latter intersection for many years had a watering trough for horses and cattle that roamed outside their nearby pastures. The water was from an artesian well drilled in the intersection of Five Points; its purpose was to provide water for the new De Soto Hotel. A main was run down Main Street to the corner of Palm Avenue, at which point the water was forced to a tank on the hotel roof.

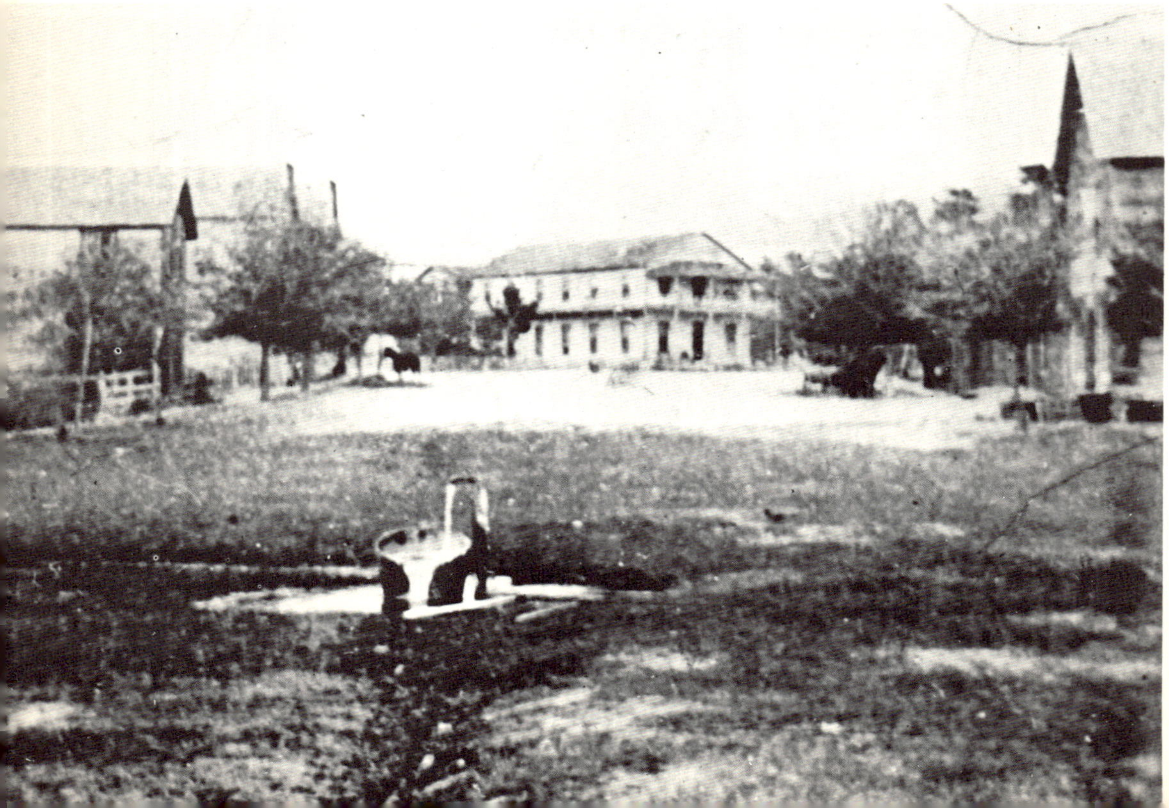

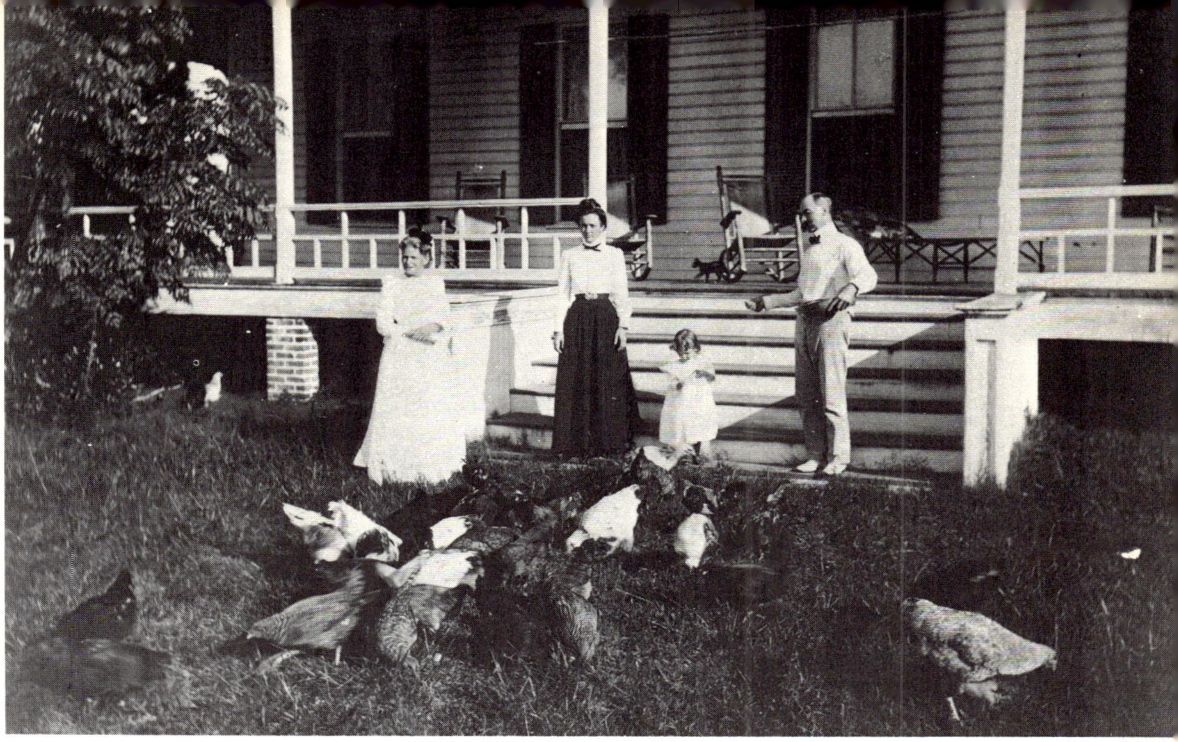

RURAL ATMOSPHERE OF DOWNTOWN SARASOTA is evident in this photo of guests at the then-fancy Belle Haven Inn on the bay. Chickens were no problem but livestock downtown were. A favorite hog wallowing pond, to the disgust of merchants, was the intersection of Main and Palm with its overflowing water trough.

CONVENTIONS WEREN'T SEEKING OUT Sarasota back in 1894, but a strong Baptist population south of the Manatee River wanted to convene somewhere and Sarasota seemed a good place. It had several public buildings such as the Sarasota House, the De Soto Hotel and The Inn, and the village was a relatively new place few people had seen. So combining religious fervor with a vacation, the delegates took over The Inn and became Sarasota's first convention.

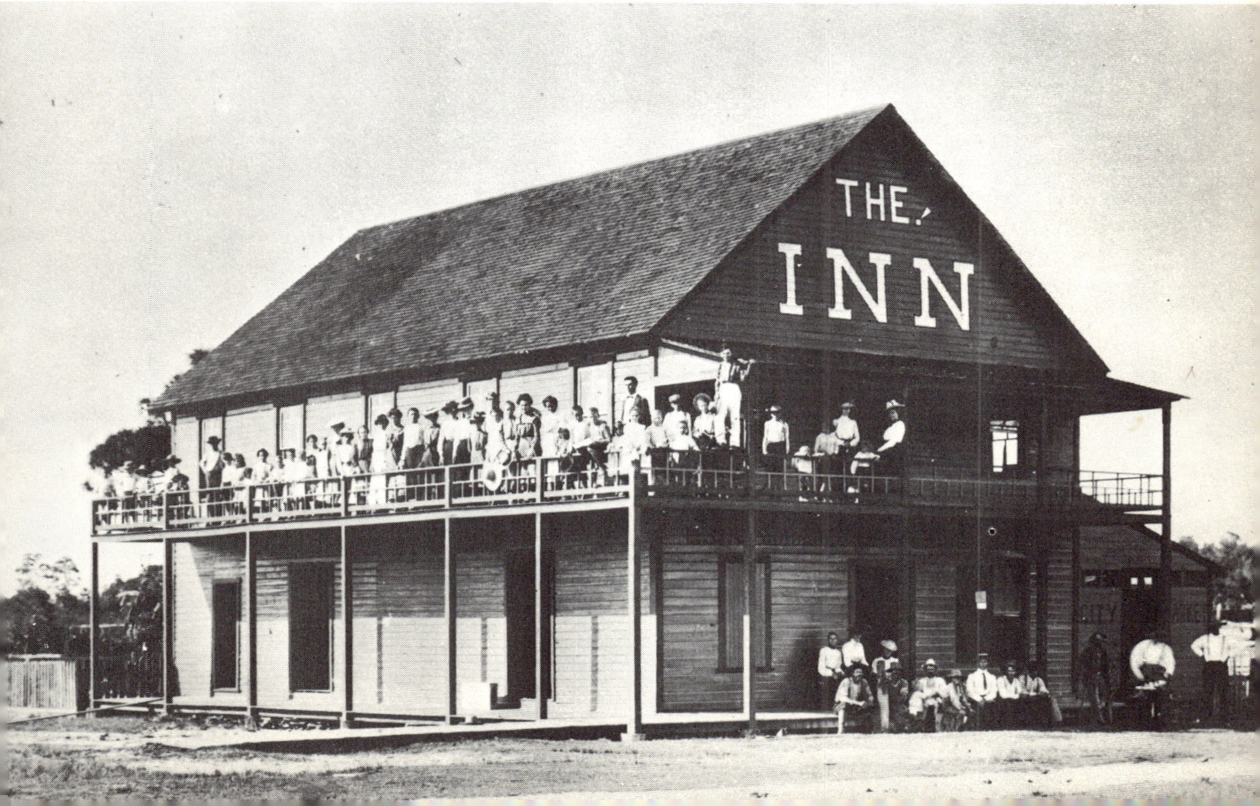

STEAMER *Mistletoe* became one of the area's first scheduled means of transportation in 1895 when a Tampa fish dealer, John Savarese, began making three trips a week to the Sarasota Bay area. Renewal of Sarasota's fishing industry occurred at this time because the Federal government had just finished dredging out shoals in Sarasota Bay north toward Tampa Bay. Shallow draft steamers now could easily make the run in protected waters. Besides hauling fish and ice, the *Mistletoe* carried passengers. Fare between Tampa and Sarasota was about the same the captain paid for 100 pounds of fish—$1.

WITHOUT A RAILROAD, the area's only commercial contact with the outside world was the pier at the foot of Main Street. It was the first structure built by the Florida Mortgage & Investment Co., the Scot syndicate. Harry Higel, one of the area's most dynamic leaders at the turn of the century, bought the wharf and adjoining land in the 1890s for $1,500. First building on dock in this 1899 photo is Dave Broadway's Pavilion, famous for its seafood lunches. Sign on post reads: "Launch Gertrude, for charter by week or day, trips to the Gulf Beach, terms reasonable, apply at office on dock."

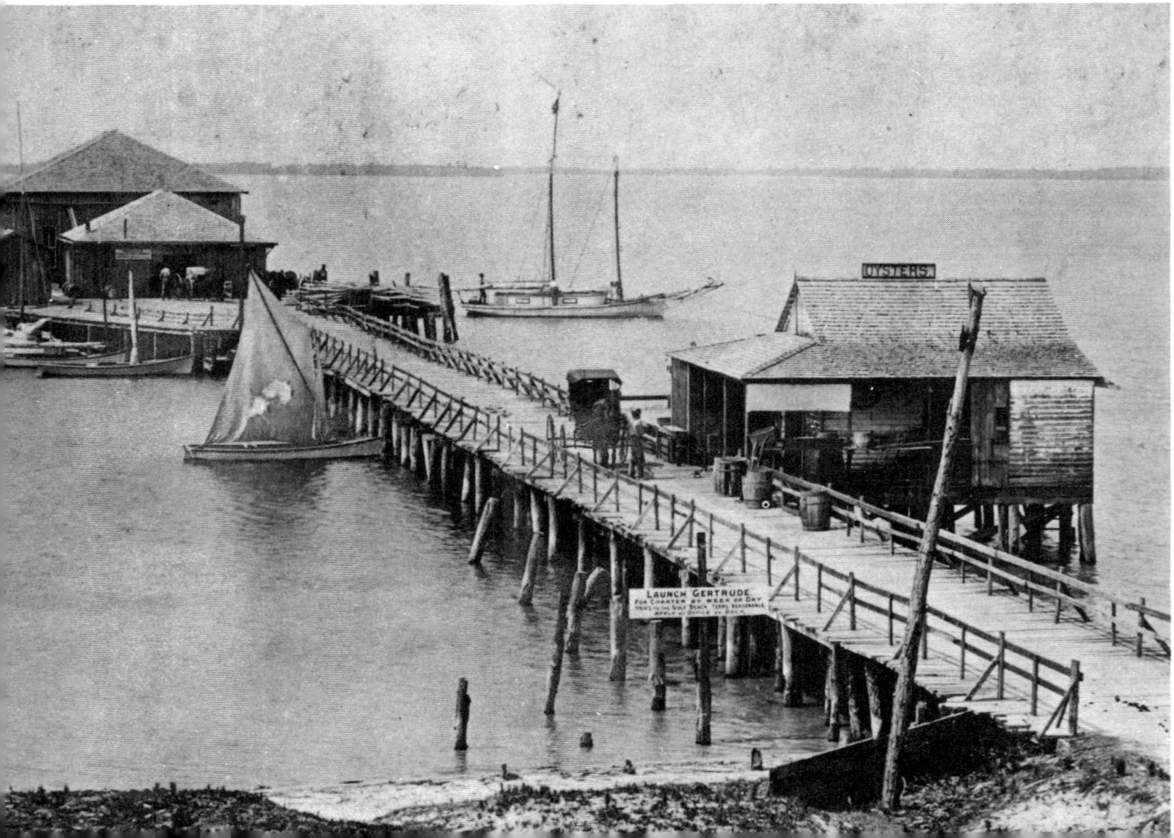

Sarasota from 1900 to 1919

THIS BUCOLIC SCENE of lower Main Street in 1900 belies the boom that was beginning in downtown Sarasota at the time. Most talked about event was the installation of the first telephone line in November 1899. Two phones were put in—one at the post office at Main and Pineapple, the other at Harry L. Higel's office down on the pier. The first call came from a real estate salesman in Manatee for the publisher of the *Sarasota Times*, extending congratulations. During this time George Blackburn built his new hardware store (*left*) at Main and Palm; Coarsey, Turner & Co. opened a general merchandise store at Main and Pineapple; H. B. Harris announced he had just opened up a barber shop, and real estate advertising stepped up its offer of 40-acre tracts on the outskirts at $3 an acre, and downtown bayfront lots at $200—cash!

HOME OF THE *Sarasota Times*, opened in 1899 by Cornelius Wilson and his wife (in doorway) on Main Street between Palm Avenue and Five Points. Wilson had been publishing the *Manatee County Advocate* but felt the Sarasota area was about to take off again and wanted to ride up with it. He was right, partly because there was no place for Sarasota to go but up. Not more than a dozen families lived in the "town plat" area in 1899, and the area's entire population, counting the Fruitville and Bee Ridge areas, hovered around 300. Wilson never missed an issue of his tabloid, and when he died in 1910 his wife continued publishing until 1923, when she sold out to T. J. Campbell and J. H. Lord.

BIG BUSINESS in 1902 was handled at the general store of Highsmith, Turner & Prime on lower Main Street. Selling everything from diapers to caskets, Prime reported doing "a mighty good business but very little of it for cash." He recalled one year selling $100,000 worth of goods and taking in only $1,000 in money, the principal mediums of exchange being alligator hides, furs, sweet potatoes, chickens, and other produce. The partners then would convert this to cash by shipping all the stuff to market by boat.

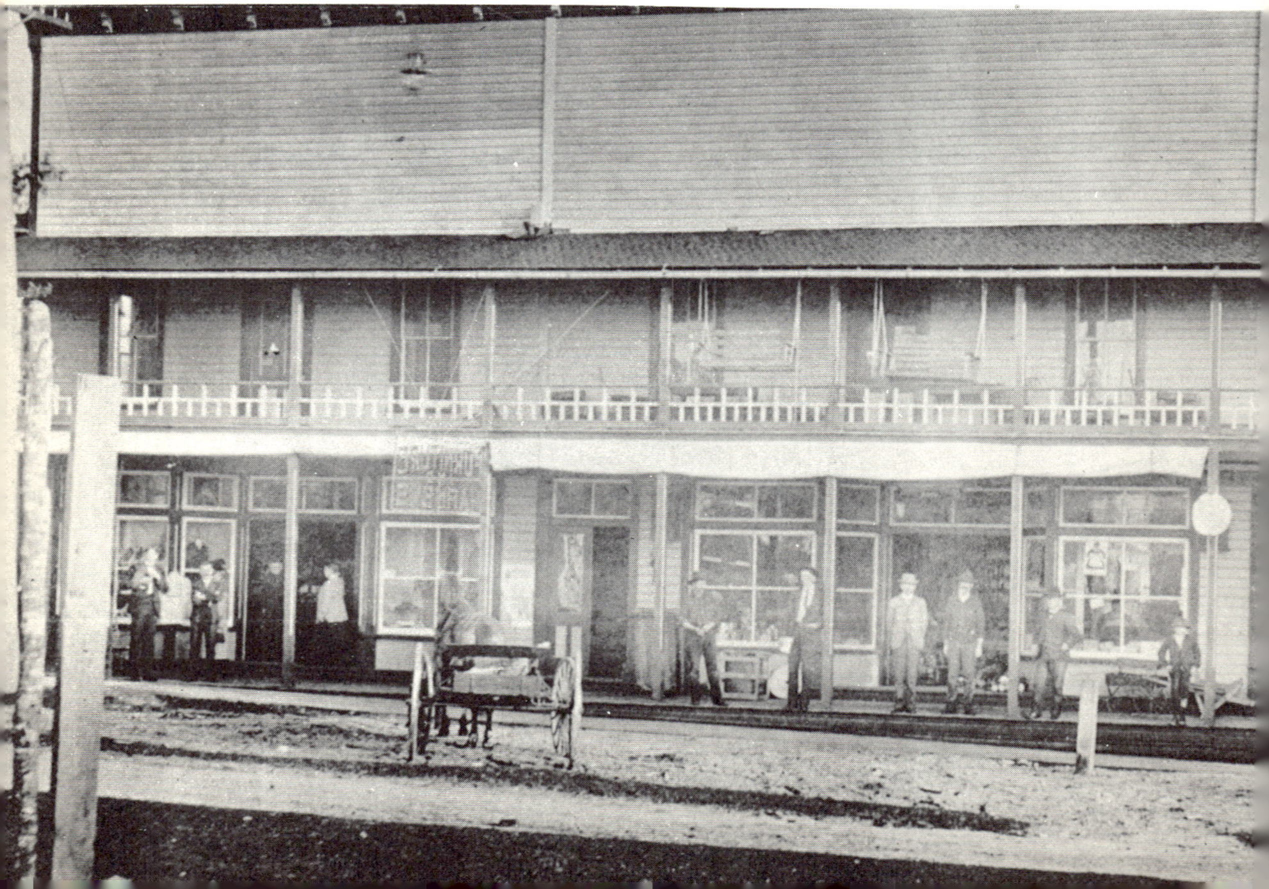

DARING FOR THEIR TIME, but only a step ahead of the fashions of the early 1900s. Not many bare arms and bare legs were seen on the beaches in the old days, for beauty often was judged by the whitest, not the tannest, of skins. In fact, few ladies went to the seaside without an umbrella and a wide-brimmed hat.

ONLY A TWO-HOLE COURSE but one of the nation's most famous is being played in this 1900 photo. Col. J. Hamilton Gillespie, the Scot shown wearing knickers, brought the game to Sarasota from his native land in 1886. That year he built the mini-course eastward from the present Mira Mar Hotel site to where the Federal Building now stands. By 1902 he felt the course inadequate and made plans for a full nine-hole course.

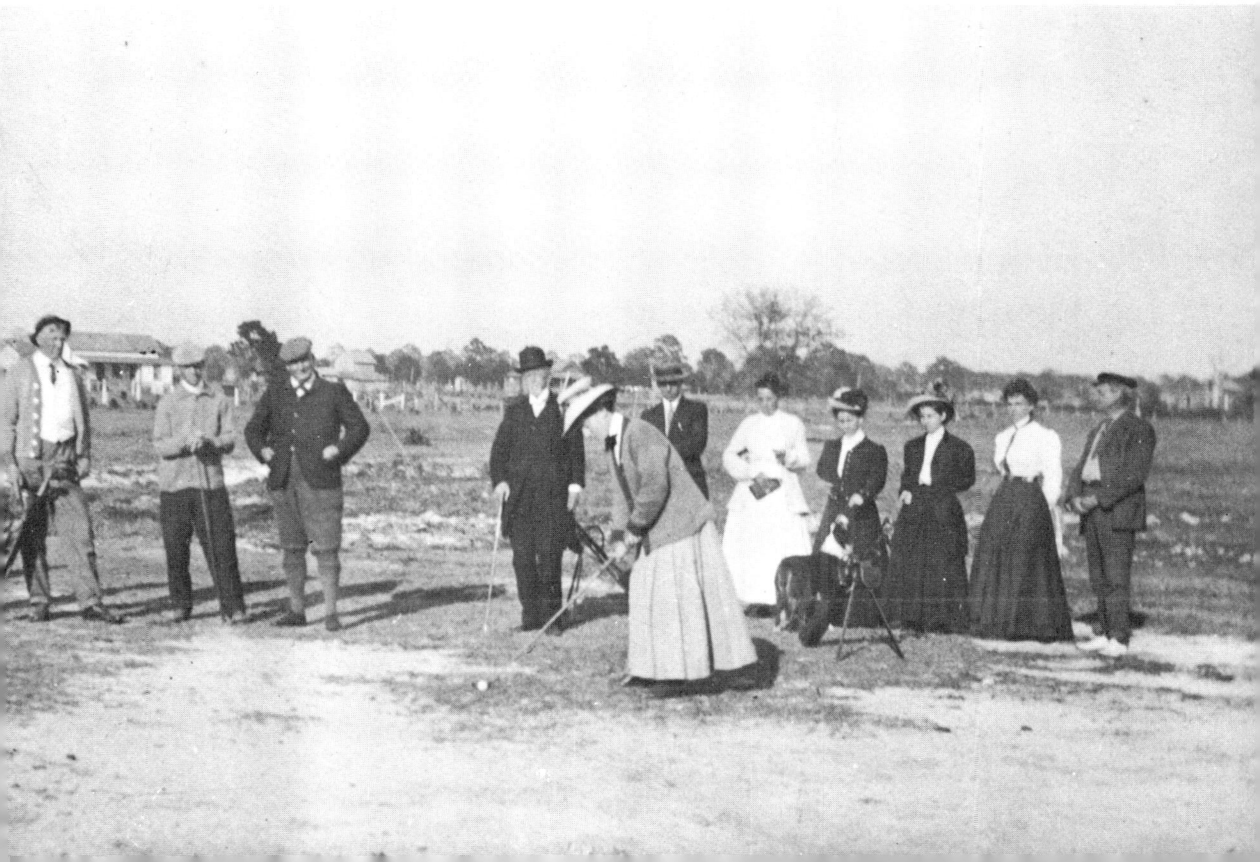

A CHORUS OF "AYES" echoed out of Harry Higel's wharf office one night in October 1902, signalling "incorporating the village into a town and fighting for improvements we need so badly." The 1903 Legislature validated the incorporation, and Sarasota began its official history, starting with the election of Col. J. Hamilton Gillespie as its mayor. Sarasota even began to look organized, what with stores and houses filling both sides of Main Street from Five Points to the pier. This 1905 photo (*above*) shows one of the town's first purchases–a street lamp hanging over the fountain at Five Points. It was one of three kerosene lamps, bought for $3.75 each; the others hung at the foot of Main and at the railroad depot. At left is the Bank of Sarasota, adjacent to Jim Flood's barber shop that soon would become the Badger Pharmacy. The town's first library in 1907 was on the second floor of this building. *Below*: lower Main Street, viewed from the pier looking toward Five Points, taken the same year. Sarasota House is seen at end of street.

FISH HANG FROM THE SHROUDS, over the gunnels and on lines in the water, on Captain Louis Roberts' fishing boat in Sarasota Bay in 1900. Fish were so thick in the bay, said one pioneer, that as you rowed across the bay the oars would club them. Lewis Giles was reported to have boated a tarpon seven feet long weighing 216 pounds where these men are fishing. In background, on end of pier, is Col. J. Hamilton Gillespie's bathhouse.

THE "SLOW & WOBBLY" was what local citizens called Sarasota's first railroad. A home-grown venture by Col. J. Hamilton Gillespie, who felt a railroad into the village would spur growth, the train ran slow and wobbly, between Bradenton and Sarasota, and only when there were enough people to pay a fare for sitting on the two flat cars behind the engine that made up the Manatee & Sarasota Railway and Drainage Co. In two years, it literally fell off the track. A real railroad, the United States & West Indies Railroad & Steamship Co. (a subsidiary of the Seaboard line), began laying track from Tampa through Bradenton into Sarasota in 1902. The photo (*below*) shows construction going on between Palmetto Junction and Sarasota. In March 1903 the first train—a Pullman, a baggage car, and the engine (*above*), pulled into the Sarasota station, built on a pair of lots at Lemon near Main. The event did not attract a crowd, only about 50 people, but village leaders could see its great significance. In fact, when the news hit the village in 1902 that the railroad was coming, the village leaders launched plans to incorporate into a town. In 1912, a rail line to Venice was added. Business south was dismal, and by 1921 the Venice segment was abandoned.

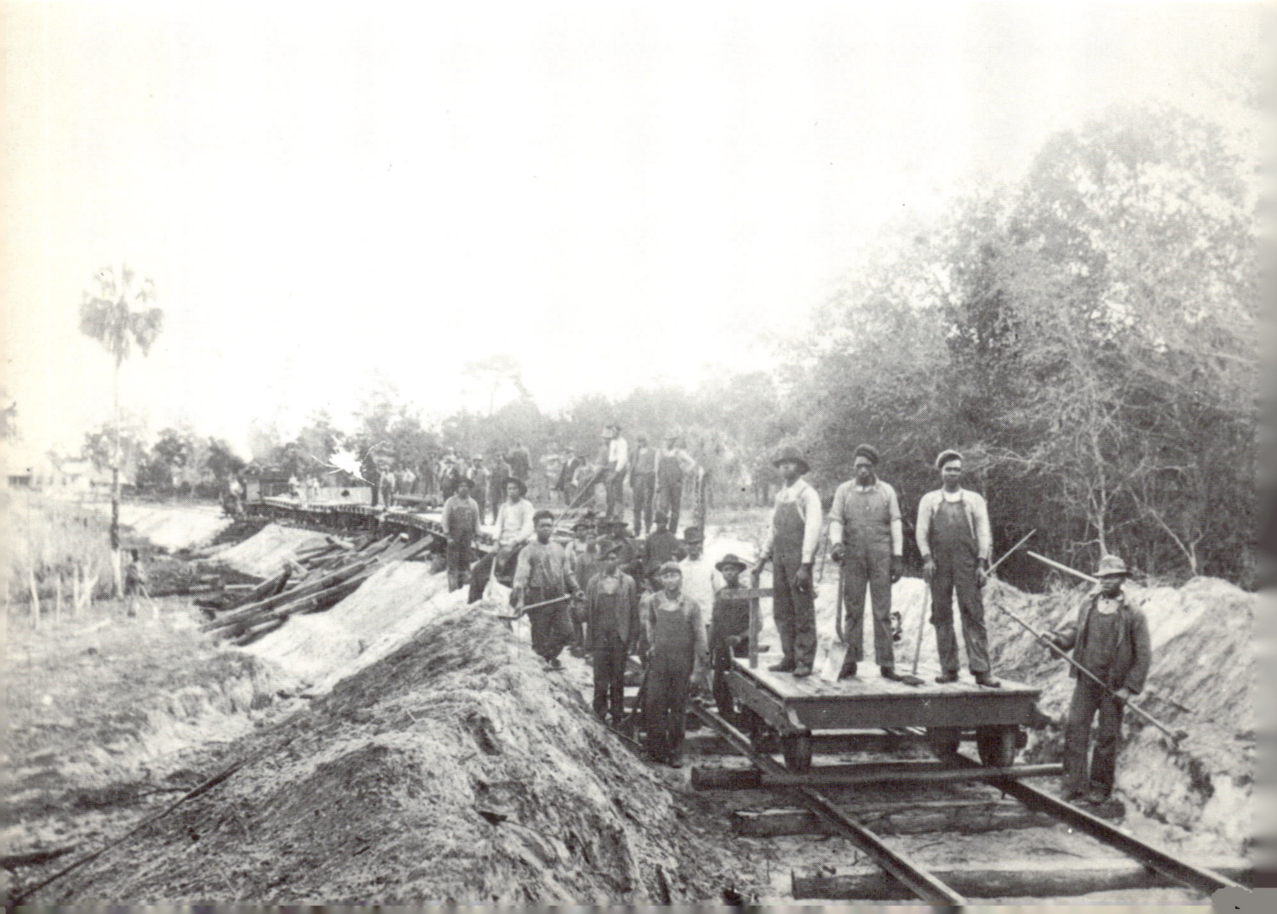

THE HEAT OF FLORIDA'S SUMMER made the beaches off Sarasota popular with the townsfolk, even though access was only by boat. This bathing scene at the turn of the century is on Siesta Key in the Pass. It was customary for all stores in town to close Thursday afternoons during the summer months so that folks could go to the beaches.

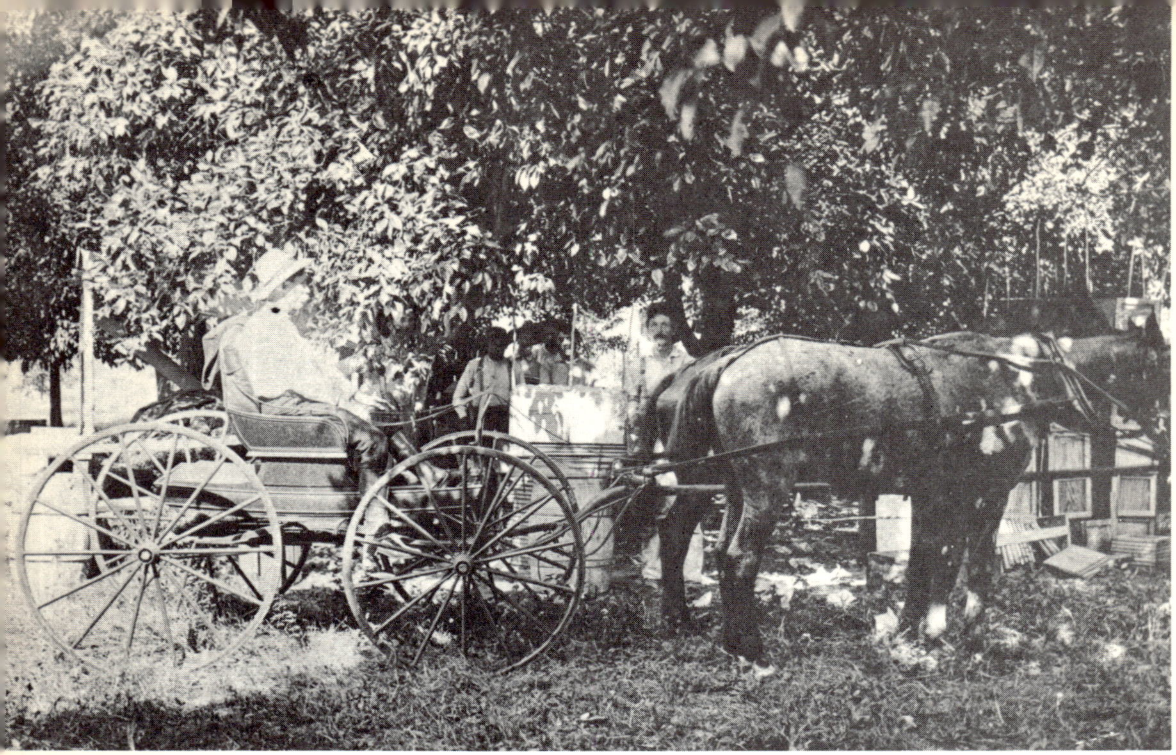

NO ONE KNEW the Sarasota area better than A. B. Edwards. Born in 1874 in what is now the northern part of the city, he felt so strongly about the beauty of the Sarasota Bay region that he wrote personal letters to the big railroad officials around the country asking them to forward to him names of persons inquiring about Florida. They did, and he personally sent every one what today would be called a public relations letter. He held several city offices, including that of first mayor under the city charter in 1914. But he never really got out of the real estate business after opening up the first such office in the town in 1903. This picture, taken at that time, shows him making his rounds in search of property for sale.

COUPLE FROM BUNGALOW HILL, Mr. and Mrs. Humber, posed in the foreground of this 1903 photograph showing rental homes on Central Avenue owned by J. H. Lord, a wealthy Rhode Island transplant who was bent on buying up as much of the Sarasota Bay region as he could. The intersection above is Pineapple and Central. Bungalow Hill later became known as Sarasota Heights, and was an area south of Hudson Bayou. It actually incorporated as a separate town in 1917, prompting charges from Sarasotans that the Heights' folks were a bunch of "tax dodgers." Not enjoying "big city" improvements and progress, Heights' residents in 1925 let themselves be annexed by Sarasota.

THE SCHOOLHOUSE that served the town's children became so overcrowded in 1903 that parents demanded a new and larger one. Estimated cost was $3,500. Funds were raised, and this two-story five-classroom building was put up on Main Street east of Pine in the summer of 1904. It served the town's needs until 1913.

FISH HOUSE SPUR was laid out by the United States & West Indies Railroad immediately after it brought its main tracks into Sarasota in 1903. The spur was put down west on Strawberry Avenue across Gulf Stream Avenue out onto a dock. The fish house above was the first of several to cluster around the tracks. In later years, when the spur was not being used, John Ringling sometimes parked his private railroad car on the dock.

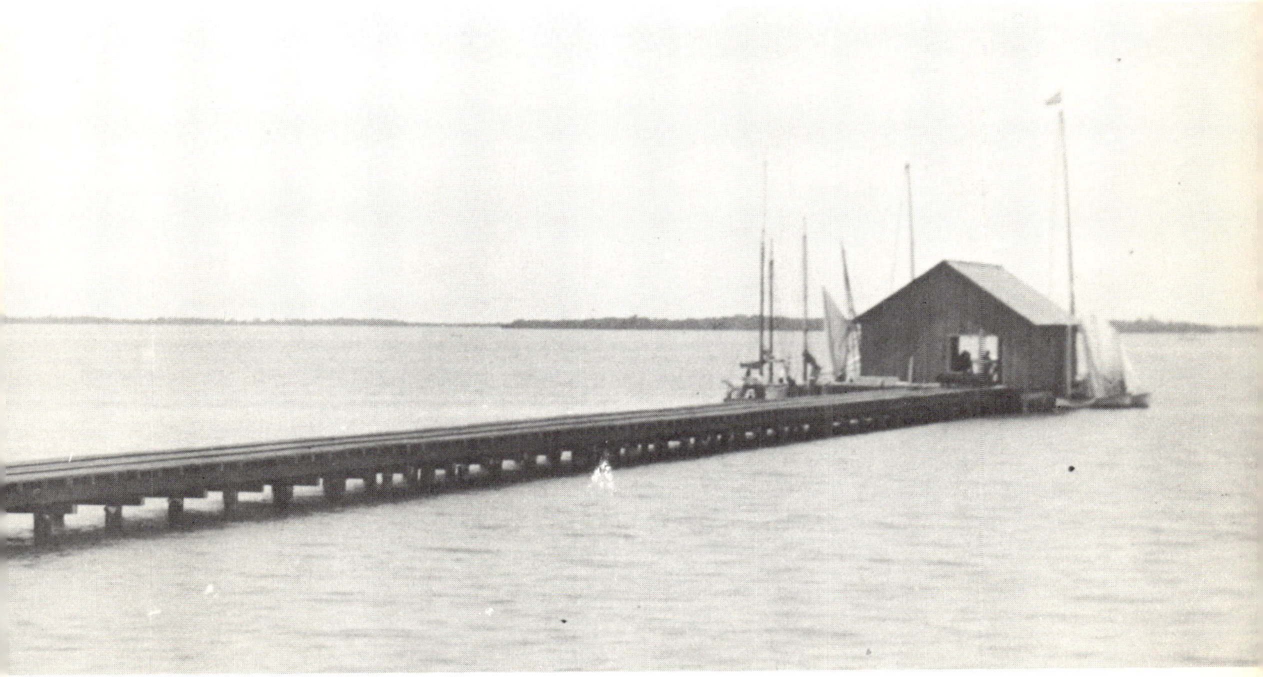

BACK FROM AN AFTERNOON OF FISHING with their catch in 1904 are Dr. F. W. Schultz, his wife, and a friend. They are passing through Five Points. Under construction in the background is the present Badger Pharmacy building. The house in rear belongs to J. B. Turner, who ran a general merchandise store. The new Methodist church is at left.

THE BADGER DRUG STORE, a famous landmark to Sarasotans for more than 50 years, had its beginning in 1905 at Five Points. It was named by Dr. F. W. Schultz for his hometown state, the Badger state of Wisconsin. On sidewalk, from left, are Bill Edwards, Mack Christie, Spencer Olson, and Jim Halton.

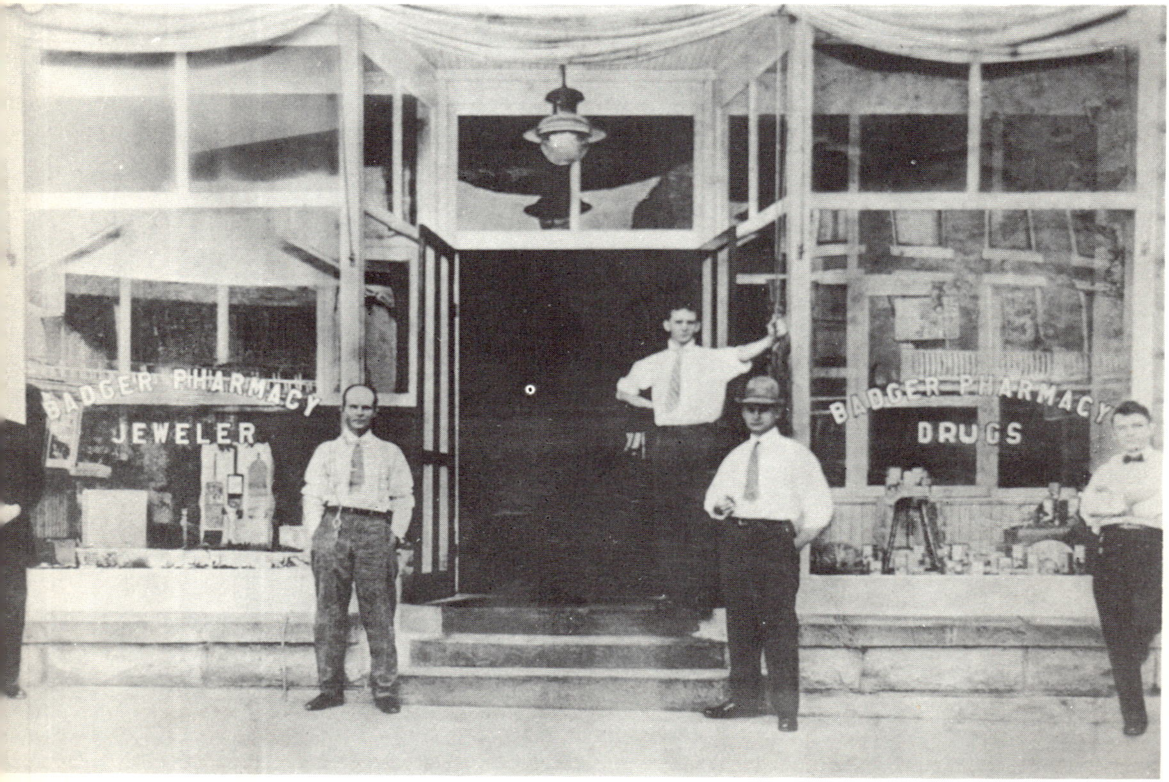

METHODISTS are often recognized as having the first organized church in the Sarasota Bay region. In the early days services were held in a frame building at Five Points with circuit-riding preachers like Revs. George Glazier and E. F. Bates coming down from Manatee. By 1906 the congregation had progressed to buying this building, and adding a belfry and steeple, at Main and Pineapple. The church and site were sold to J. H. Lord five years later—for $1,600—and the Methodists erected a new structure on Pineapple. The Methodists always have had a "downtown" church. Hamming it up for the photographer, four telephone workmen pose atop a pole while stringing line.

EPISCOPAL CHURCH OF THE REDEEMER began in 1904 with only 12 members in a small building on Pineapple. Two years later, with help from prominent members Dr. Jack Halton (left) and Col. J. Hamilton Gillespie (right), the building was moved to Strawberry and Palm and remodeled. It was moved again in 1908 to South Orange Avenue and Morrill Street, where it stood for four decades until a new edifice was completed on South Gulf Stream Avenue.

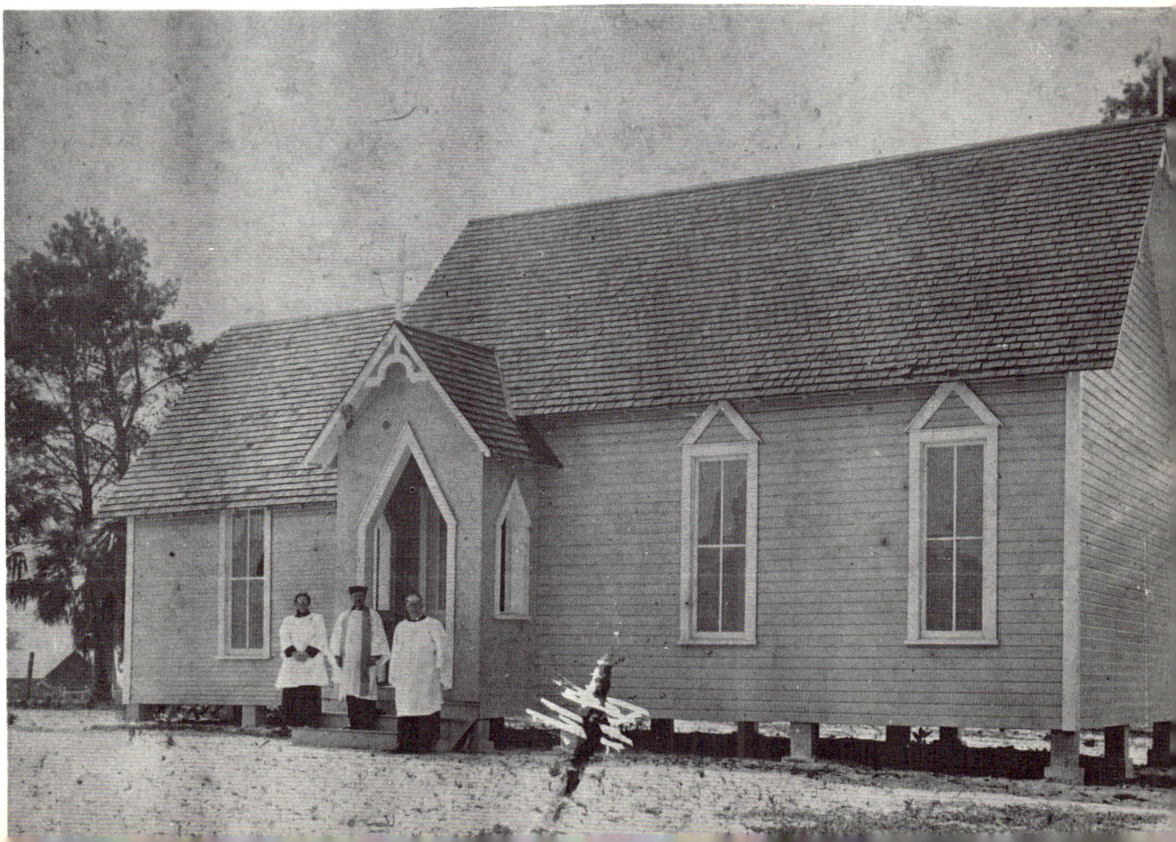

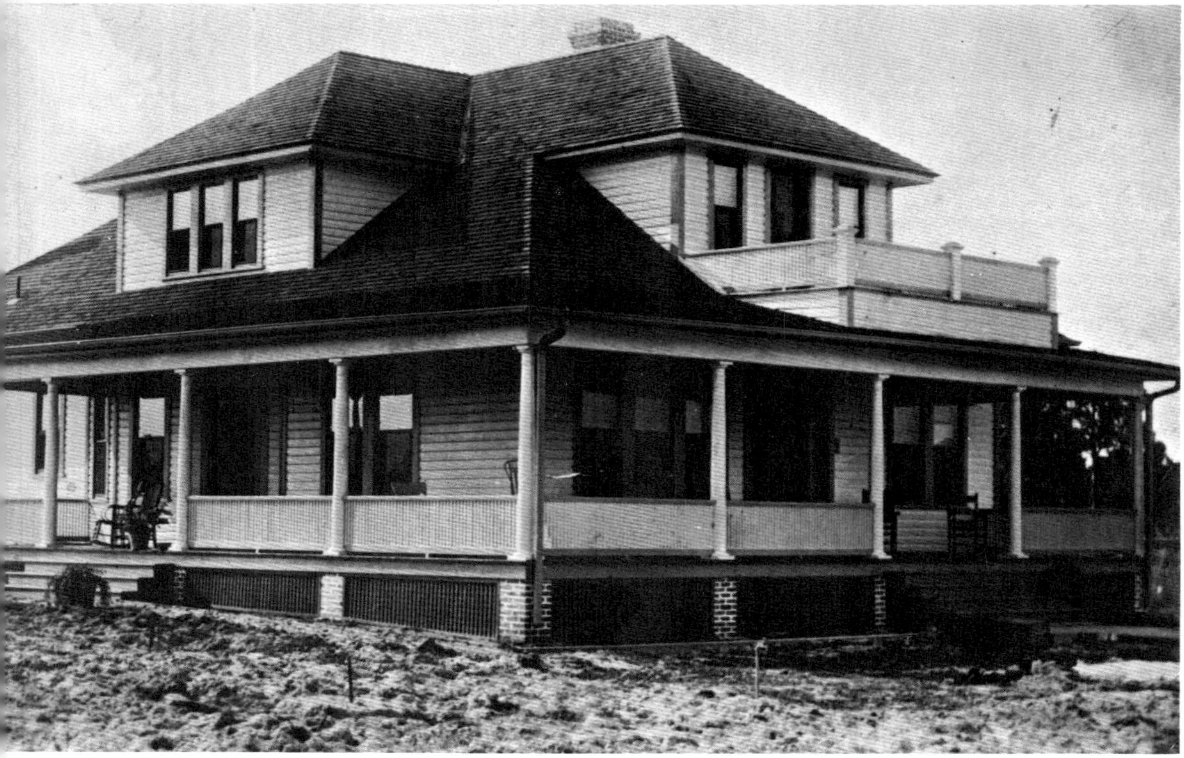

HOME OF THE FIRST MAYOR of the Town of Sarasota—Col. J. Hamilton Gillespie—still stands but in a renovated and expanded condition. It is now the central section of the present Robarts Funeral Home at 22 S. Links Avenue. In front of this home, facing east, the Colonel laid out his golf course in 1905.

REPUTATION FOR SURVIVAL must be claimed by houses occupied by Col. J. Hamilton Gillespie. One became Robarts Funeral Home, and this one, on Morrill Street, also remains. It is part of the Prew School. That's the Colonel with his second wife (on porch).

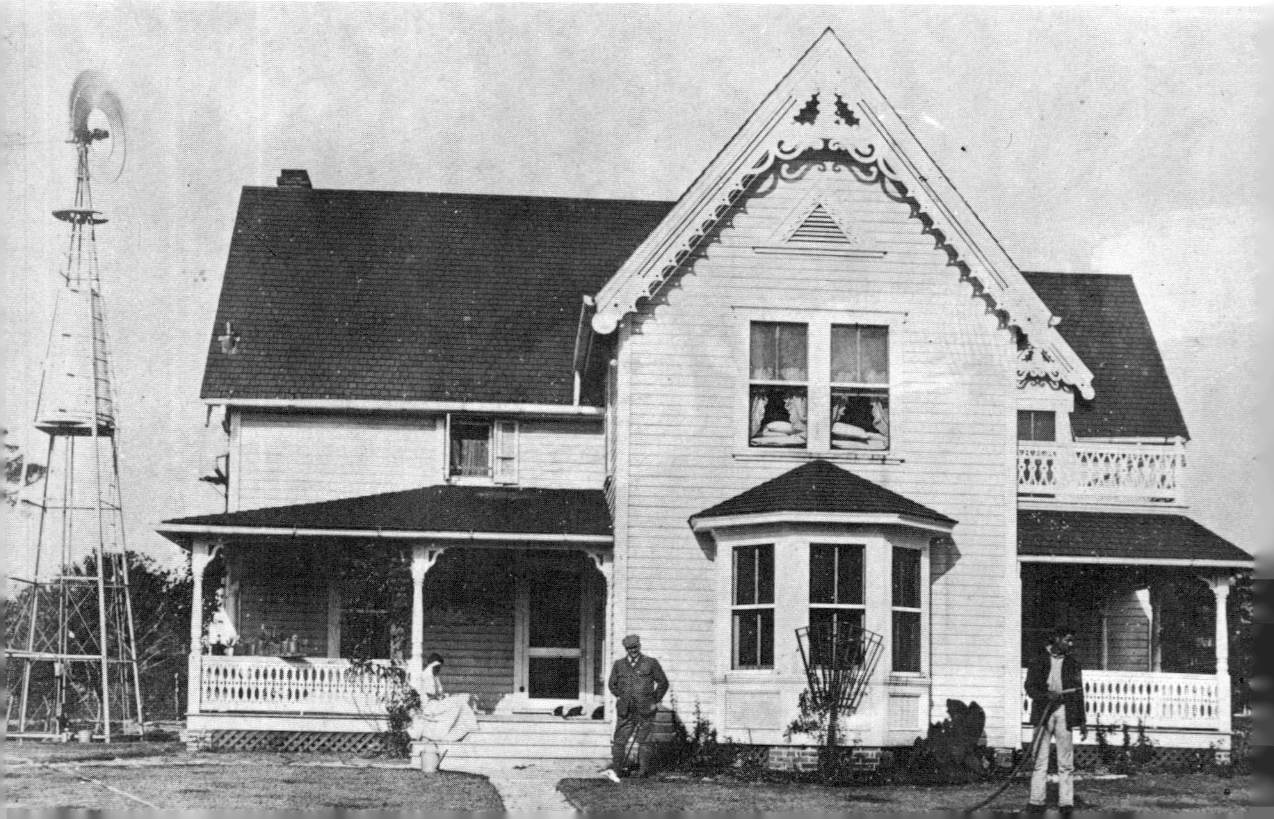

GROWING UP IN SARASOTA in 1906 had its delights. To young Victor Grantham, it was hitching up his calf to a wagon and riding down lower Main Street. The *Sarasota Times* office is in the background.

THE STEAMER *Vandalia* took over the regular runs between Sarasota and Tampa because hard times hit in 1907 and the three-times-a-week trips by the *Mistletoe* were canceled by Tampan John Savarese. Sarasotan Harry Higel bought the *Vandalia* only to continue the scheduled transportation of fish, ice, and travelers between the two towns.

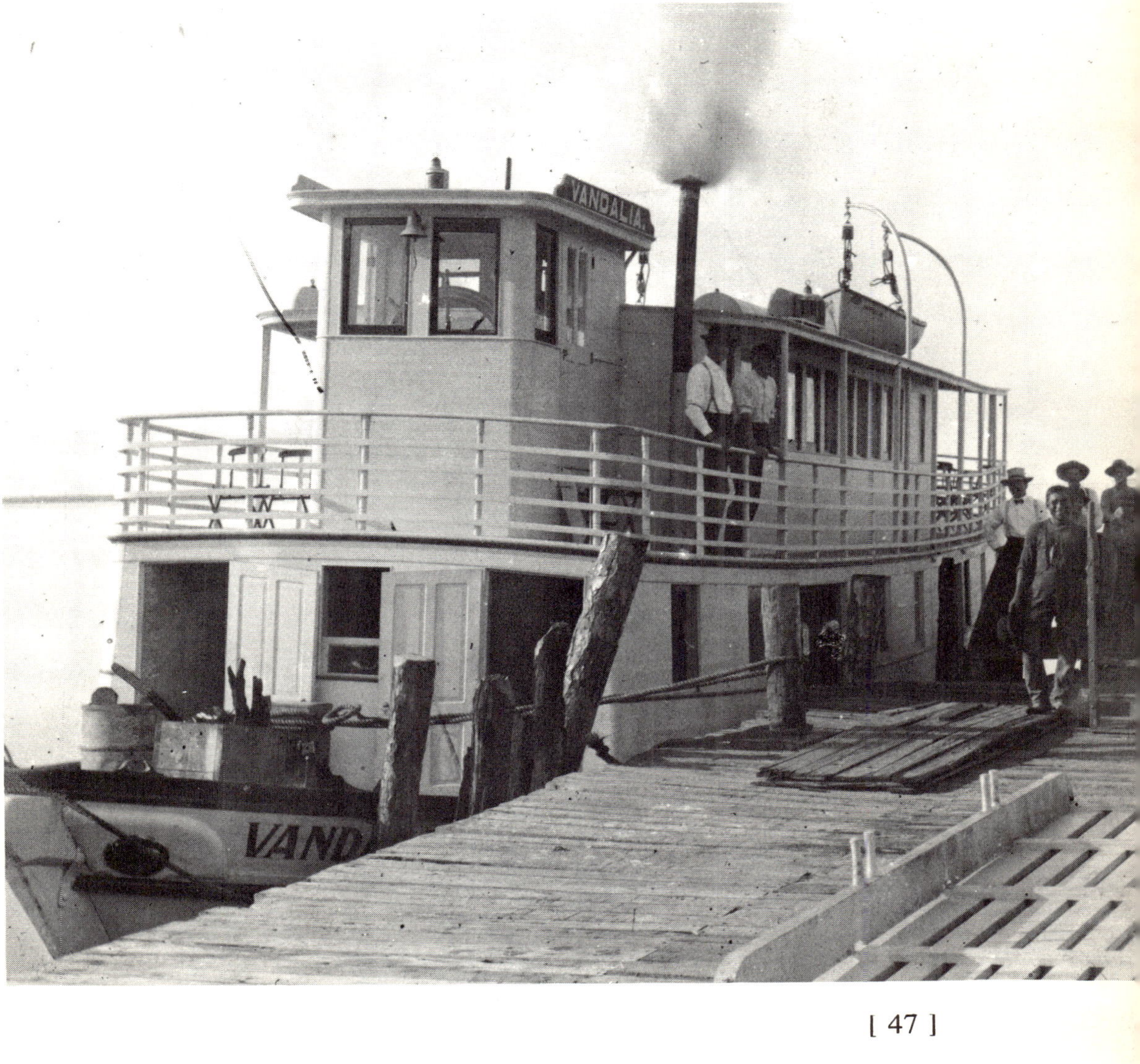

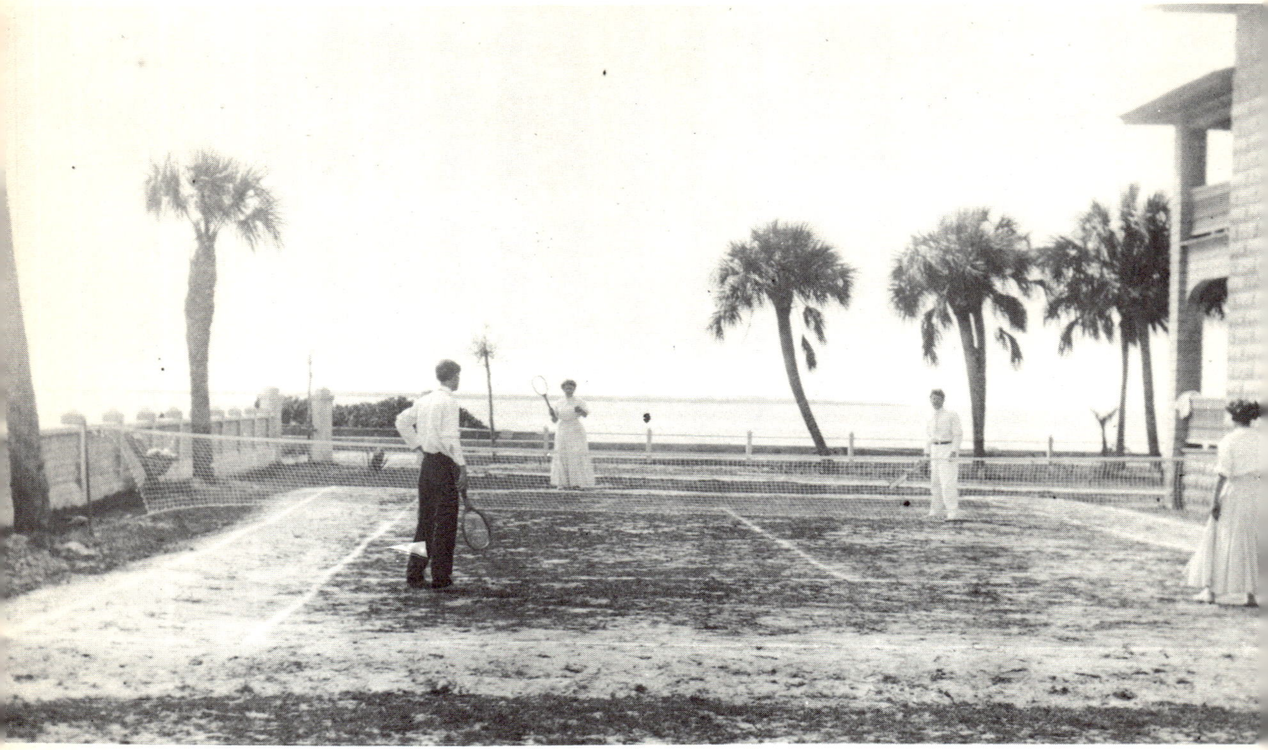

A GAME OF DOUBLES at the Halton Sanatorium in 1908 (*above*). An afternoon of golf about to get under way in 1908 (*left*). Col. J. Hamilton Gillespie and friends are sitting on the steps of the course clubhouse he built at Golf and Links Avenue. The Elks Club for many years occupied the site, but its building was torn down for a parking lot next to Robarts Funeral Home.

THE MARSHAL AND HIS FAMILY. L. D. Hodges served as town marshal and police chief from 1908 to 1921. He was succeeded by S. Tilden Davis, the city's chief until his death in 1937. Two years after the area separated from Manatee County and became Sarasota County, Hodges was elected sheriff.

HOMESTEADING ON GULF STREAM AVENUE back in the early 1900s was not much different from homesteading back in the hinterland. The John Iverson family here has just returned from a hunting trip through the nearby woods; the bagged game hangs on the front porch pillars. For a change in diet, the Iversons apparently kept a seine handy (against porch), for fish were unusually abundant across the street in the bay.

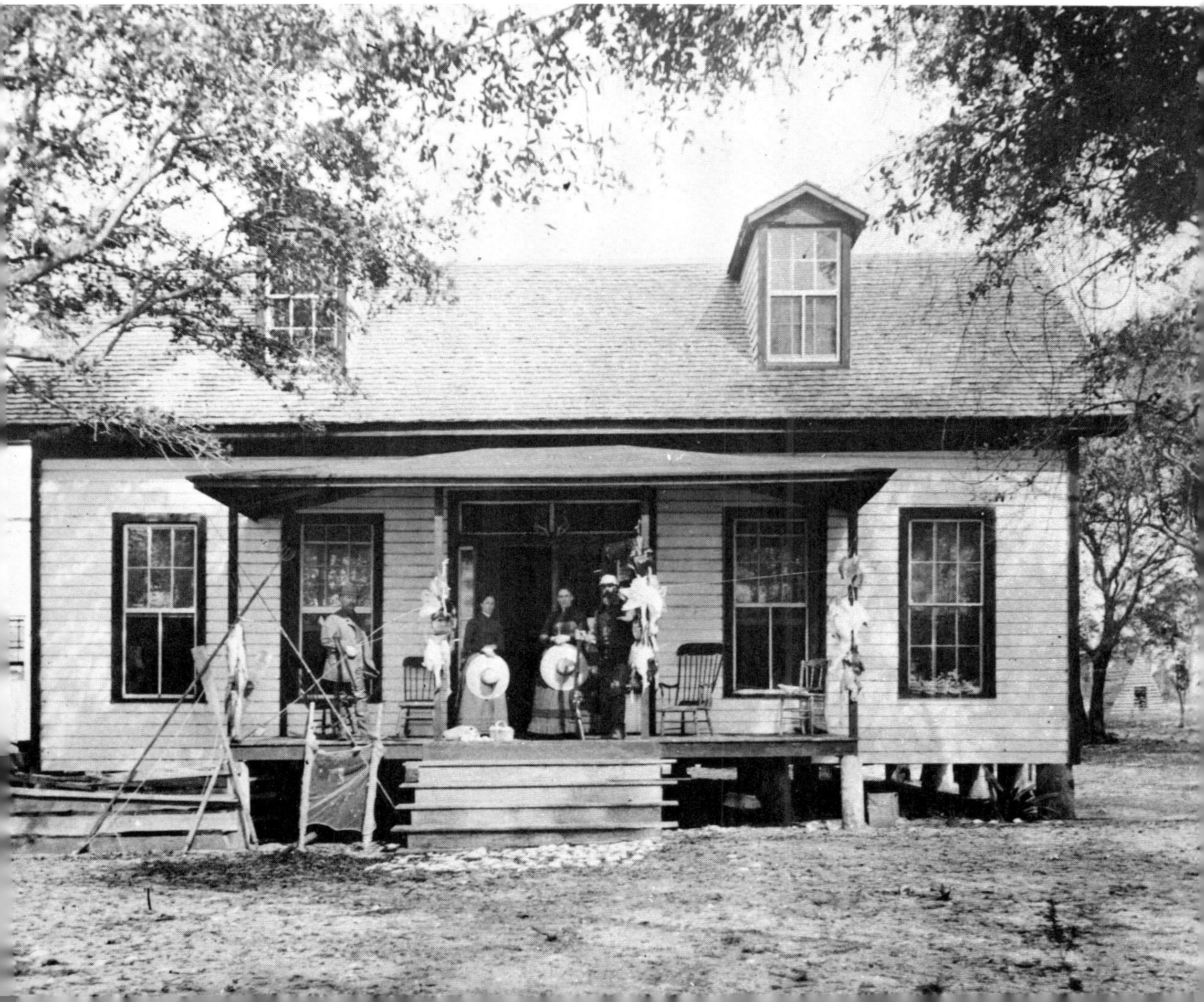

MORE FAMOUS FOR one of its guests than as a place for the ailing was the Halton Sanatorium, built by Dr. Jack Halton in 1908 on North Gulf Stream Avenue. When Mrs. Potter Palmer, well-known Chicago socialite, expressed an interest in visiting Sarasota, the recently built sanatorium was considered the most decent building downtown in which she might be housed, as nearby Belle Haven Inn was badly run down. So Halton's place was quickly renovated and refurbished. Impressed with the "refreshingly quaint" town and apparently comfortable in the sanatorium, Mrs. Palmer stayed long enough to buy a 13-acre tract for what later became "The Oaks," an adjoining 200 acres, another 80,000 acres east of the town and in the Myakka area, and even property in Hillsborough County. Her coming proved to be one of the three or four most important events in the history of Sarasota, for it attracted other wealthy people, publicized the town as a winter resort, and instilled a new life and pride in Sarasotans that stimulated the town's growth and activities.

WITHOUT A FIRE DEPARTMENT, the town of Sarasota threatened to go up in smoke in 1908. The Bay View Hotel on the northwest corner of Main and Palm, only two years old, caught fire, and in minutes the 16-room wooden structure crumbled, shooting sparks across the rooftops of other frame buildings. Without a volunteer fire department, not even a community hose, the townspeople watched and prayed. Nothing else caught fire.

TWO SARASOTA CYCLISTS in the early 1900s.

STICKNEY POINT was a grand place for picnics even back in 1908. "Uncle Ben" Stickney, who homesteaded on Sarasota Key, now named Siesta Key, was a social individual and often invited people to his woods for a get-together. Among those attending this one were Postmistress Carrie Abbe (left); the publisher of Sarasota's first newspaper, Cornelius Wilson (fifth from left); and Professor T. W. Yarbrough (wearing hat), principal of the Sarasota public schools.

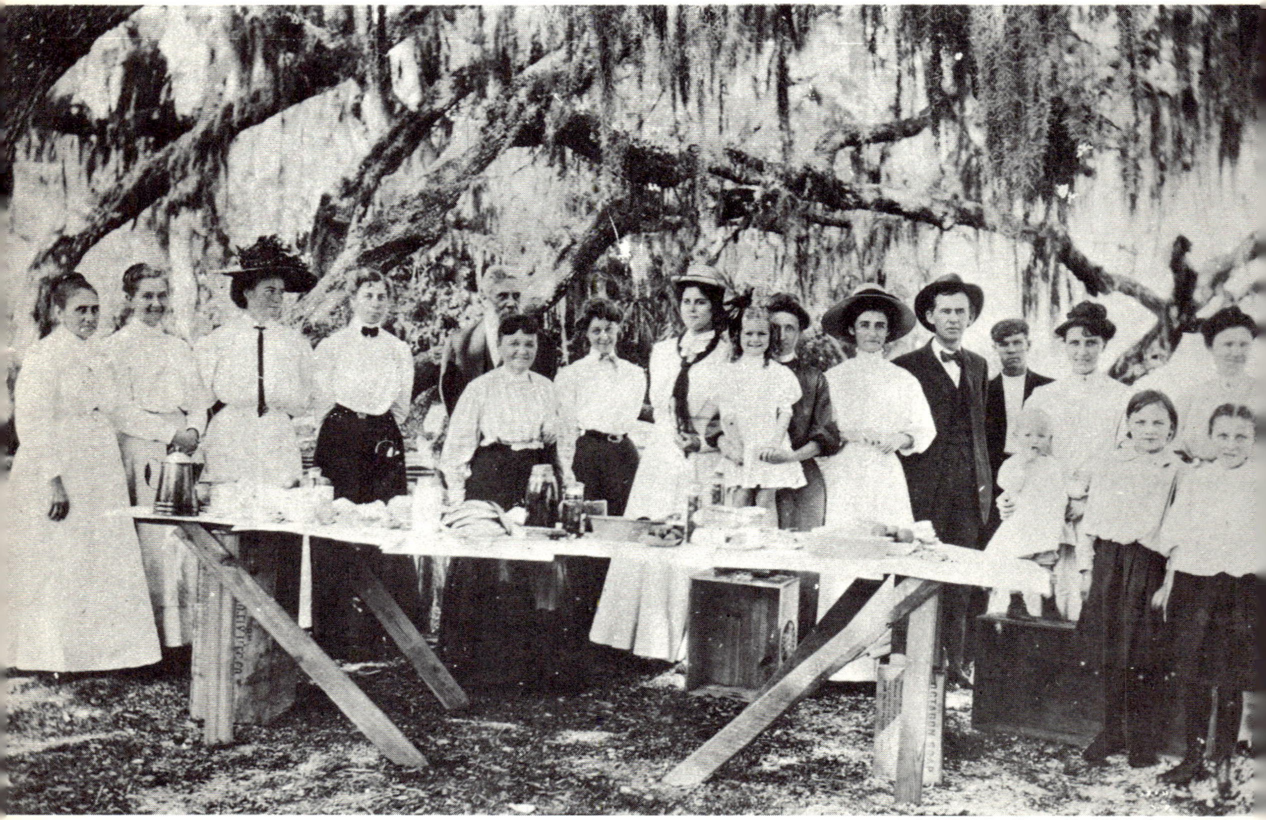

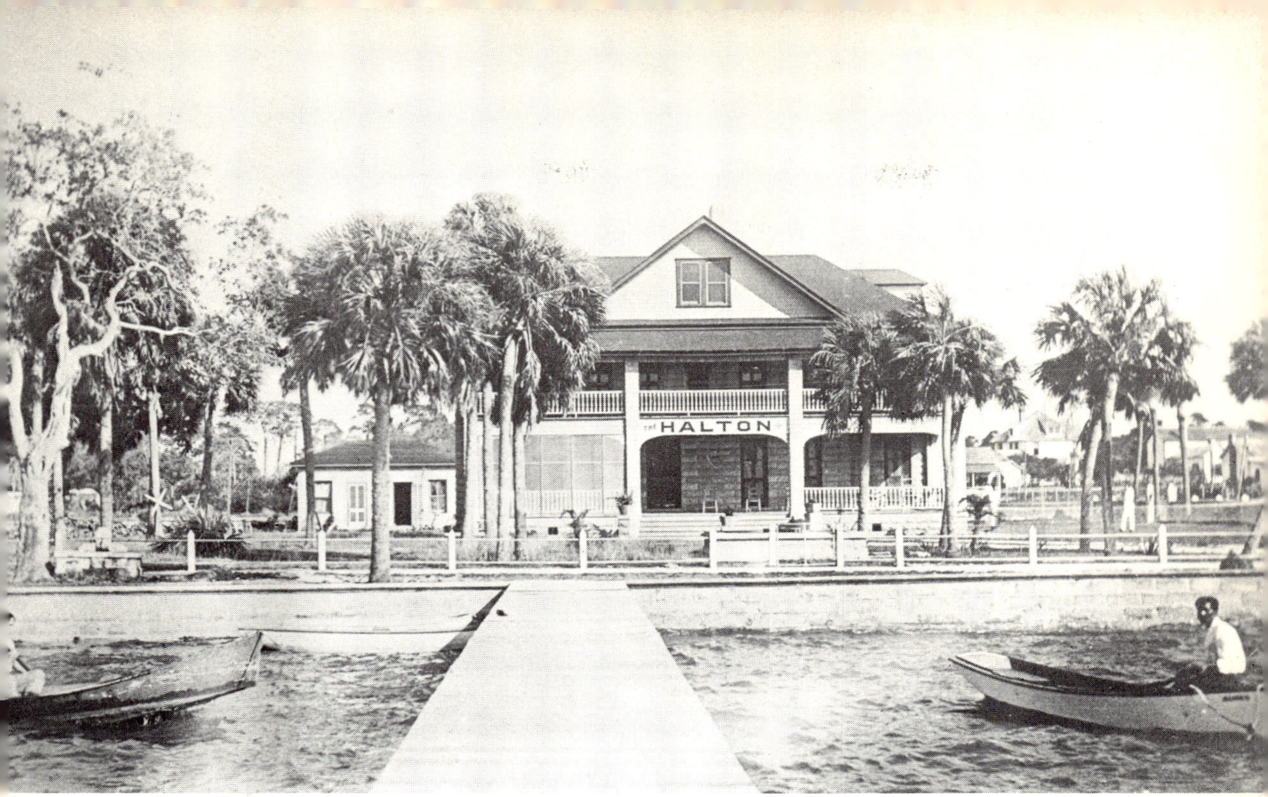

MANY FINE BUILDINGS erected in Sarasota in the early 1900s remained for decades, their use and occupants changing frequently. The Halton (*above and right*), for example, opened in 1908 as a sanatorium. In an emergency in 1910, it served as the guest quarters for Mrs. Potter Palmer of Chicago. Then it became an apartment, then the home of Owen Burns, a persuasive and wealthy promoter from Chicago, and finally the Admiral Bayfront Hotel. The landmark was torn down in the 1960s.

FIRST AUTOMOBILE in Sarasota was bought in 1909 by Dr. Cullen B. Wilson as a Christmas present to himself. It was a 20 horsepower Reo of the roadster type. Wilson had to drive to Tampa to pick it up. The trip, one-way, took five hours—from 9 a.m. to 2 p.m., "including time lost by getting on wrong roads and a lunch in Bradentown."

BUSINESS BLOCK on lower Main Street in 1909 housed Blackburn's hardware store, a tailor shop, the office of dentist S. S. Curry, and J. B. Chapline's real estate business. It is now the First Federal parking lot.

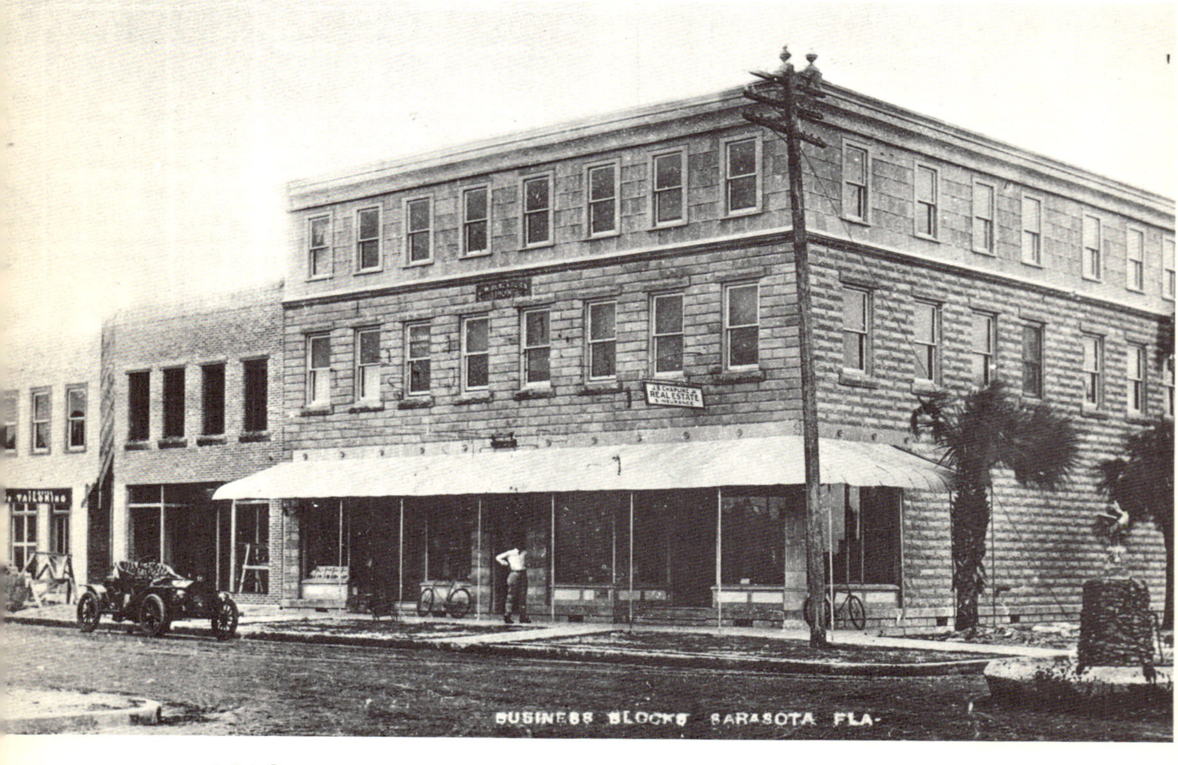

BUSINESS BLOCKS SARASOTA FLA.

"HER HEART IS IN TROPICAL SARASOTA BAY," wrote a Chicago newspaperman after interviewing Mrs. Potter Palmer (*right*) upon her return visit from Sarasota. Mrs. Palmer, the wife of the Chicago financier and developer, was enticed to Sarasota by a real estate ad that spoke of rich land to be purchased at low prices, and the picturesque charm of the region. During her visit, in the company of her father, Colonel H. H. Honore, and her two sons and brother, the Palmers purchased more than 80,000 acres, so enthused were they with the "delightful climate and general ideal conditions." Included in their purchases was a home site near Osprey on Little Sarasota Bay. The home was called "The Oaks" (*above and below*), and became her winter residence, flanked by homes for her sons. Mrs. Palmer had planned "The Oaks" as a temporary residence; she had intended to build one day a grand chateau. The Palmers maintained year-around interest in their lands, forming the Palmer Farms Growers Cooperative and the Palmer Farmers experimental station, developing a large celery farm operation and model cattle ranch, and organizing the Palmer Bank. Much of Myakka State Park is comprised of lands sold or donated to the state by the Palmers. In 1918, Mrs. Palmer died at "The Oaks." Her decision to come to Sarasota and help develop the area is considered one of the most significant forward steps in Sarasota's history.

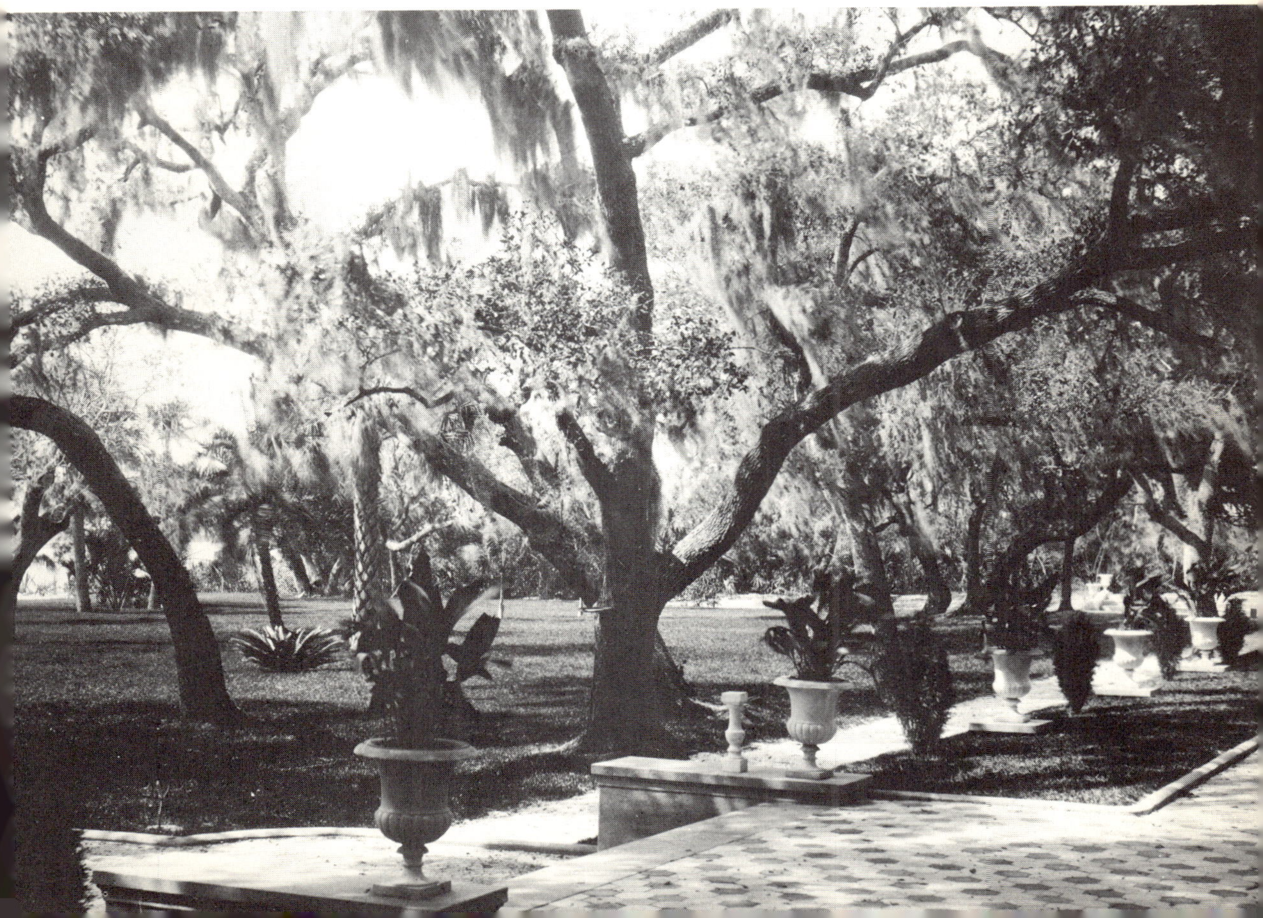

CATTLE PROVOKED A NEAR WAR in the early 1900s because cattlemen refused to confine their animals. The result was that cows, hogs, and goats sometimes trampled down people's yards and even littered Main Street. Mayor Hamden Smith finally took the bull by the horns, so to speak, and

proposed an ordinance banning the grazing and roaming of animals within the town limits. After a bitter argument between townspeople and cattlemen, the ordinance was approved and downtown began looking less like the West and more like a city.

THE MOST SIGNIFICANT PERSONALITY IN SARASOTA HISTORY, John Ringling, arrived for the first time in Sarasota in 1911. He and his wife Mable purchased the C. N. Thompson home in 1912 and lived there until the completion of Ca'd'Zan in 1926. The circus, his extensive real estate holdings on Longboat Key, St. Armand's Key, Bird Key, Lido Beach, Shell Beach, and the purchase of the John Ringling Hotel, made Ringling into one of the world's 25 wealthiest men in the mid-20s, with $180,000,000 in assets. A longtime admirer of the fine arts, Ringling built the John and Mable Ringling Museum of Art, opened in 1931. After Mable's death in 1929 and the devastating blow of the Depression, Ringling's holdings became entangled in financial chaos. His creditors were "closing in like hounds on a fox." Owen Burns took him to court on charges of fraud connected with the purchase of the El Vernona Hotel, but Ringling won the case. On December 19, 1930, Ringling remarried, to wealthy widow Emily Buck, and on their wedding day he borrowed $50,000 from her. Their "civil contract" was ended when John won his divorce from her, but it cost him $201,211.95 in attorney fees. Shortly after, Emily married Ringling's attorney. Ringling's health began deteriorating; in addition, he learned that directors of his business affairs had neglected to pay income taxes and had removed his authority "on or off" the circus lot. The final blow came just before his death, when he was informed that his mansion and its furnishings would be sold at public auction to pay off creditors. He died on December 9, 1936, six days before the auction. His sister, Ida, spent 10 years unraveling her brother's money matters, then turned over the home and museum to the state of Florida in 1946.

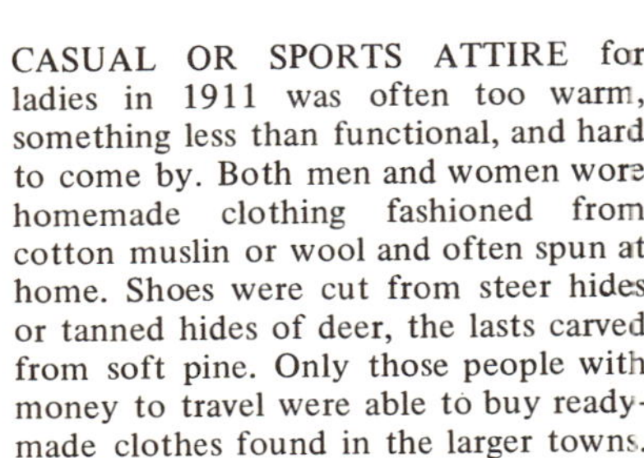

CASUAL OR SPORTS ATTIRE for ladies in 1911 was often too warm, something less than functional, and hard to come by. Both men and women wore homemade clothing fashioned from cotton muslin or wool and often spun at home. Shoes were cut from steer hides or tanned hides of deer, the lasts carved from soft pine. Only those people with money to travel were able to buy ready-made clothes found in the larger towns.

INDIAN BEACH, north of Whitaker Bayou and along Sarasota Bay, truly was one of the most beautiful wooded waterfront areas in Sarasota. The Indian Beach Land Company around 1913 did not spare the superlatives in publicizing it, either, publishing a 60-page booklet of photographs, essays, and testimonials about the area. The booklet made the most of name-dropping: "In this beautiful subdivision are 93 of the prettiest located lots to be found on the entire bay, nearby the palatial homes of wealthy northern tourists who spend their winters here. Among those in our immediate vicinity are the Ringling Brothers of circus fame; Col. C. N. Thompson of Buffalo Bill's Wild West; D. L. Wooster, wealthy manufacturer of Cincinnati; Mrs. Admiral Jack Philips, whose husband will be recalled as the commander of the battleship *Texas* of Spanish war fame, and Mrs. Potter Palmer, Chicago society leader, which aggregate over a million of dollars." The booklet then urged the reader to take advantage of having such good neighbors by buying a lot "for small monthly payments you won't miss."

HORSING AROUND with the town's new hook and ladder wagon in 1911. The photo was taken in front of J. W. Harvey's blacksmith shop on Main between Lemon and Orange.

FORERUNNER OF PIPED-IN WATER for businesses and homes was this "Economy Water System" built about 1911. Before this date, the town had to depend on water from wells and cisterns. There were no sewers. Residents approved a $20,000 bond issue in 1911, and before the year ended the business section and central residential section had both water and sewers. The water was obtained from a well drilled near the experimental system above at Lemon and State.

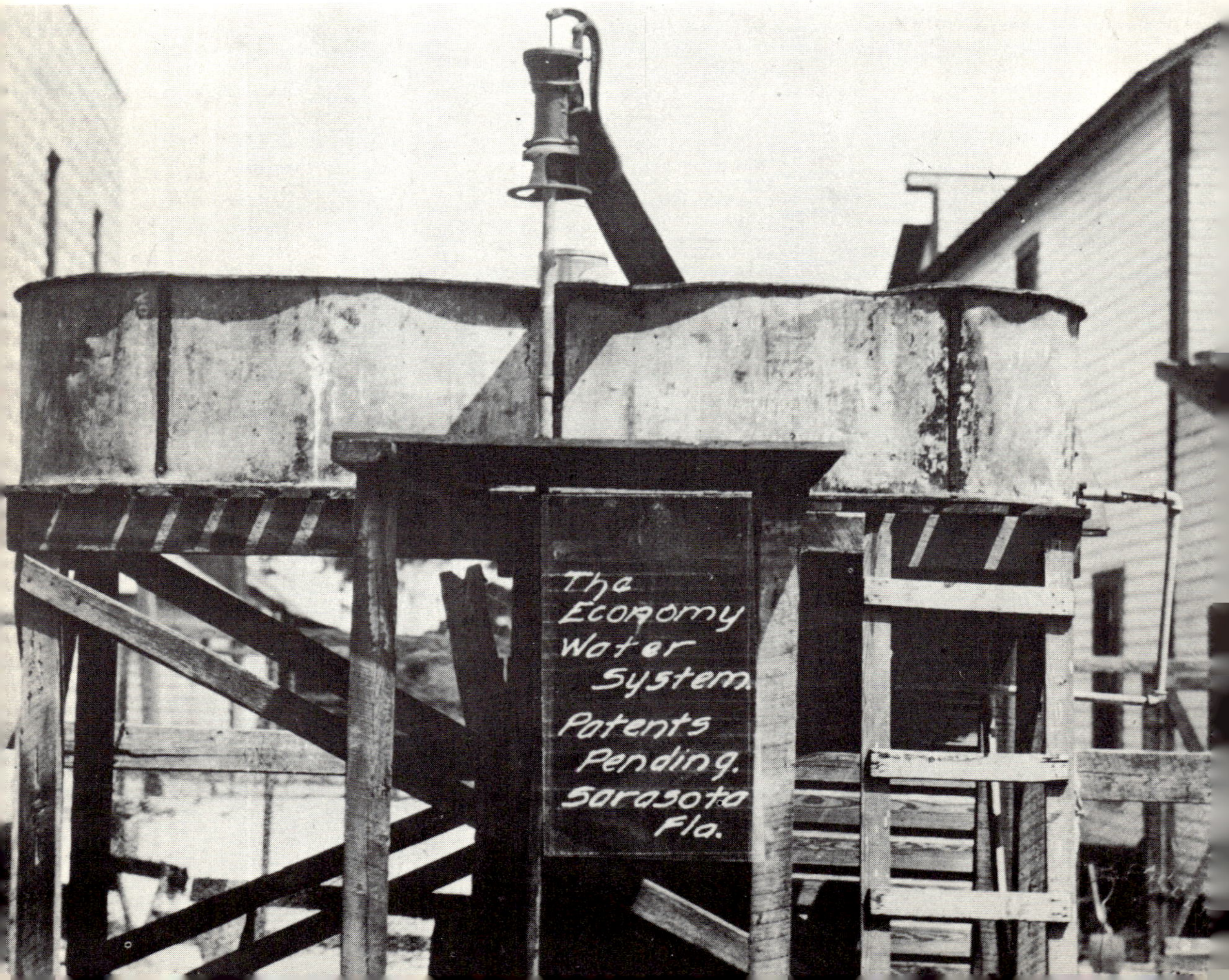

The Economy Water System. Patents Pending. Sarasota Fla.

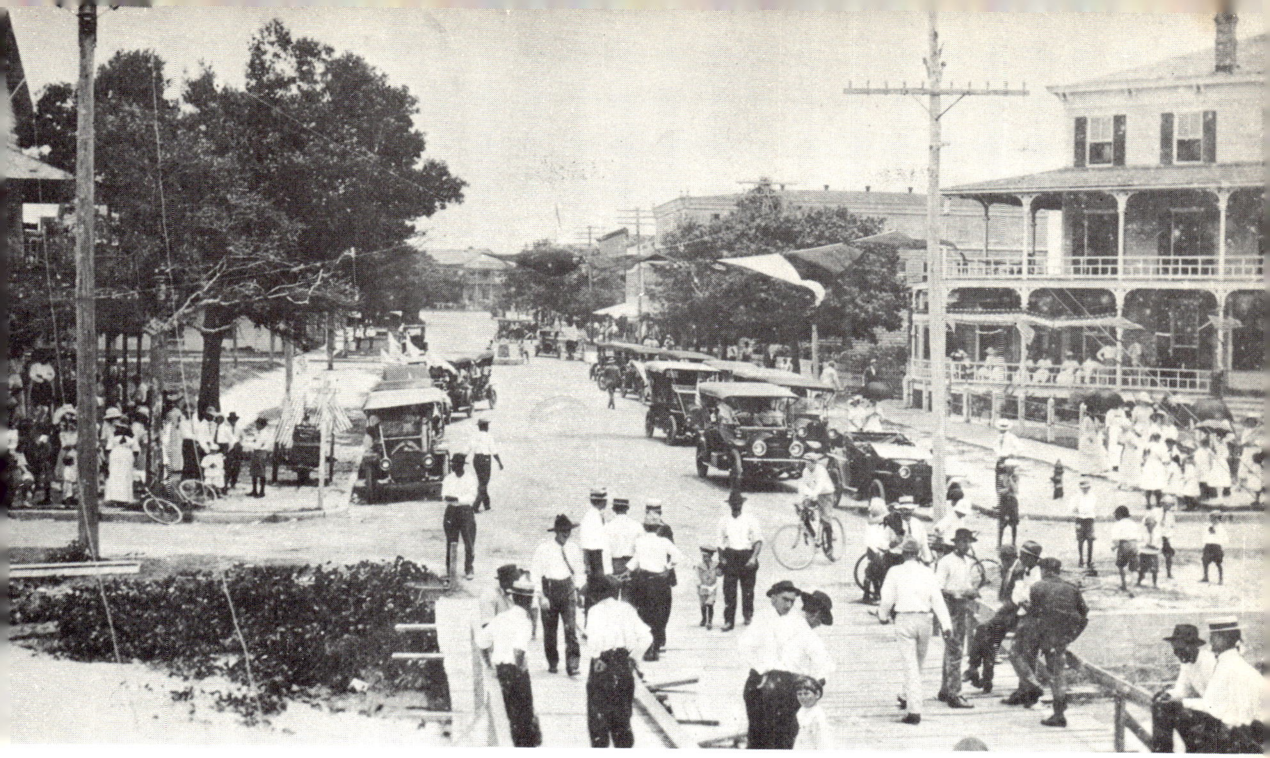

AWAITING A PARADE in 1912, the menfolk mingled in the street and on the pier while the women clustered about the Belle Haven Inn at right. The view is looking toward Five Points up lower Main Street from the pier. Sarasota still was two years away from being designated a city, but great progress had been made since its incorporation as a town in 1903. Sidewalks and curbs were in, telephone lines up, water and sewer lines were being installed, and a seawall along Gulf Stream Avenue was ordered poured. The plentiful water oaks cooled the street, but no one ventured out without a hat or parasol.

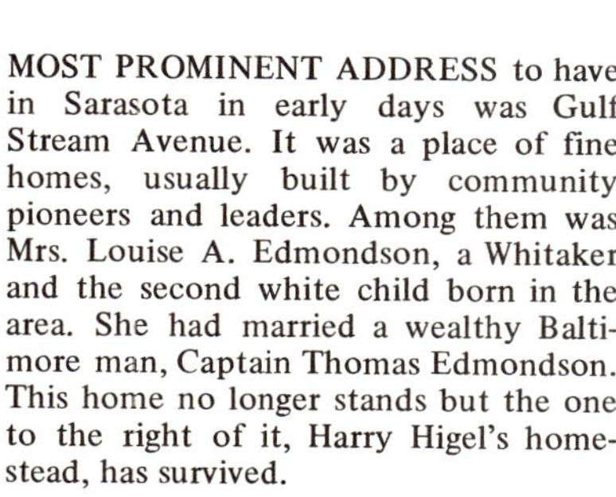

MOST PROMINENT ADDRESS to have in Sarasota in early days was Gulf Stream Avenue. It was a place of fine homes, usually built by community pioneers and leaders. Among them was Mrs. Louise A. Edmondson, a Whitaker and the second white child born in the area. She had married a wealthy Baltimore man, Captain Thomas Edmondson. This home no longer stands but the one to the right of it, Harry Higel's homestead, has survived.

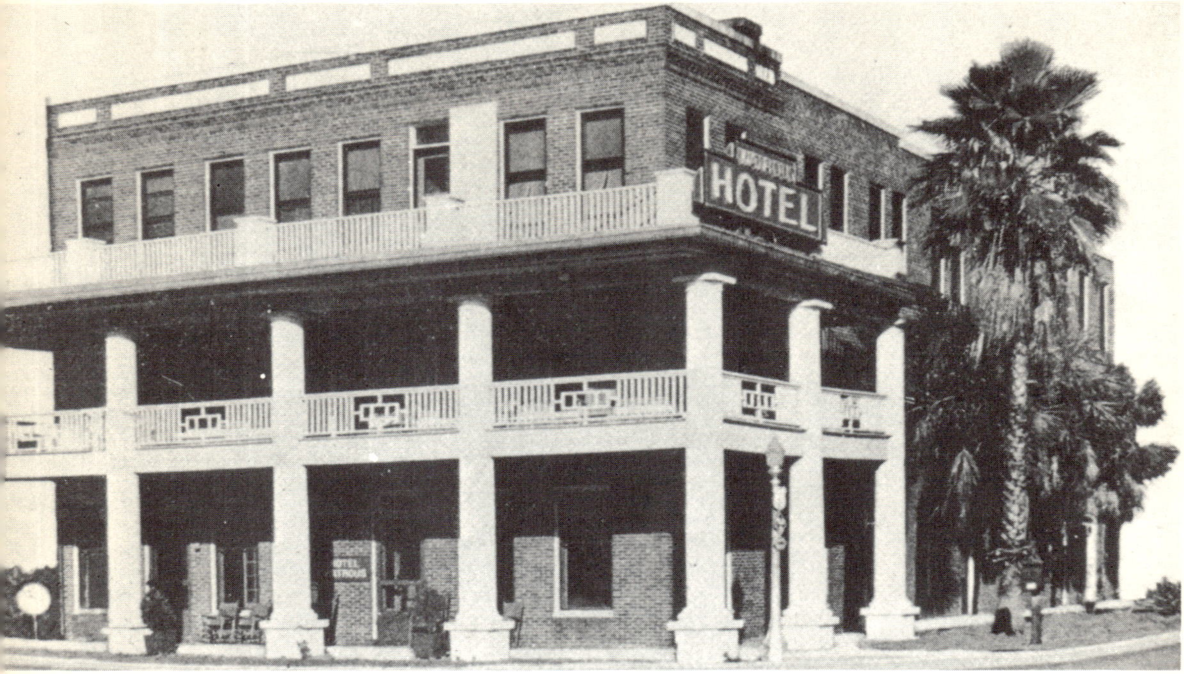

A MAJOR HOTEL and improvement to the downtown in 1912 was construction of the Watrous Hotel on the northwest corner of Main and Palm. It later became the Colonial Hotel, and finally was torn down.

FIVE POINTS LANDMARK for 38 years was the Sarasota House, built at Main and Central in 1886 as a rooming house by the Scot land company. Last owner of the hotel was J. H. Lord, who bought it for $3,000 in 1903. The previous owner paid $500 for it three years earlier. Lord kept the Sarasota House until 1924, when he tore it down for the site of a bank, the First Bank & Trust Co., now the Palmer National Bank & Trust Co.

A FULL THREE STORIES HIGH, the Tonnelier Building in 1912 became the town's tallest and most modern building. Occupants were the Palms Hotel, with 38 rooms, and the Palms Theater, the first indoor theater in the area. Considered fireproof because of its brick veneer walls, the Tonnelier building failed to prove it when the city suffered its worst fire in 1915. An old wooden structure at Main and Pineapple, used as a town meeting hall and church, caught fire, and flames leaped down the north side of lower Main Street. A shoe repair shop went up, then a 5 & 10 store, then a fruit stand; flames hesitated only briefly against the walls of the Tonnelier before consuming all three stories. Adjoining the Tonnelier was the *Sarasota Times* building. Its presses were too big to be moved, but the fire never got to them. Volunteers contained it, without the help of the city's new fire engine; it was on order but not yet delivered. Damage was estimated at $100,000.

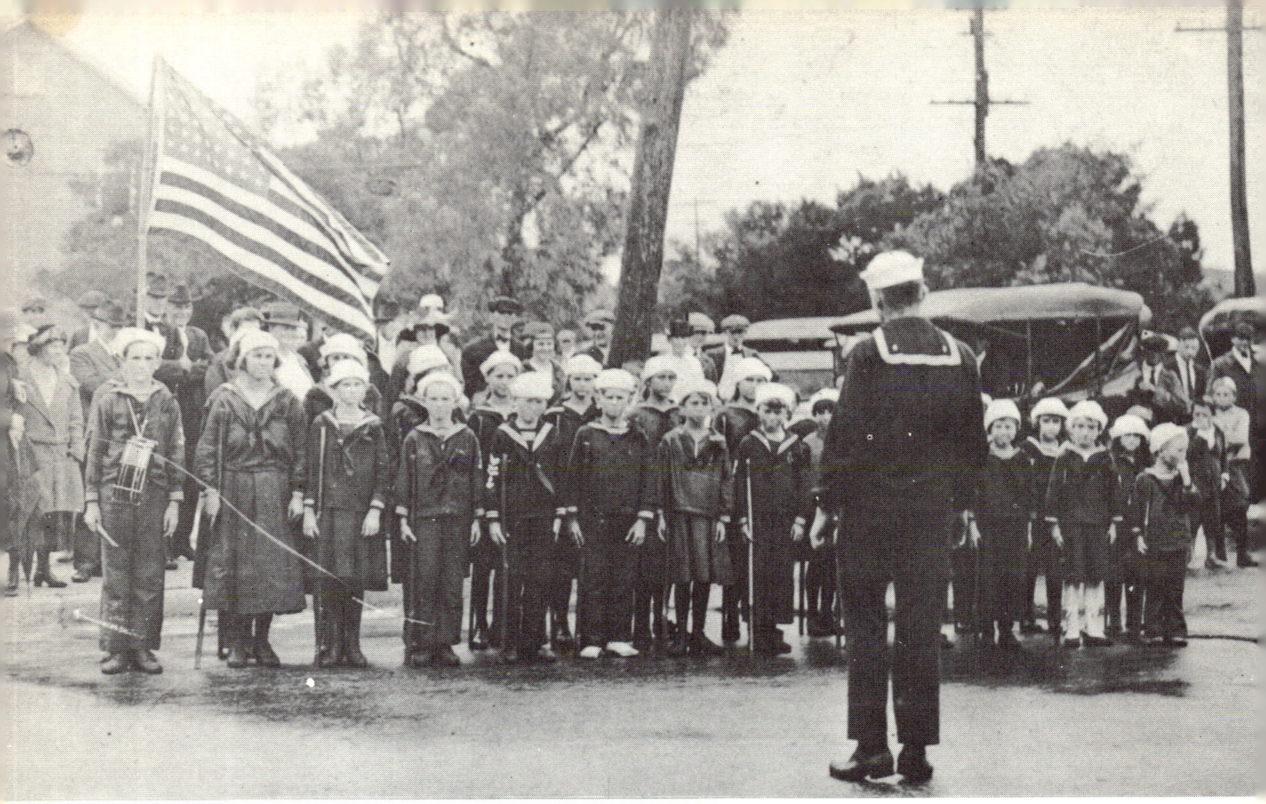

SEA SCOUTS seemed a logical organization in a town nearly surrounded by water. These youngsters were piped aboard the membership roll in the club's first year—1912.

THE TOWN OF SARASOTA as first glimpsed by travelers coming into the area by steamer. The large building is the Belle Haven Inn, formerly the De Soto Hotel, with a new wing. The small cottage in front of it was home to the Hugh K. Browning family, Scot colonists. At left, beyond the lower Main Street pier, is the Halton Sanatorium.

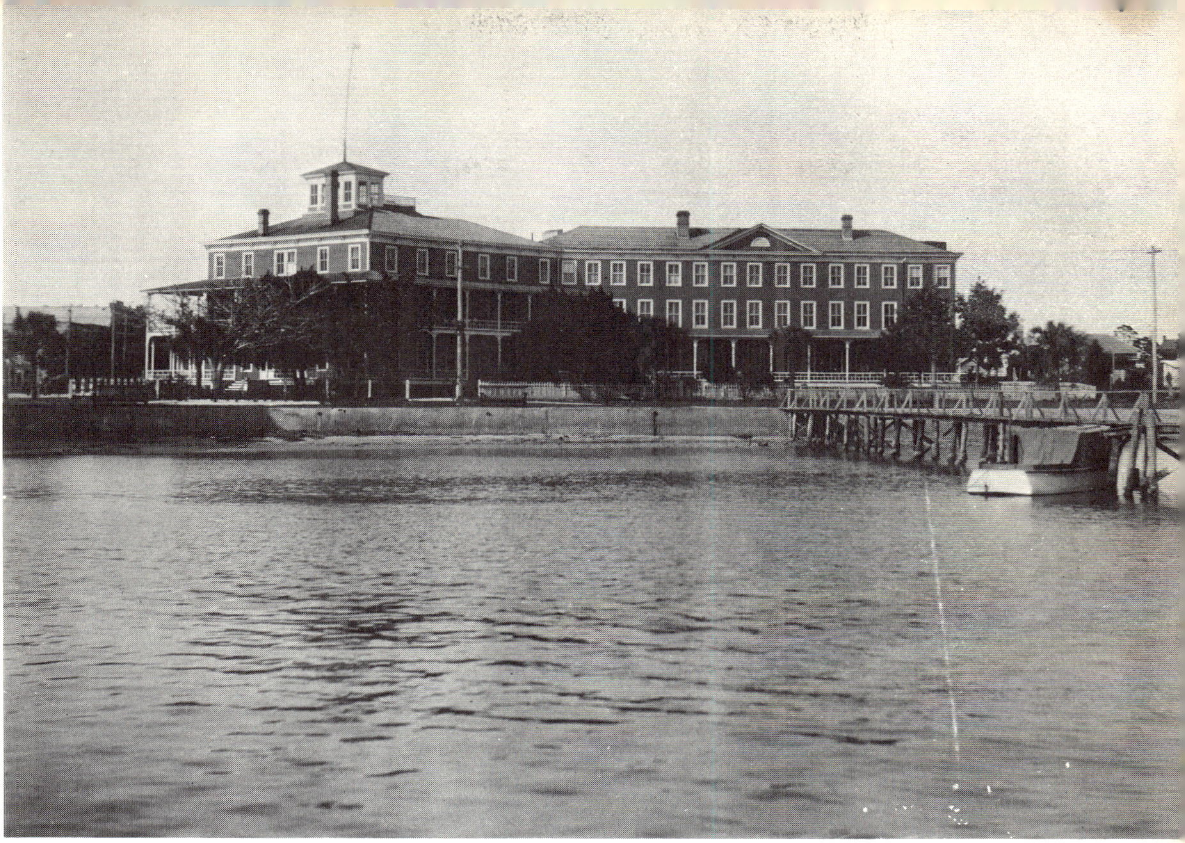

THE BELLE HAVEN INN with its new wing was considered the area' s finest winter resort in 1913, despite frequent changes of ownership and complaints that the cesspools were so inadequate that dinner guests could not get through their meals. The Inn sold in 1914 for $35,000, and then during the boom in 1925 for a reported price of $500,000.

HE BELLE HAVEN INN

SARASOTA. FLORIDA

Has been thoroughly renovated and is under new management. Large, airy rooms, single or en suite, with or without fire, and private sulphur baths. Large spacious verandas, overlooking beautiful Sarasota Bay. Is situated immediately on the bay shore, and is in sight of the rolling Gulf of Mexico. Large pretty lawns and pretty park. Tennis and croquet, also free row boats for the guest. Fishing, boating and bathing the best, hunting good. House open all the year round.

Rates by the day $2.50 to $3.50. Special rates by the week and for families. For further information apply to ***H. S. SMITH, Proprietor***

OBVIOUSLY NOT ESCAPE-PROOF was the Sarasota jail in 1911, nailed together at Lemon and 2nd Street. Hot summer days in the jail were reported worse than capital punishment.

SOUTH GULF STREAM AVENUE in 1912, looking north. Because seaweed and debris often littered the shore along Gulf Stream, the town council decreed in 1910 that seawalls must be built at the expense of the property owners.

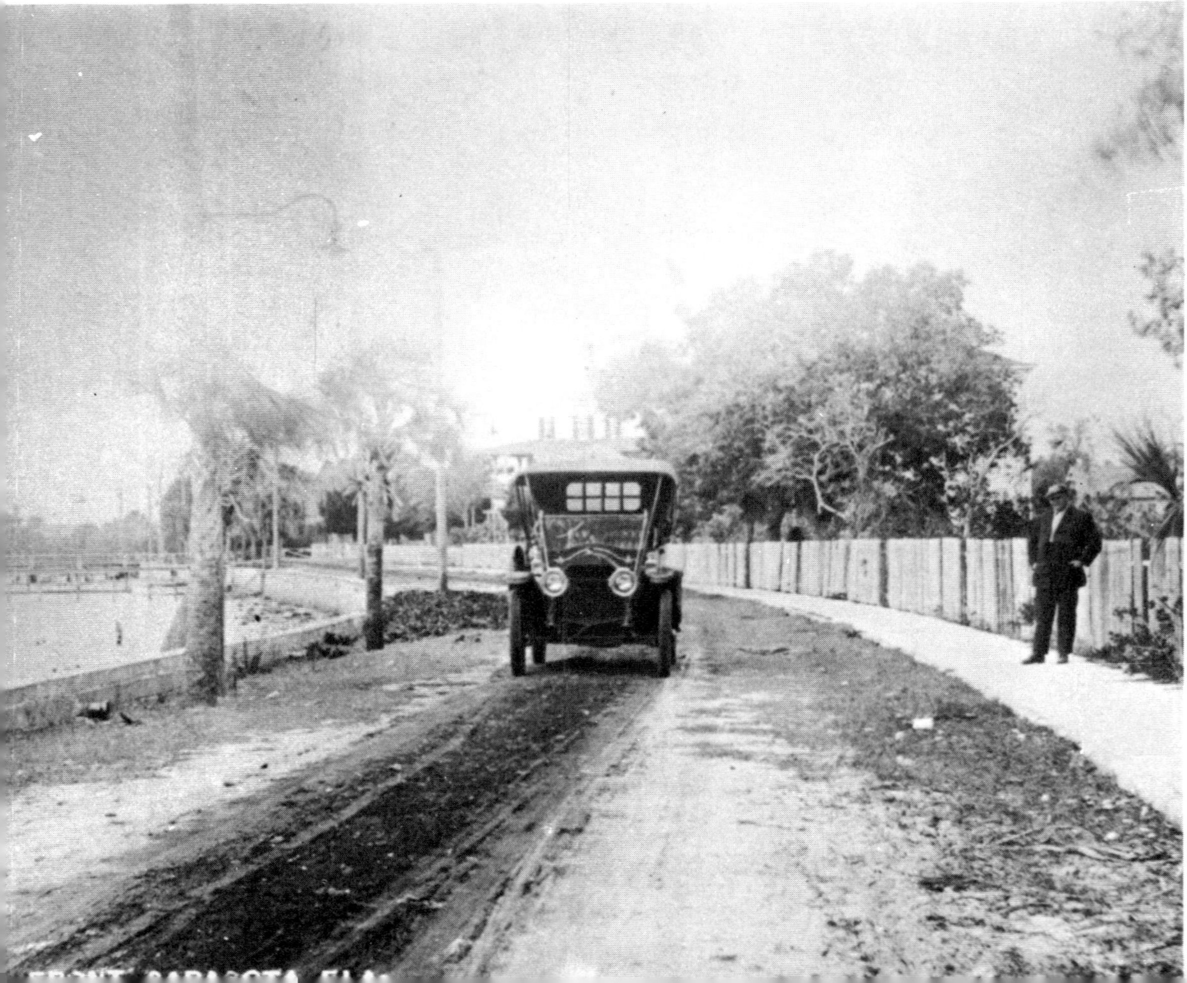

BOASTING CAPITAL OF $25,000, the First National Bank of Sarasota opened in 1913. It was organized two years earlier by Owen Burns, as the Citizens Bank of Sarasota.

SARASOTA HIGH SCHOOL, a "grand all-brick" building costing $23,000, was erected in 1913. It contained 11 recitation rooms and an auditorium, enough to take care of the town's needs at least 10 years, said school officials. But when the Fall term began, more than 350 children enrolled, and the school was overcrowded the first day. Some grade shuffling was done and the following year the school no longer was just a high school, but a junior high and elementary school as well. And the old, abandoned wooden school it replaced was put into use in back of the new brick school. Grades 1-3 were held in the old school, and 4-12 in the new building. The unexpectedly large enrollment was not the school's only problem; teacher turnover plagued it, also. Salaries were blamed, the teachers contending they couldn't live on the $50 to $55 monthly pay.

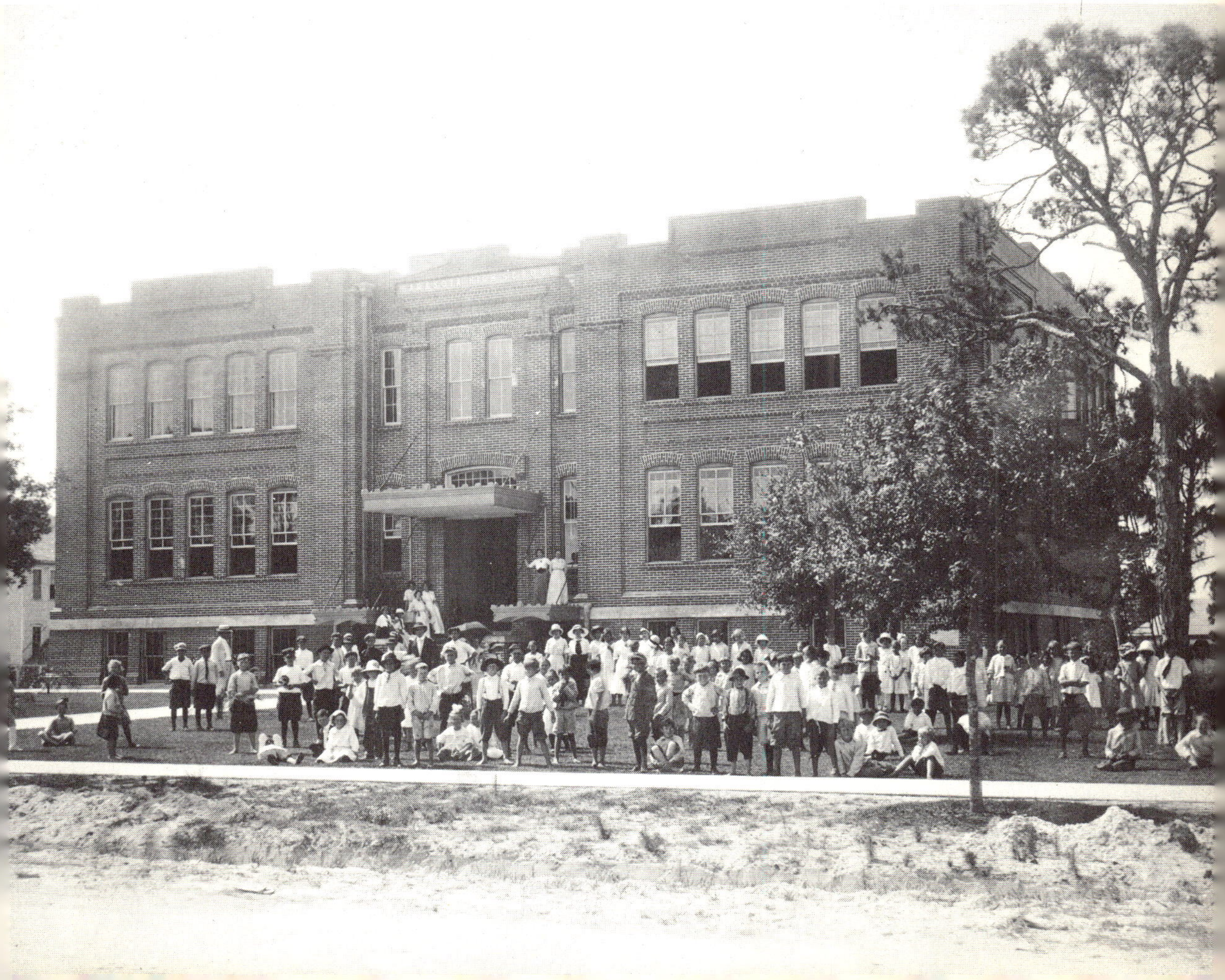

A PUBLIC WORK DAY was declared November 6, 1913, by Mayor Harry Higel to beautify the newly created park at the foot of Main Street on South Gulf Stream Avenue. Owen Burns and George L. Thacker supplied loads of black dirt, with Burns turning over his team of mules (*above*) to do the heavy clearing work. While the men graded the sandy area and spread on the rich top soil, the ladies (*below*) planted plugs of grass and flowers and served refreshments at the Belle Haven Inn. Workers' thirsts were alleviated by youngsters who had formed a drinking-water bucket brigade.

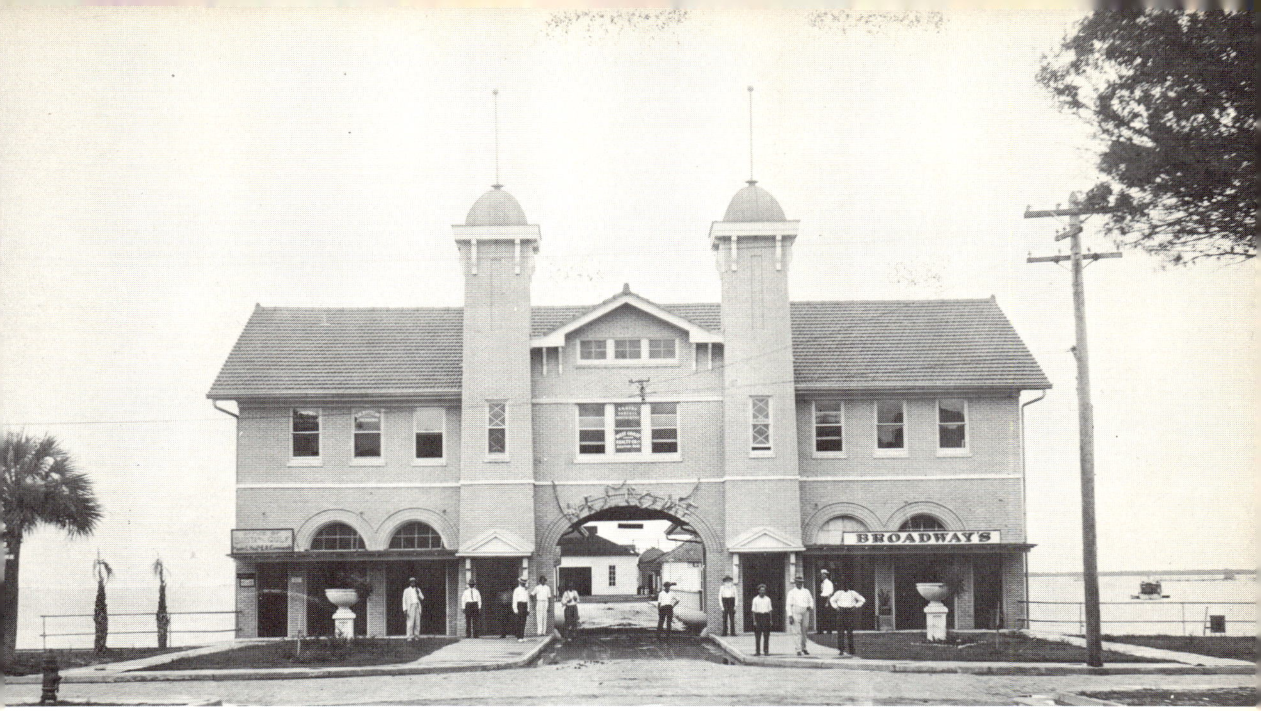

THE HOVER ARCADE, more familiar in later years to Sarasotans as City Hall, was put up in 1913 by Dr. W. E. Hover and his two brothers from Ohio. They bought the entire pier from Harry Higel, who had offered it to the town for $5,000 but was turned down. The Hovers put $20,000 into the project, extending the pier and erecting the archway building at its entrance. One wing was designed for a moving picture house, the other housed Dave Broadway's restaurant and ice cream parlor. Four years later the city did buy it for a City Hall; it paid the Hovers $40,000.

SARASOTA YACHT AND AUTOMOBILE CLUB immediately became a social hub upon completion in 1913 on North Gulf Stream Avenue. The club's history, however, goes back to 1907 when Harry Higel built the first Sarasota Yacht Club on the north end of Siesta Key. Too remote, the clubhouse never became popular. A two-story boat house on Cedar Point was purchased, therefore, by the club's incorporators in 1912. It served its purpose until the members could buy the 100-foot lot on Gulf Stream Avenue with the square-tiered building shown above. When John Ringling bought up real estate in 1917, one of his first acquisitions was the club and its grounds, including Cedar Point. Mable Ringling, his wife, remodeled the building in 1923 in order to convert it into the Sunset Apartments. Fifty-one years after its opening, in 1964, the building was leveled.

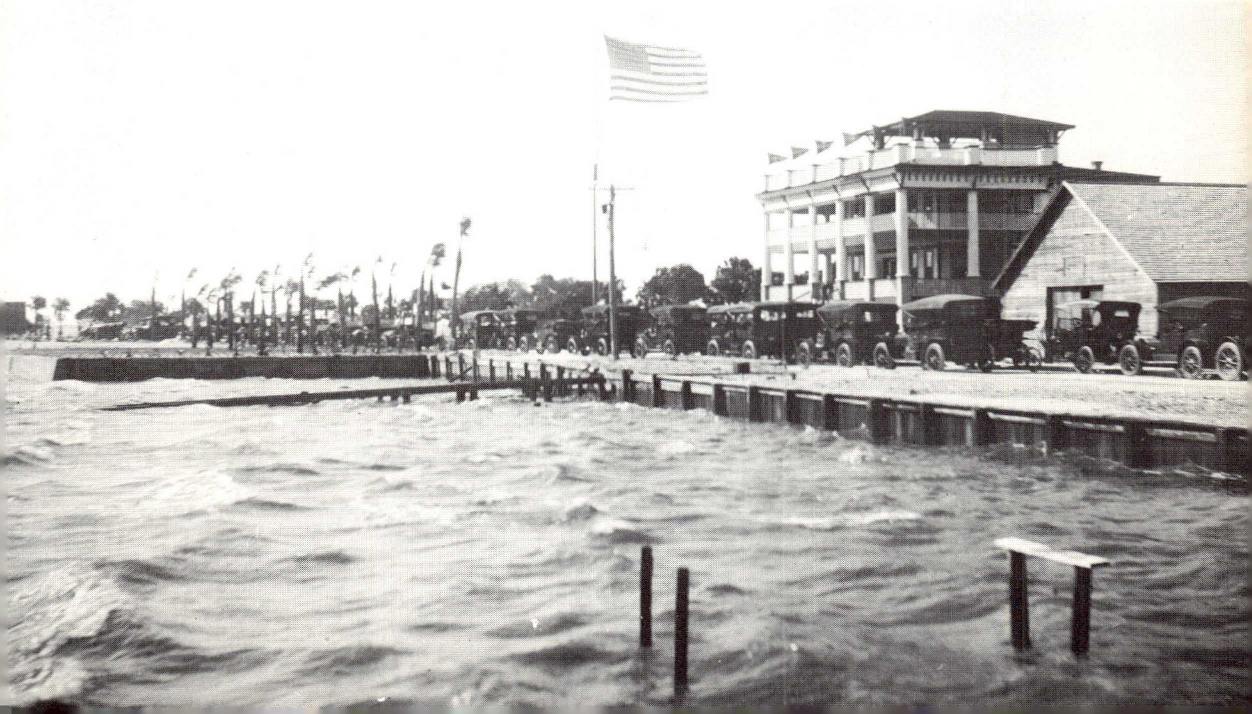

METHODIST Church on South Pineapple Avenue (*center*), built in 1914 at a cost of $10,000. St. Martha's Roman Catholic Church (*left*), erected in 1911 on Adelia. First Presbyterian Church (*right*), dedicated in 1913 on Orange Avenue.

BOUNTIFUL CATCHES OF FISH like this were often used by real estate and promotional men in advertising booklets to sell the Sarasota area to northern visitors. The 1914 photo, taken in front of a newly completed Bay Island Hotel on Siesta Key, includes many town notables: A. B. Edwards (second from the right) and then Mayor Harry Higel (third from the right).

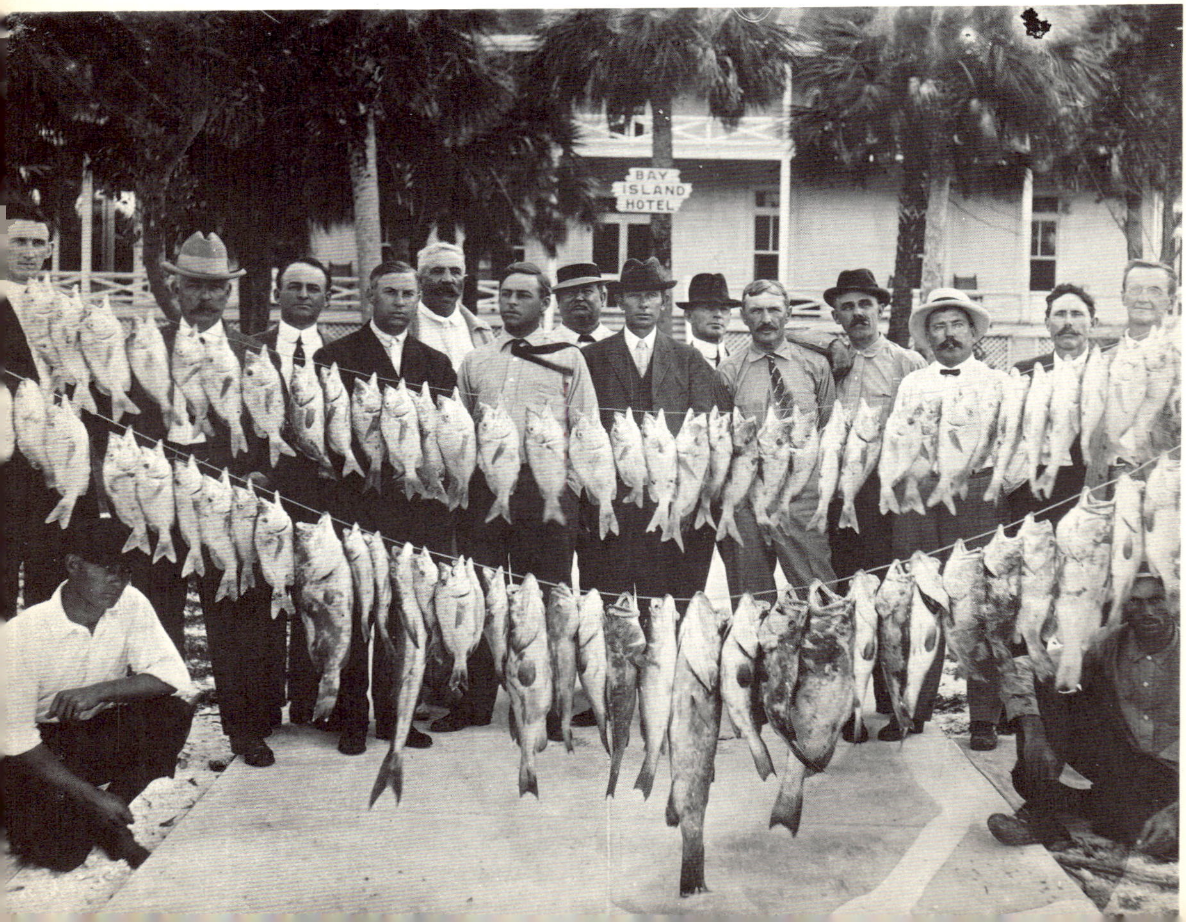

FRUITVILLE ROAD, a rather scenic drive in the old days, was not much good in the rainy season. Actually, none of the roads south of Tampa before 1911 were satisfactory to residents, and Sarasota officials decreed in 1914 that it was time to provide an adequate road system in the rural area. A bond issue was proposed, approved by voters, and by 1916 construction was underway on nine-foot wide roads to the east toward Fruitville and Bee Ridge, south toward Osprey and Venice and north toward Bradenton.

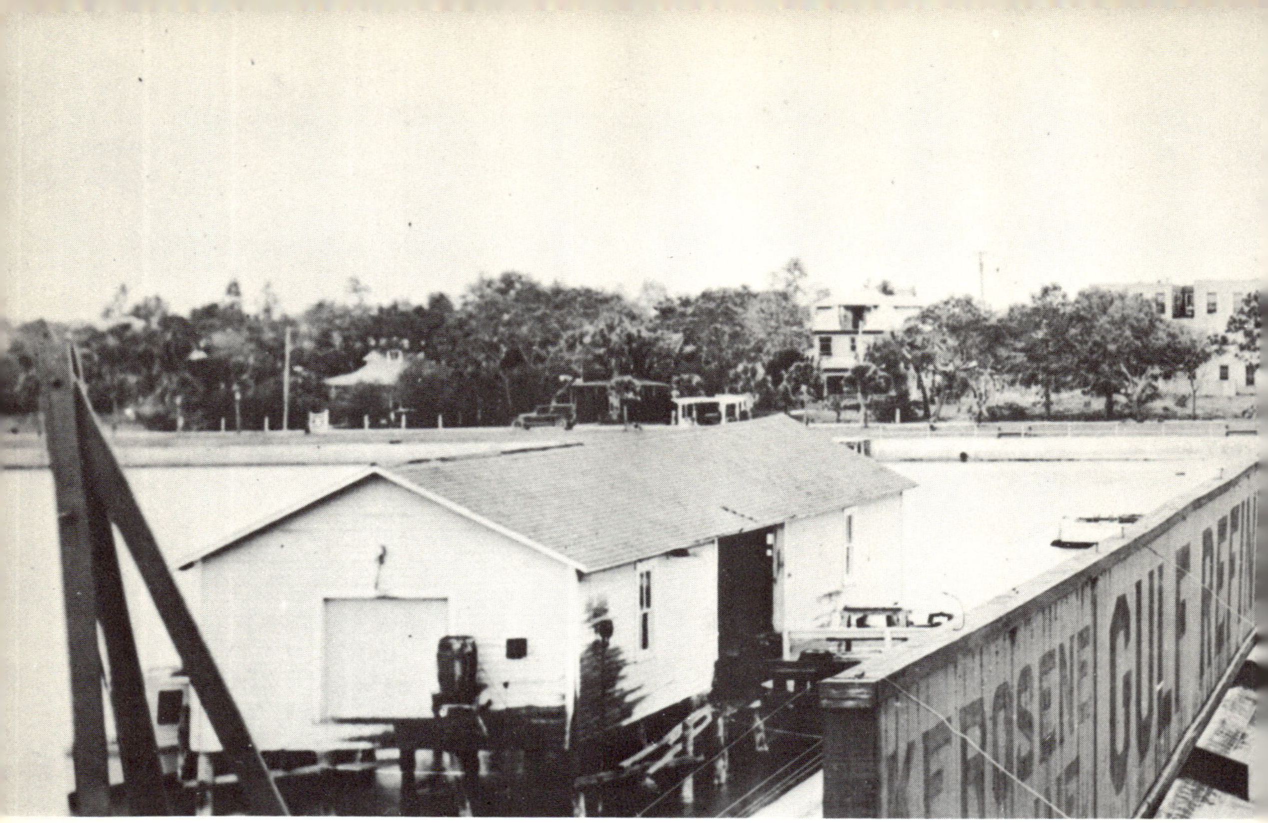

COMMERCE FIRST DEVELOPED out on the piers in Sarasota Bay so that by 1916 the wharf at the end of lower Main Street (*above*) took on the appearance of an early-day industrial park. It housed machine shops, fish houses, auto and motor supplies, and even a refining company. The 1921 storm washed away most of businesses.

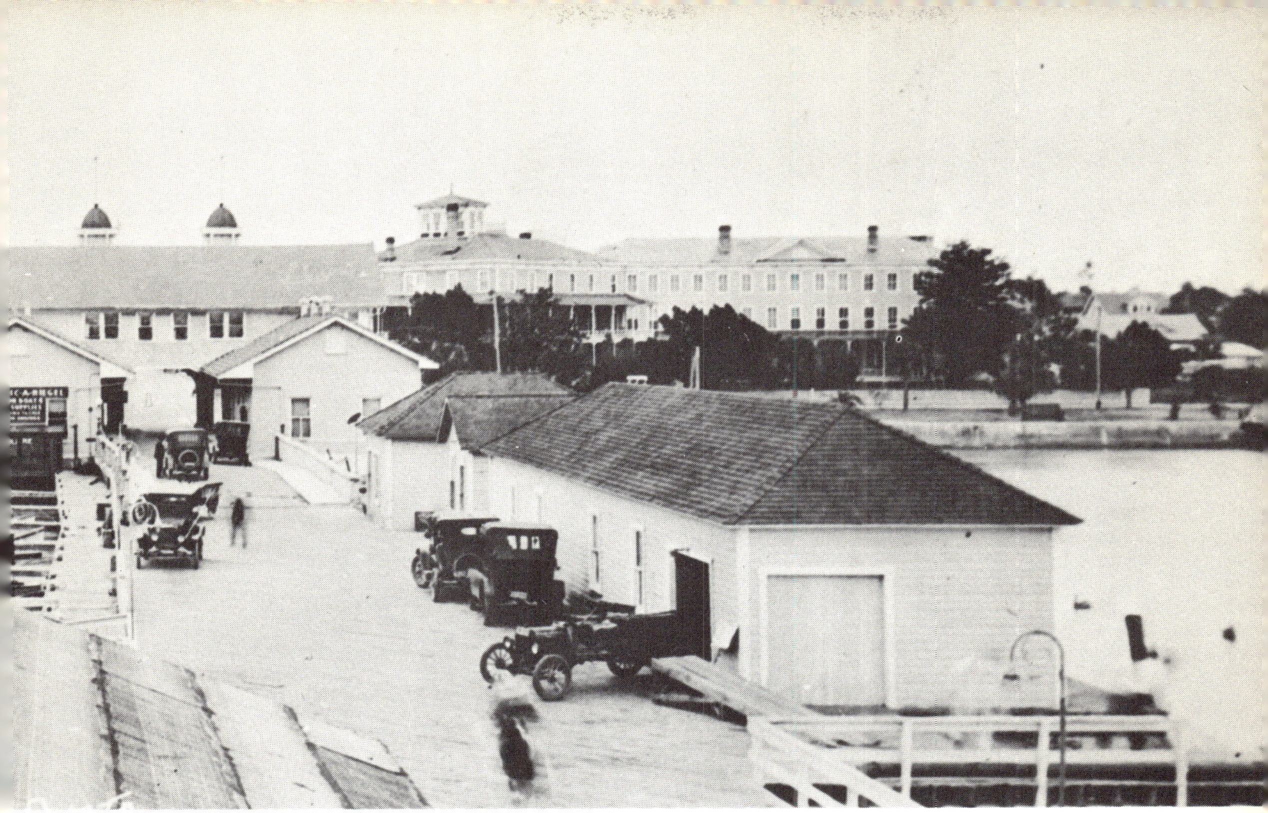

A NEW YACHT BASIN (*below*) for Sarasota in 1916 was created at McClellan Park. Donors were the McClellan sisters, here waving to the first boat out of the basin.

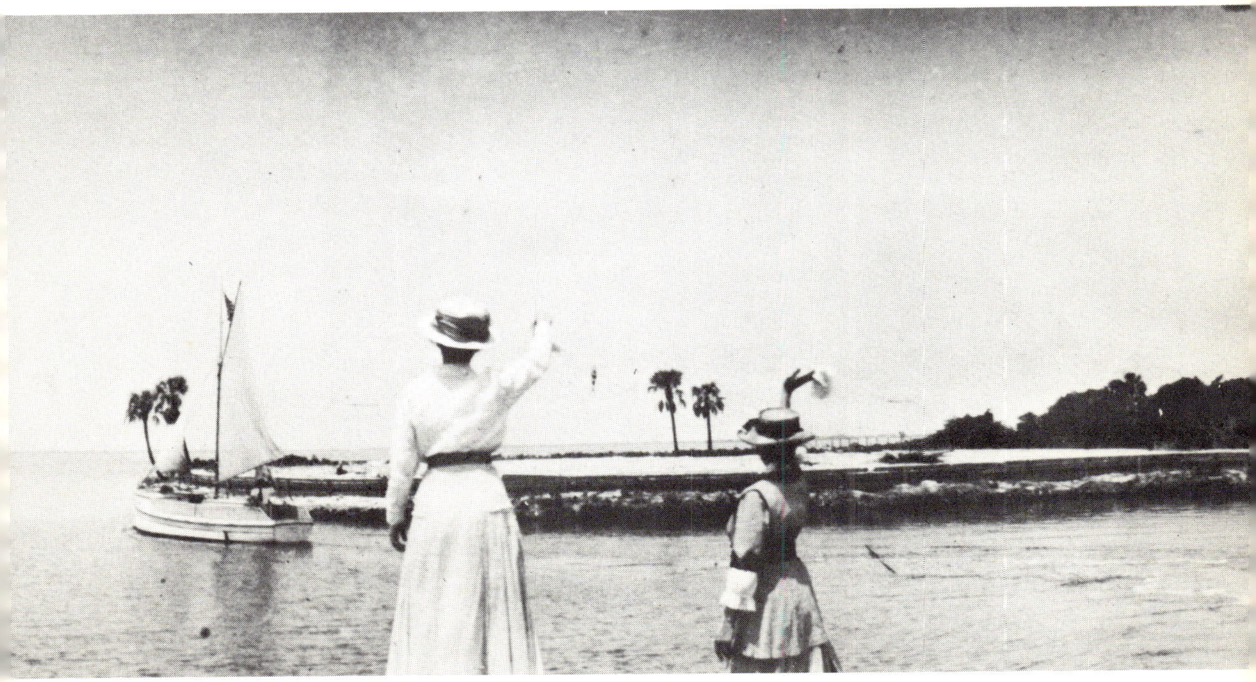

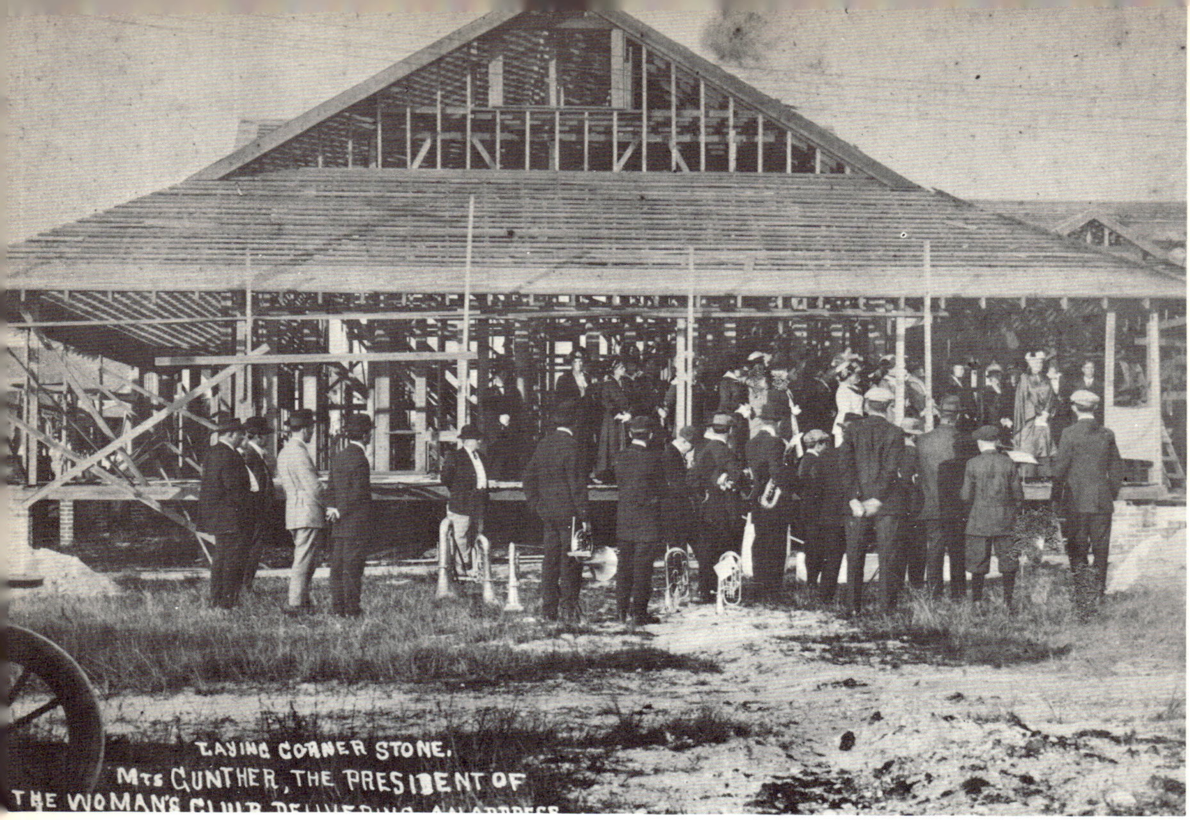

LAYING CORNER STONE.
Mrs GUNTHER, THE PRESIDENT OF
THE WOMAN'S CLUB

THE WOMAN'S CLUB has been active in community service ever since 1913. Its own biggest moment occurred in 1915 when the cornerstone was placed for the clubhouse on Palm Avenue and Park. City officials, even the band, turned out for the occasion (*above*). Among the notables attending (*left*) were Ralph Caples (left) and the club's president, Mrs. F. H. Guenther (third lady from left). Charter members numbered 63. The clubhouse still stands on its original site.

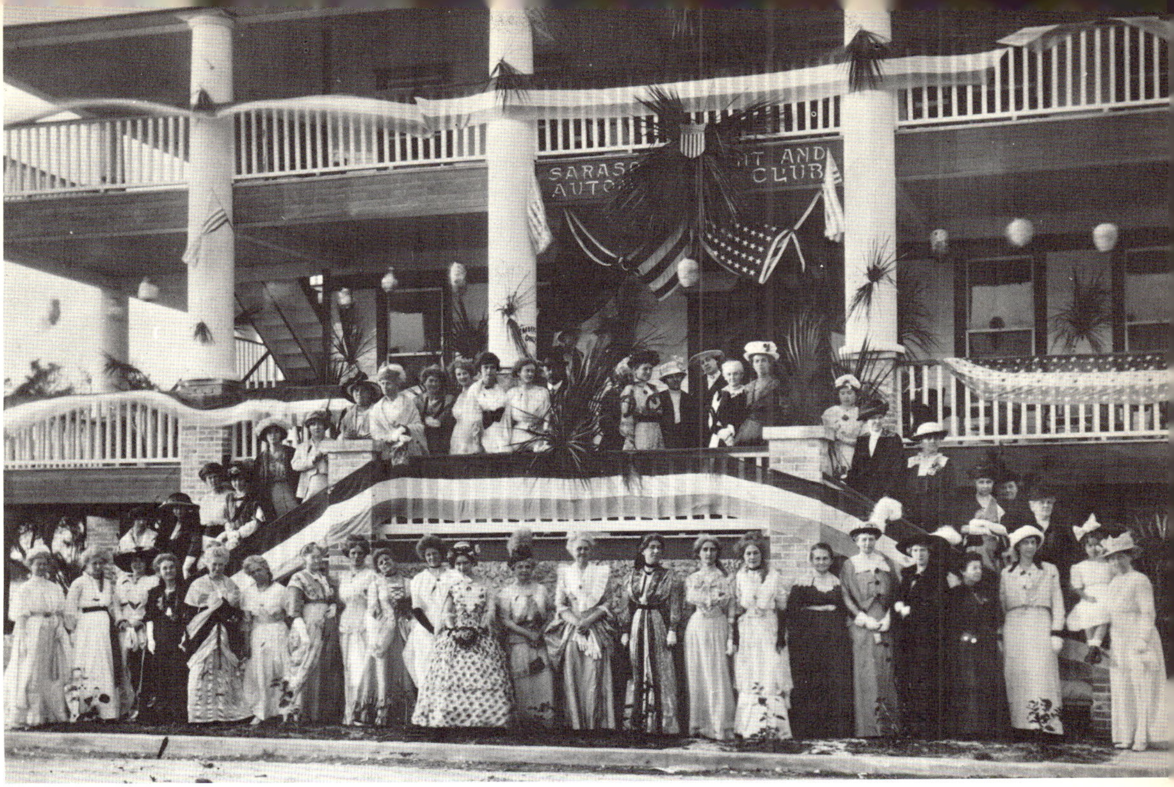

THE TOWN'S LADIES needed a place for meetings and socials in 1914, a year before their own Woman's Club house was built, so they gathered either at the Sarasota Yacht and Automobile Club (*above*) on North Gulf Stream Avenue or the two-story wooden schoolhouse on Main. The costumes worn by the ladies reveal the event—the Colonial Tea.

MOTHER GOOSE PARTY given at the Woman's Club in 1916 was one of several costume parties staged by the clubwomen. Although popular social events, such parties often were only a relaxer for the women who during the year, and for many years, worked at beautifying the city. It was the Woman's Club members who planted more than 250 coconut palms along the waterfront, that pushed the program for sidewalks and hard-surfaced roads in town, and that pleaded through the newspaper columns for residents to "plant grass and shrubs which bloom the whole year 'round."

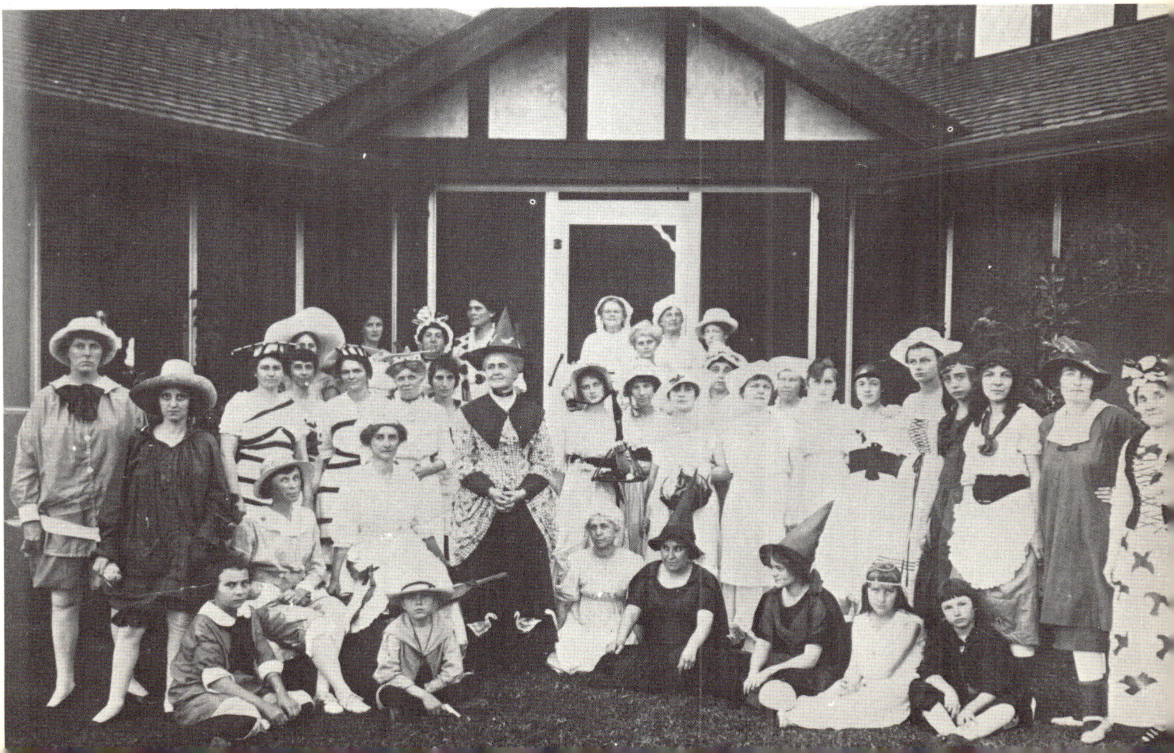

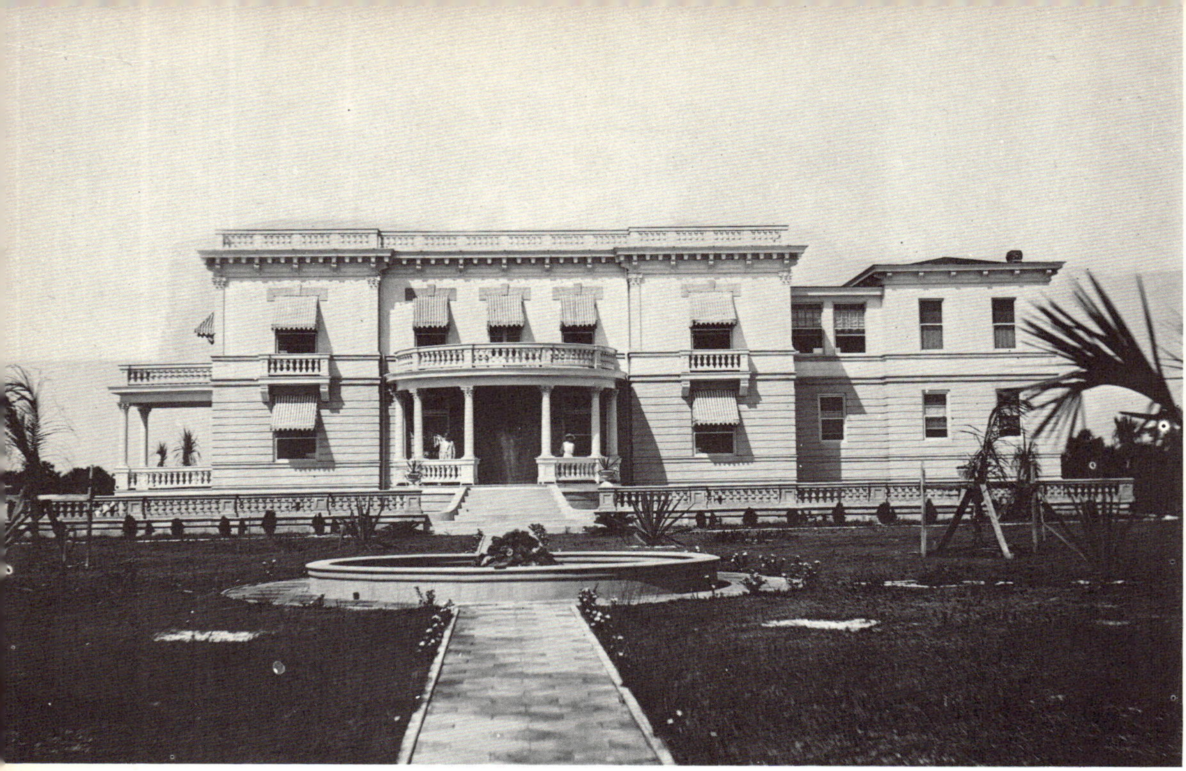

NEW EDZELL CASTLE, built in 1914 on Bird Key by Thomas M. Worcester, a retired manufacturer from Cincinnati. The Worcesters named it after the ancestral home in Scotland of Mrs. Worcester. John Ringling later bought the house and the entire key. His only sister, Ida Ringling North, and her family lived in the house until shortly before it was purchased by the Arvida Corporation, which tore it down and developed the key as an exclusive subdivision.

TRINITY COMMANDERY 16, Sarasota Commandery, Knights Templar, in 1916.

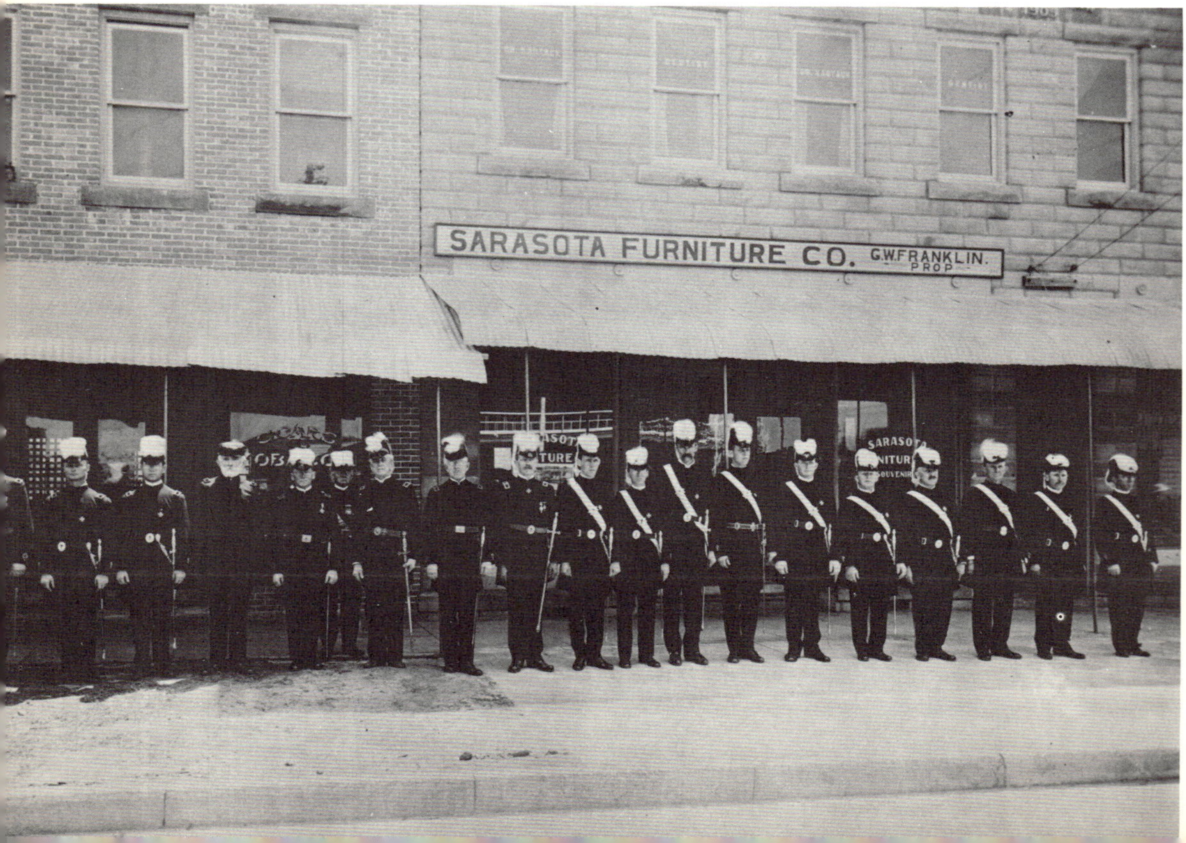

FOLKS TOOK PRIDE in fire trucks and Sarasotans were no exception. In 1915 they got a new LaFrance engine, a combination chemical pump and hose truck. The engine could pump 750 gallons a minute and throw a stream of water over a building 100 feet high.

A TERRIBLE EXPENSE to the city in 1915 but a necessary one, reported the city council, was purchase of modern fire-fighting equipment. Hit by a half dozen fires the past two years, the city acquired a $9,000 pump and hose truck (*below at right*), bringing its apparatus inventory to three pieces. A racy, low-slung speedster (*right*) was bought for Fire Chief Henry Behrens. It was for his use, in addition to his $75 a month salary.

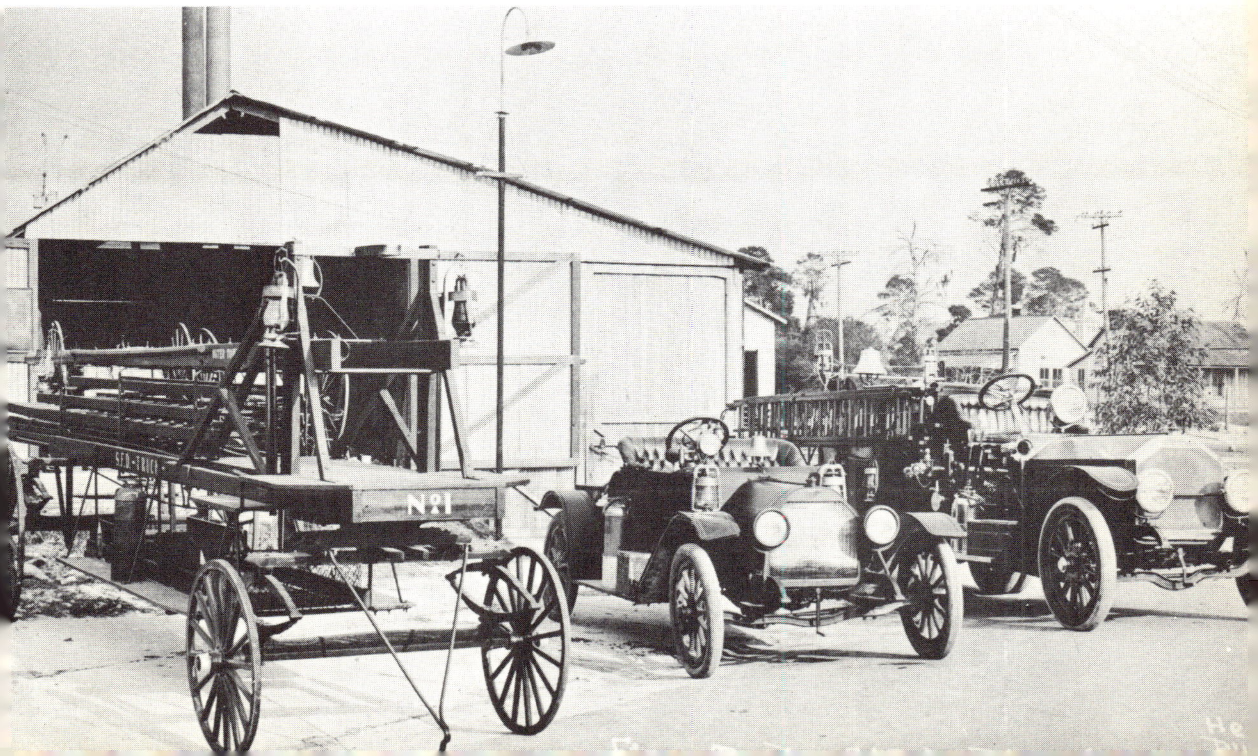

THE WOODS AROUND SARASOTA were a hunter's paradise, as the early Indians well knew. Zeke Messer (*left*) and his companions bagged these deer and turkeys south of town in 1915. Pioneers recall there never was a time, winter or summer, when one could not go out into the woods and "shoot a meal" for his family out of the nearest thicket.

THE TOURING MINSTRELS of Sarasota, accustomed to playing before full houses at home and on the road, was a non-profit group organized by Dr. Jack Halton. Performers were members of the Sarasota Yacht and Automobile Club. They often traveled to St. Petersburg and surrounding communities for benefit performances. The troupers are posing at Five Points in 1916 prior to a trip.

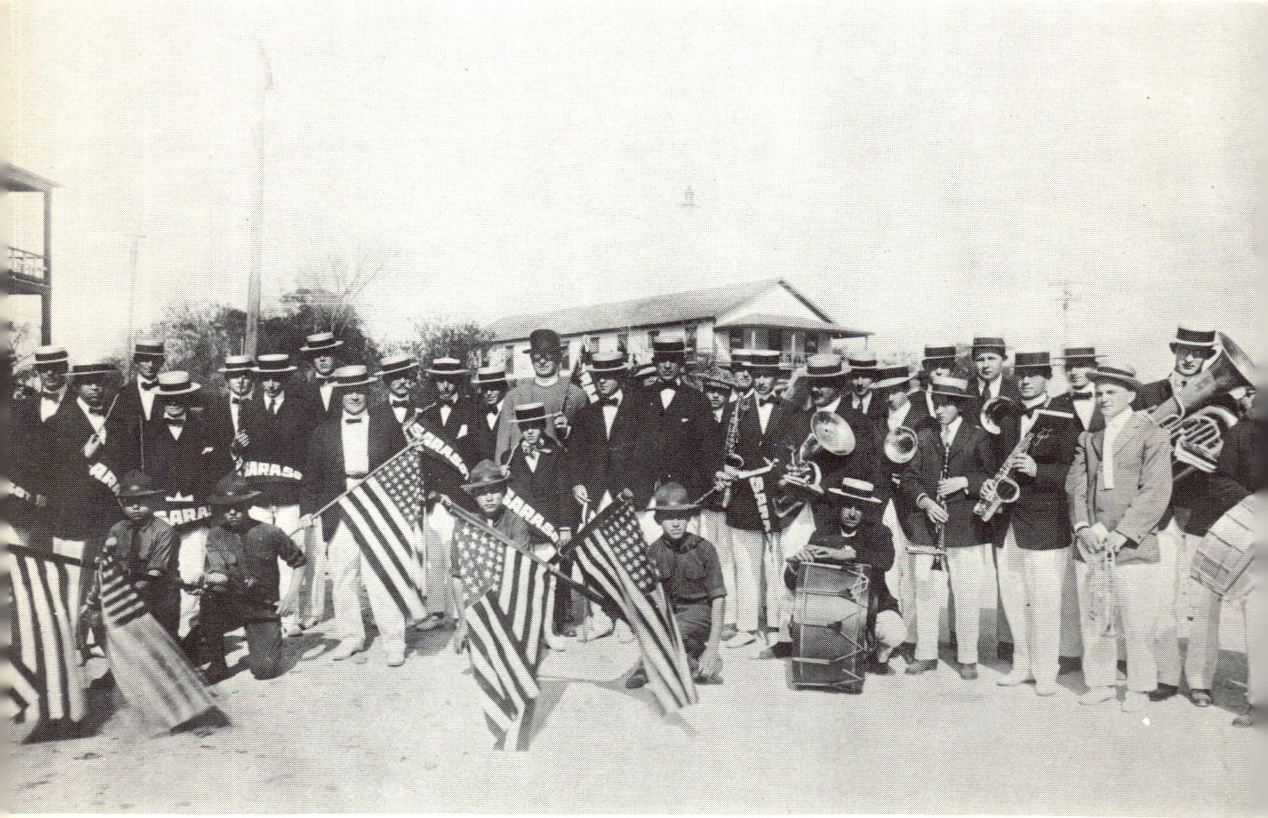

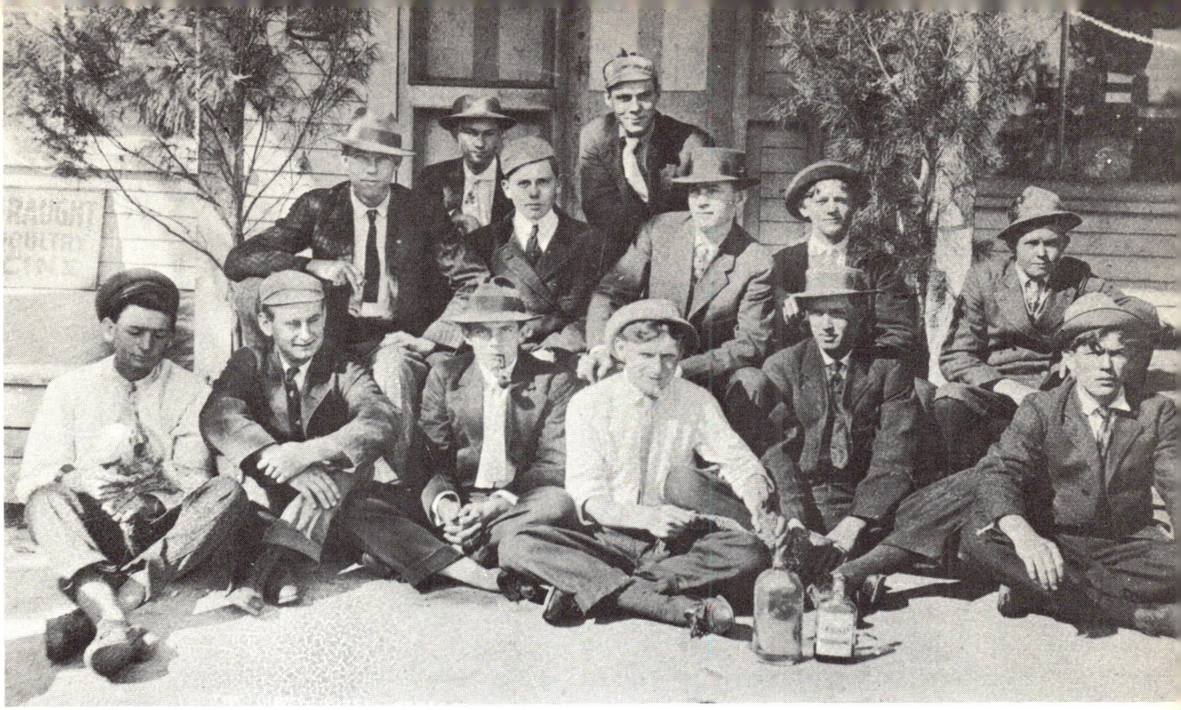

THE DIRTY DOZEN CLUB, a baker's dozen of "rascals" who enjoyed each other's company in 1916. All grew up into respectable citizens, despite the evidence here that most of them smoked, had polished off a bottle and a half of spirits, and that one of them restrains a game cock.

A FULL HOUSE greeted the opening of Sarasota's new theater—the Virginian, on the north side of Main Street where Penney's used to be. The Virginian was established because the city's only theater, in the Hover Arcade on the pier, had been purchased for a City Hall. Movie-goers remember the Virginian as becoming the Sarasota Theater and finally the Ritz Theater. The Sarasota Minstrels opened the Virginian, but two weeks later films started playing, the inaugural movie being a five-reeler called "Jimmy Valentine." An extra attraction was the first installment of the thriller, "The Strange Case of Mary Page."

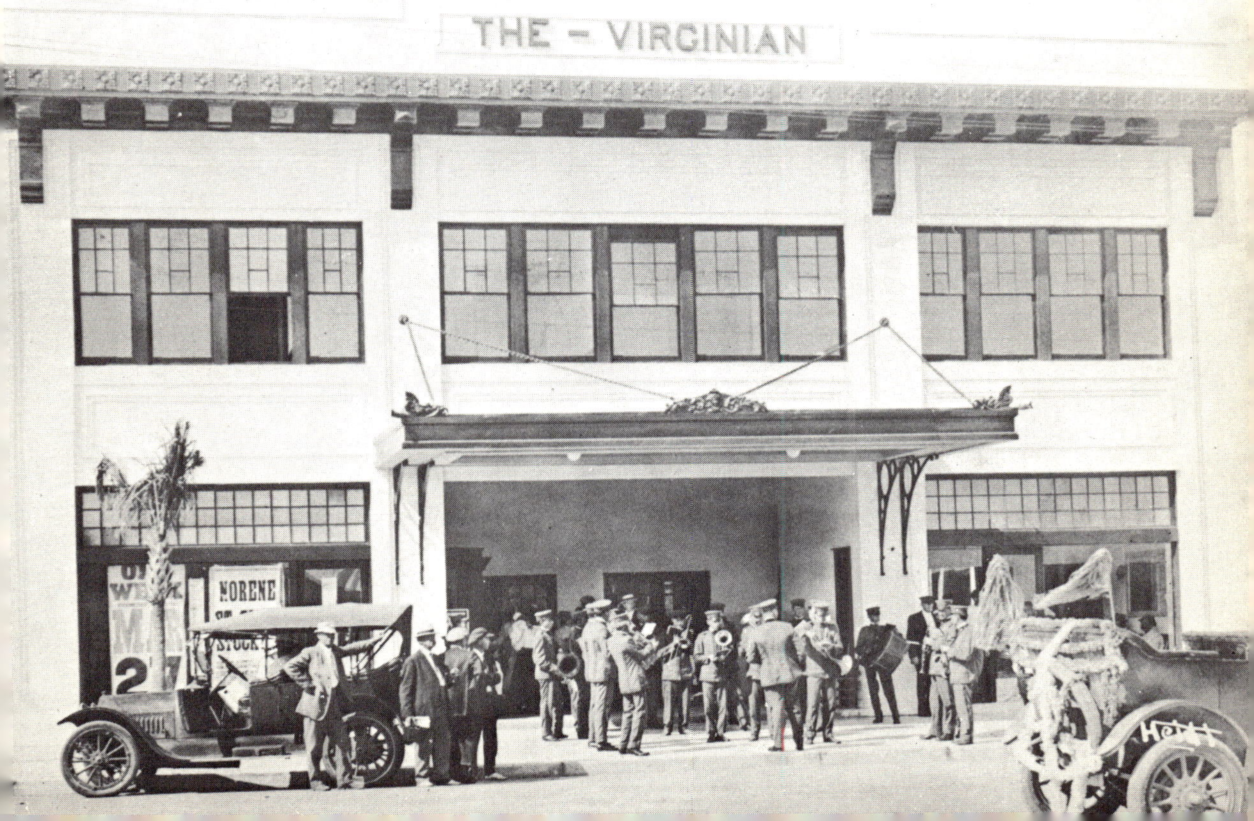

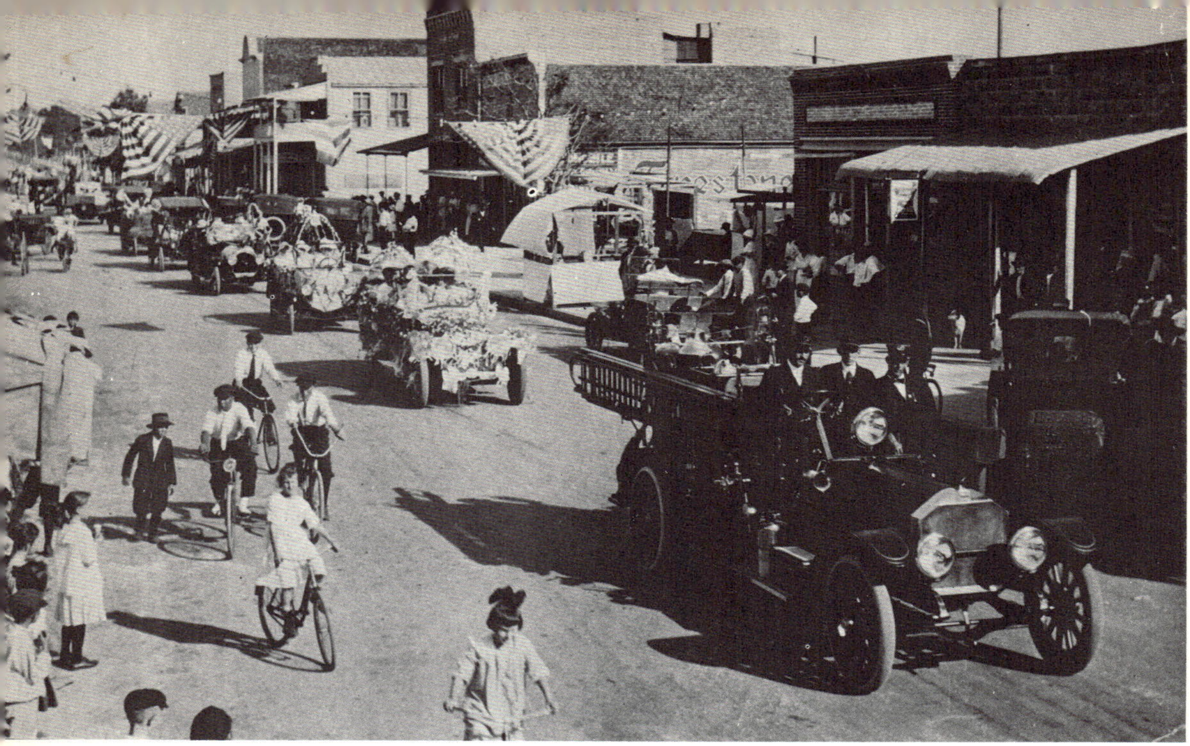

HISTORY RECORDS that explorer Hernando de Soto had no daughter but thanks to George Chapline, a winter visitor with a lively imagination, one was written into a legend that became the basis for Sarasota's annual pageant. Her name: Sara de Soto. According to the story, she was loved by the son of an Indian chief, whom she nursed back to health. When she became ill, the young Indian, Chichi-Okobee, tried nursing her but his efforts failed and she died. She was buried in Sarasota Bay, and Chichi-Okobee and a hundred warriors drowned themselves beside her. The legend caught the fancy of Sarasotans so they created a pageant around it, the first one in 1916. The pageant has been interrupted by two World Wars and a Depression, but an annual celebration has survived in one form or another. In later years the Sara de Soto theme conflicted with neighboring Bradenton's De Soto Celebration, so the city's festival now is known as King Neptune Frolics, and Sara de Soto again has become only a legend.

THE FIRST PAGEANT was an all-out effort that lasted five days (*above*). Bunting was hung, amusement rides were brought into town, concessionaires set up on Main Street, and dozens of races and athletic events encouraged the participation of the residents. Spearing the ring (*left*), a test of horsemanship, was most popular during the 1916 celebration.

A WINNER among the decorated cars in the first celebration parade.

BURIAL AT SEA, the final enactment of a Sara de Soto Pageant.

AFTER THE PARADE: a huge traffic jam at Five Points. The view is looking east on Main Street.

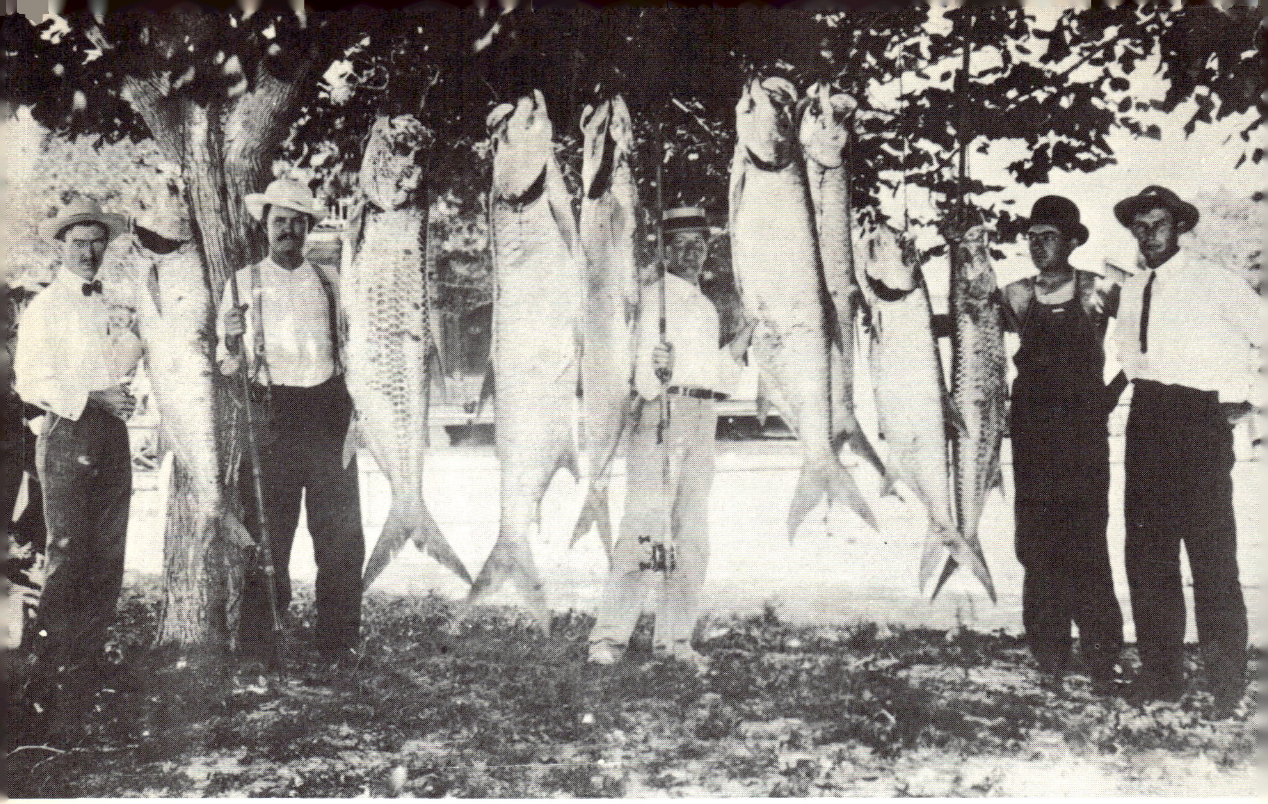

TARPON CAUGHT OFF SARASOTA boggled the minds of northerners visiting the city. Most had never seen such large fish. But to guests at the Belle Haven Inn, the sight above in 1916 was seen almost daily. Catches by people staying at the Inn always were hung in the yard at the hotel.

SUSPENDED FROM ICE TONGS, the large shark was caught by C. W. Mills in 1917. Living relatives say the shark was among the first ones hooked off Roberts Point.

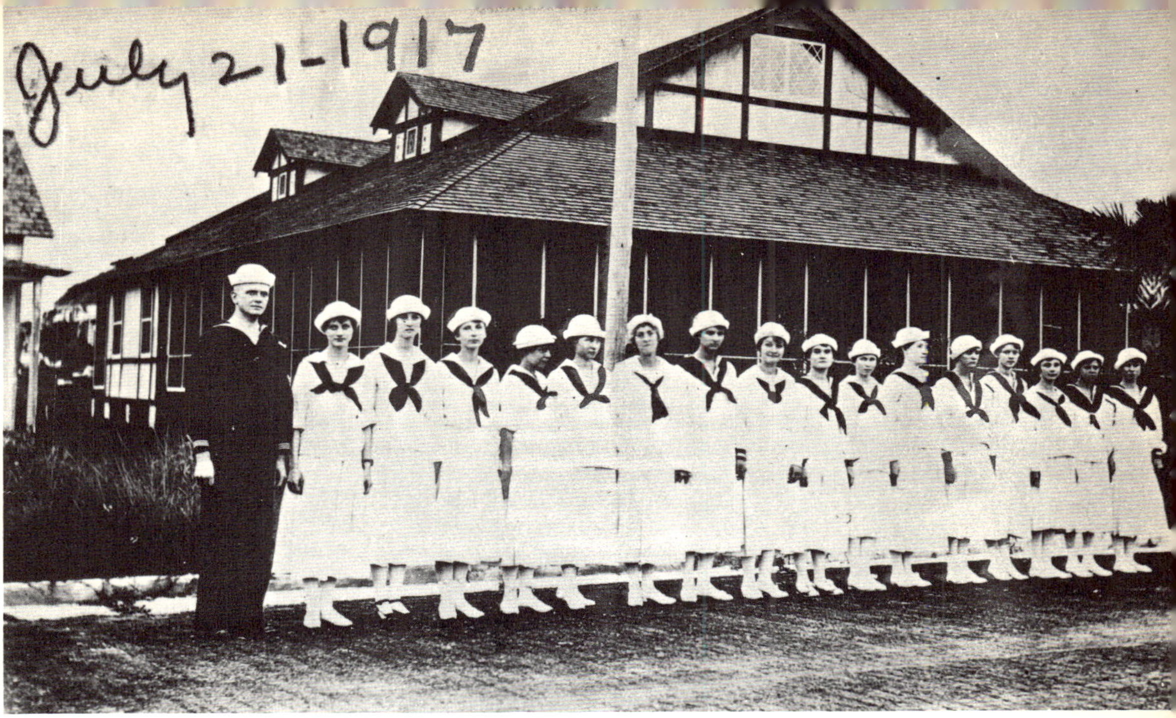

BOTH MEN AND WOMEN ORGANIZED a Naval Militia during World War I in Sarasota. The Sarasota Girls Militia above, posing in front of the Woman's Club in 1917, was trained for exhibition drills on Main Street during parades. The Drill Master is Henry Grinton. He was called "Susie" when out of earshot.

PREPARING TO LEAVE FOR WAR is the 3rd Division, 1st Battalion, Florida Naval Militia, a Sarasota group. It is photographed in 1917 at its final local muster, in front of the Sarasota Yacht and Automobile Club.

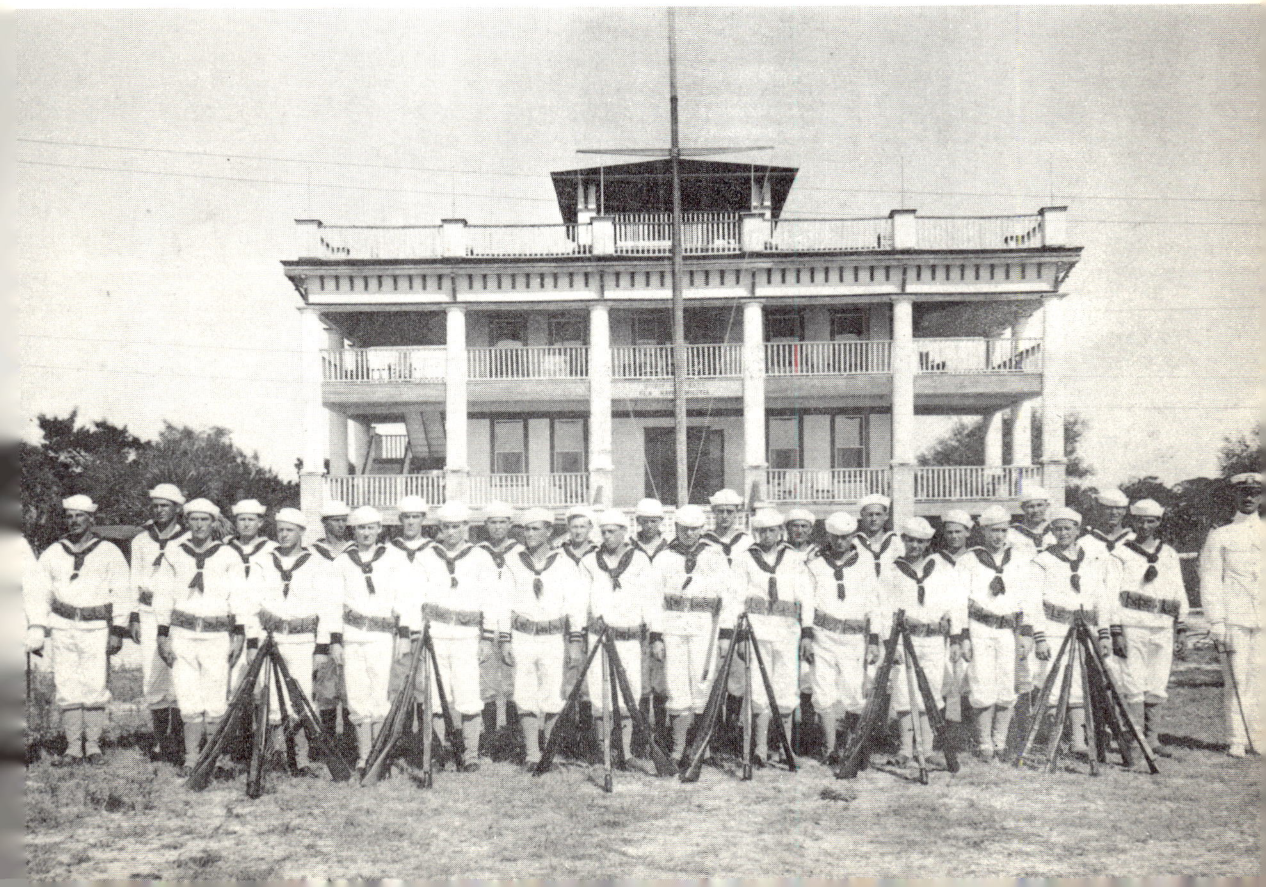

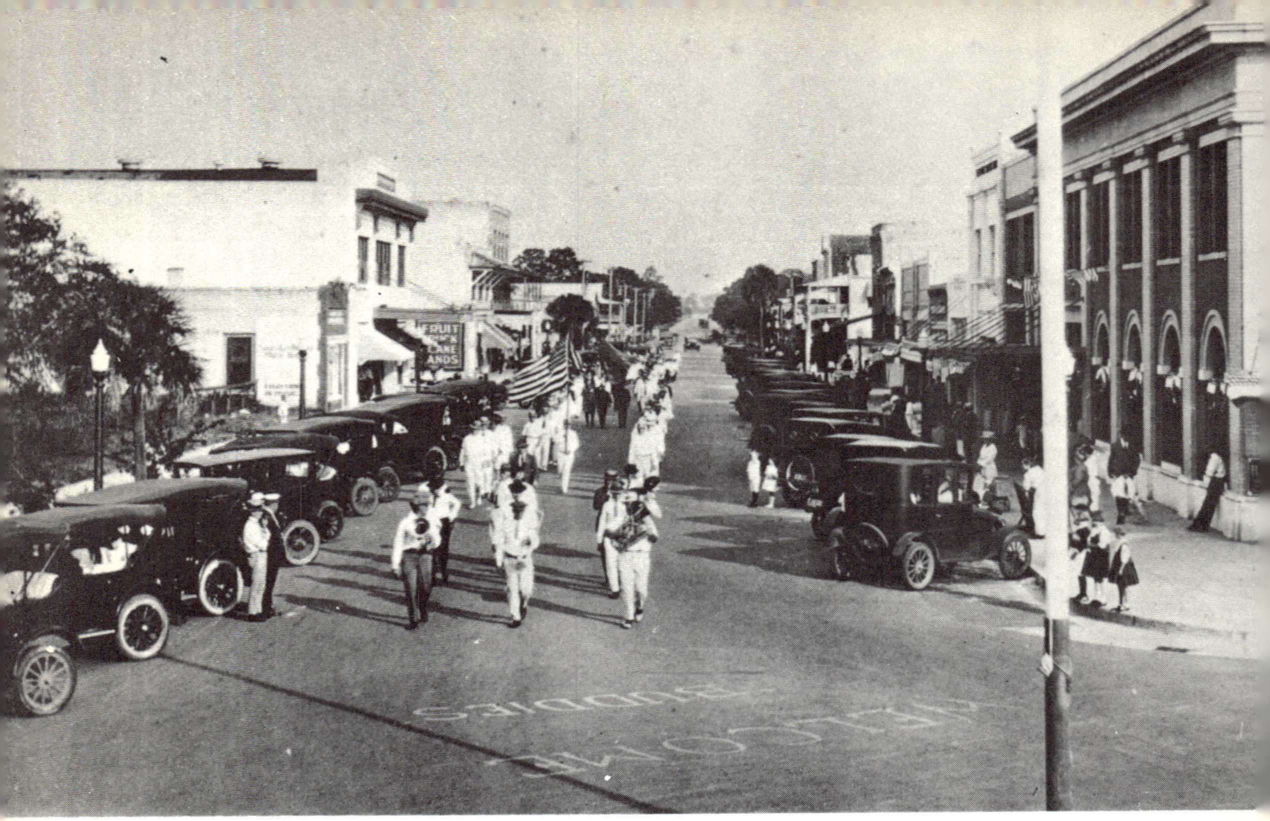

WELCOME BUDDIES, reads the sign painted on the pavement at Five Points to signify the event—a welcoming home parade in 1918 for veterans of World War I. The view is looking east on Main Street. A flag pole was installed in the intersection.

CEREMONIES AT FIVE POINTS on the first Armistice Day in 1919. More than 200 Sarasotans joined the armed forces for World War I, and all came back but one, a young soldier who died of pneumonia in camp.

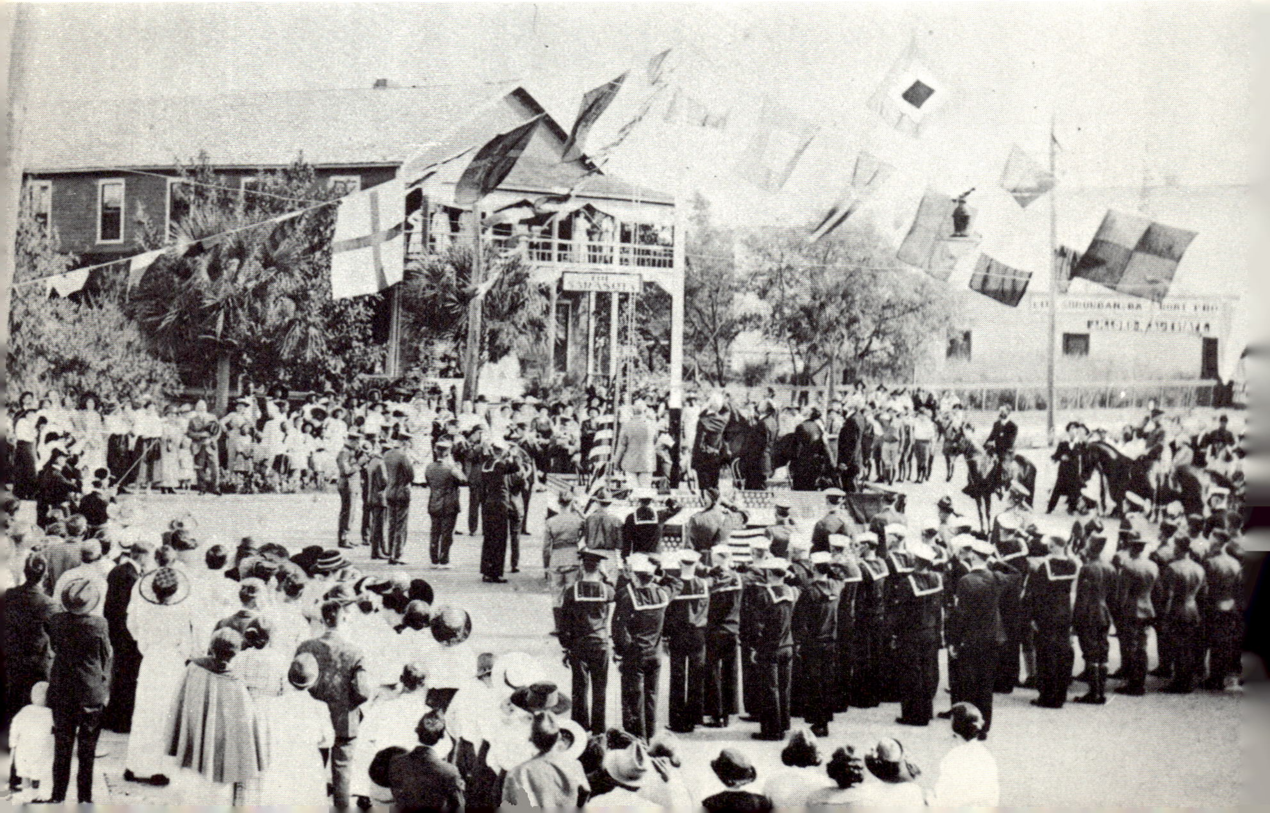

BIGGEST CELEBRATION in Sarasota's history to that time was the 1919 first Armistice Day observance. Veterans marched down the street to Five Points for speeches around the flag pole that was erected to honor the servicemen, athletic events were held at the golf course, lower Main Street was blocked off for an evening of street dancing, and the Woman's Club made plans to plant 181 water oaks on Main Street from Orange Avenue to the east city limits, a section that was later dedicated as Victory Avenue.

Facing page: SARASOTANS LOVED PARADES, and they were organized for many occasions. This one, in 1921, was to celebrate the birth of a new county—Sarasota County.

Sarasota in the 1920s

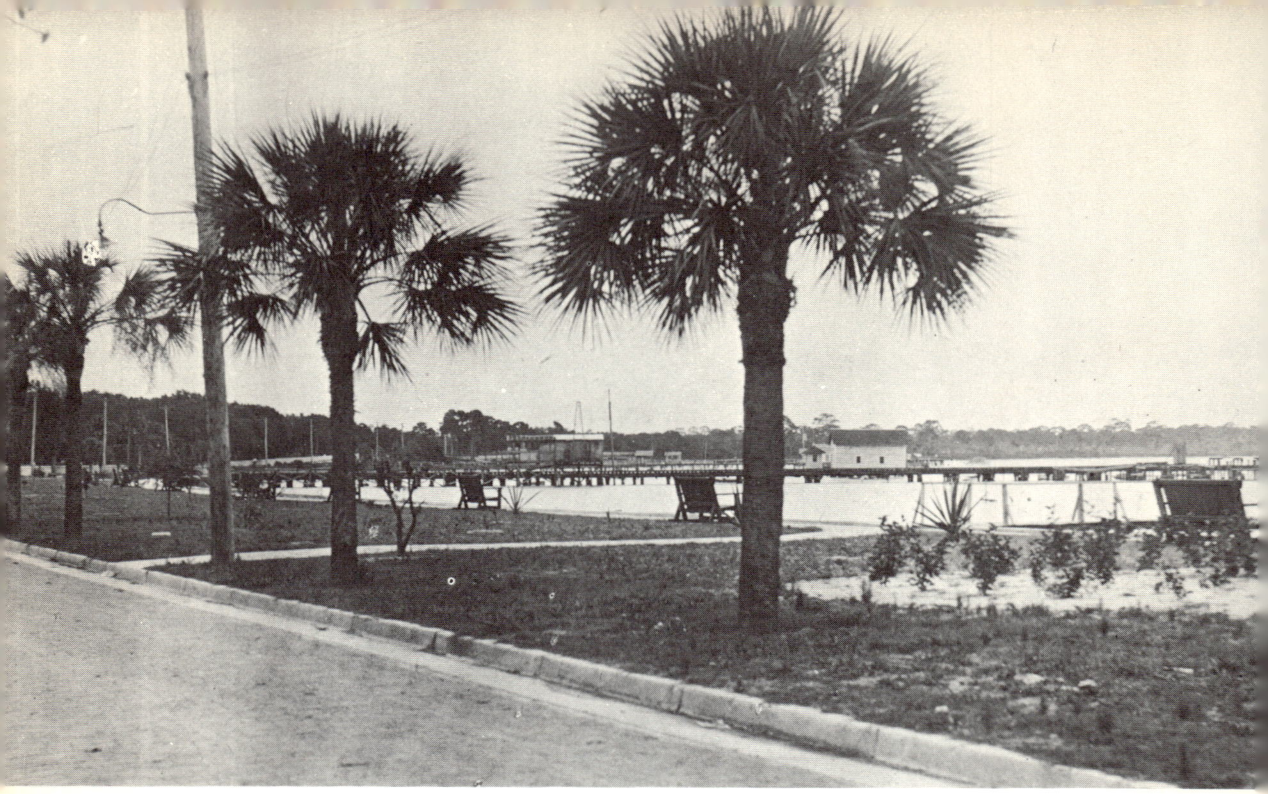

GULF STREAM AVENUE looking north (*preceding page*) and south (*above*) a few years before the storm of 1921 that destroyed most of the fishing piers. In the photo on the preceding page the Belle Haven Inn can be seen, downtown's tallest building, and the old City Hall (over the boat's bow).

THE OLD SEABOARD depot at Main and Lemon, used for decades prior to the merger of the Seaboard with the Atlantic Coast Line. Arrival of the Seaboard in 1903 touched off a building spree in Sarasota but didn't have the same effect to the south, in Venice, when a spur was built to that area in 1911. In fact, it angered the Venetians because the Seaboard ran its tracks right through the area and built its station a mile south, in the sticks, where few folks could get to it. In retribution, the people of Venice changed their town's name to Nokomis. But old-timers still attribute much of Sarasota's progress prior to the mid-1920s to Seaboard's arrival (the ACL came to town in 1924), mainly because roads into the area were atrocious. The Tamiami Trail linking Tampa with Bradenton, Sarasota, Fort Myers, and then Miami wasn't inaugurated until 1928.

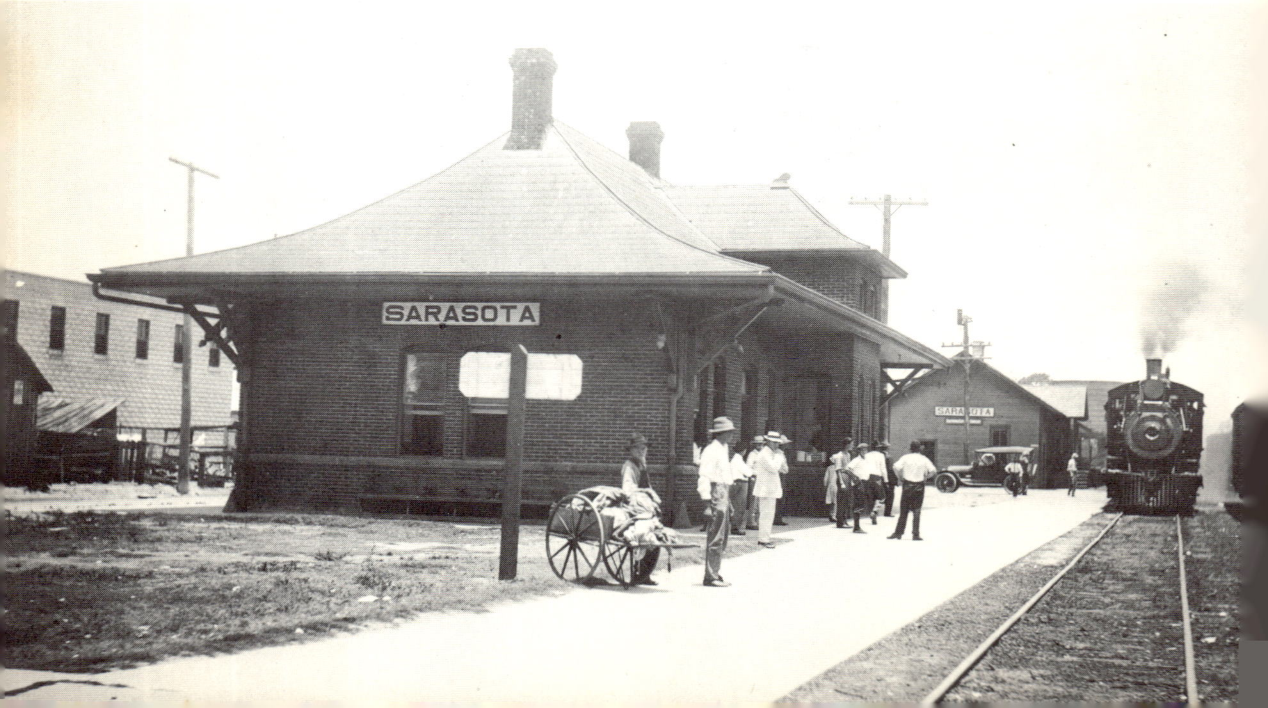

THE 1921 HURRICANE was one of the most violent storms to hit the central west coast of Florida. Although it entered the state north of Sarasota (at Tarpon Springs), it changed the face and the future of Sarasota's waterfront. The downtown area stayed dry, but water and wind splintered just about every man-made object in Sarasota Bay. The small boat houses broke up, the railroad dock disintegrated (*below*), fish houses on piers blew away (*above*) and then the piers, including most of the municipal pier. No one was killed, and damage was limited to the Gulf Stream Avenue area. Despite its unwelcomed visit, the storm provided Sarasota with an opportunity it quickly seized. It blew the city's unsightly fishing industry out of the front yard, and when the City Council voted to build a new 700-foot concrete pier, the ordinance plainly stated it would be for recreational purposes only. To assuage the fish house and machine shop owners, philanthropist and winter resident Calvin Payne paid for dredging of nearby Hog Creek, put in new docks, convinced the Seaboard to run a spur track to them, and Sarasota had what it promptly named Payne Terminal.

CALVIN N. PAYNE's gift to the city is often referred to as the finest and most invaluable gift ever received by Sarasota. An executive with gas and oil companies, Payne wintered in Sarasota from 1917 until his death in 1926. In 1921 he joined local efforts to enlarge the old Gillespie golf course by buying 60 adjoining acres. But on second thought, he gave the acreage to the city and county for park purposes. He felt that the centrally located land was too valuable for a golf course. The land has been used for the annual county fair; a section was made into a baseball park for spring training of the New York Giants, Boston Red Sox, and Chicago White Sox; and another tract became the site of the city's Mobile Home Park. When the demands for a golf course grew louder, he softened his stipulation that all 60 acres be used for parks, and permitted the city to sell off 14 acres for money to buy golf acreage elsewhere. This resulted in the beautiful Bobby Jones Golf Course. Payne's 60 acres were valued at a quarter million dollars when he donated it; today it is priceless.

FIRST GET-TOGETHER of the Sarasota Kiwanis Club, shortly after it was chartered in 1922 with 68 members.

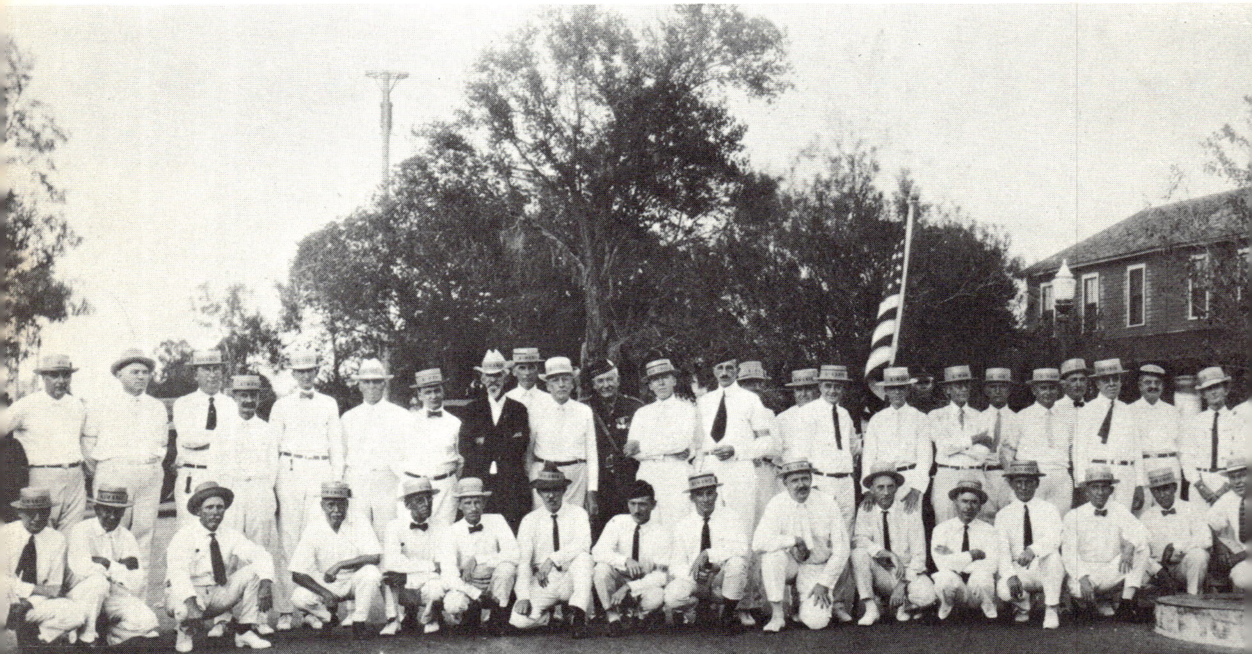

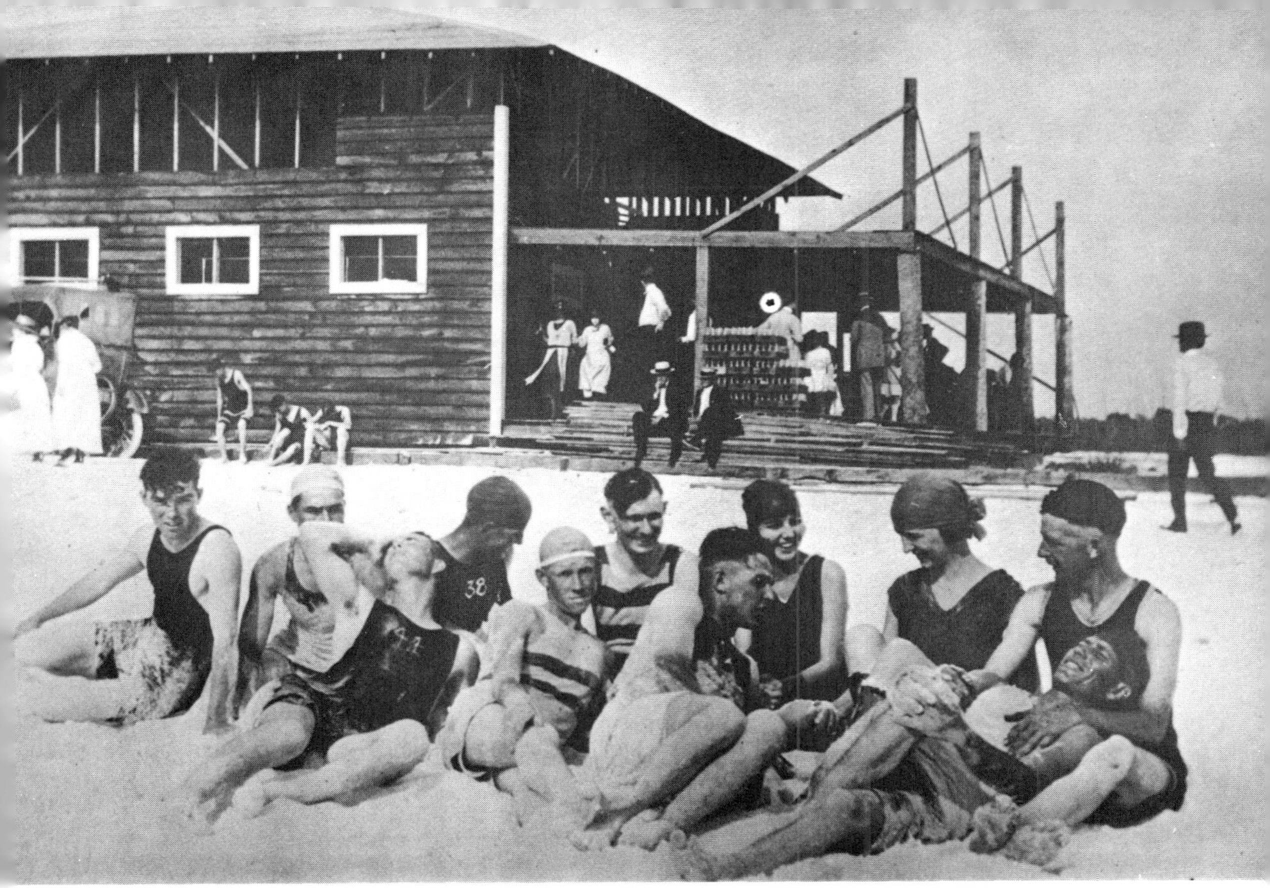

ROBERTS CASINO ON SIESTA KEY, named for key settler, Captain Louis Roberts, was the scene of many beach frolics. The Roaring Twenties, as in this 1922 scene, were a time of change, especially in the dress habits of women. Bared legs, even on the beach, were still a bit bold, but seemed only sensible in Sarasota's mid-summer heat.

LADIES OF THE RED CROSS never missed a disaster nor a parade. This is 1921, with five volunteers riding in a decorated Studebaker.

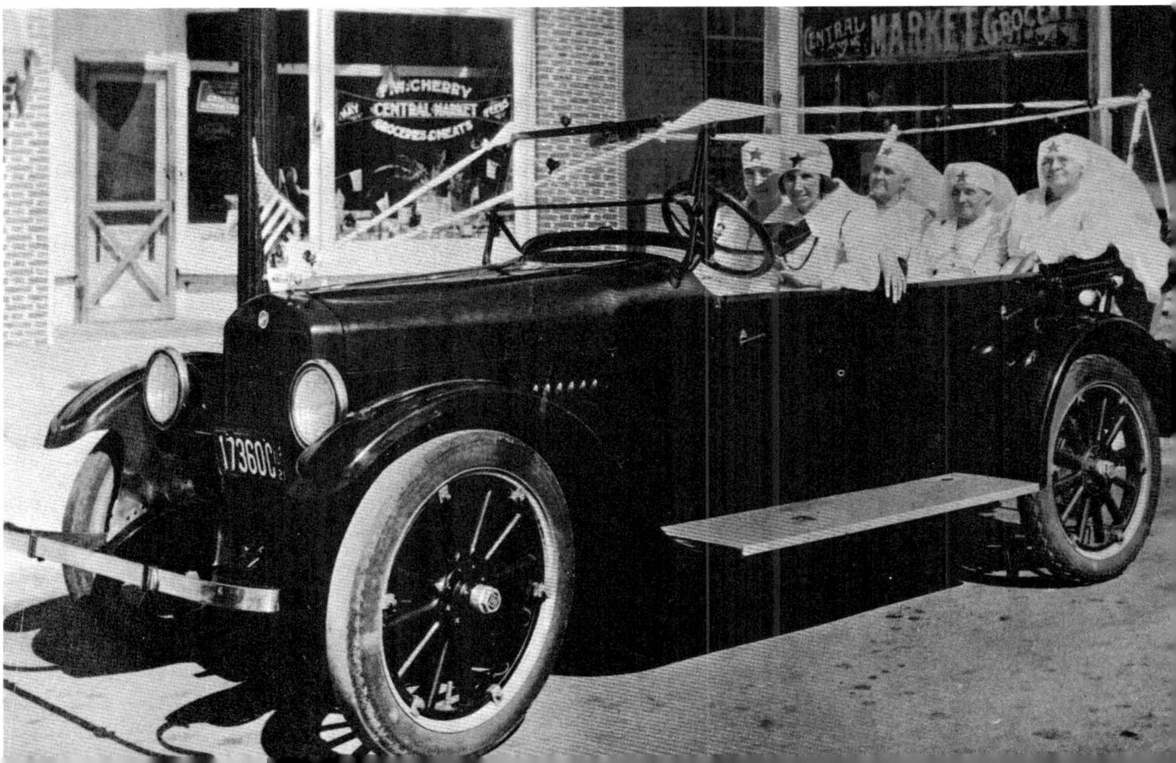

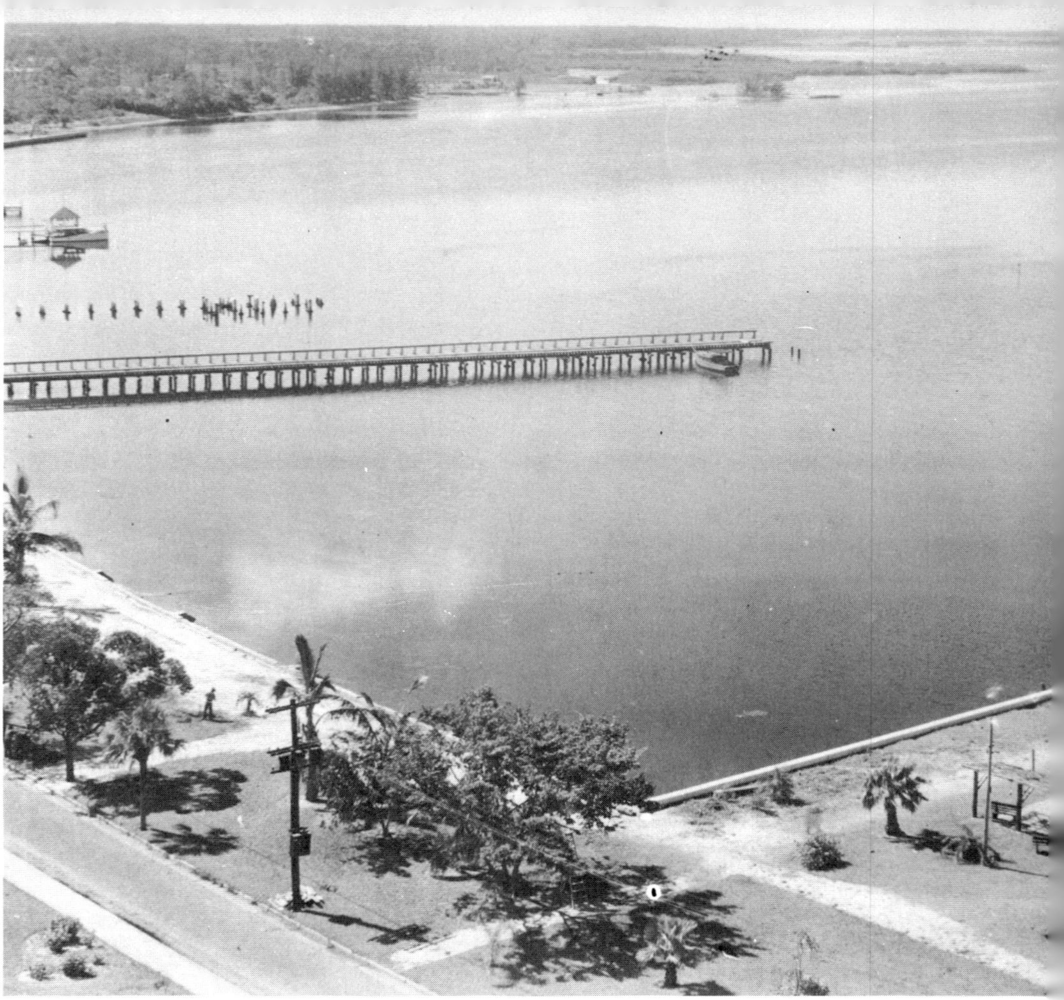

UNDEVELOPED SOUTHERN SECTION of city is evident in the 1923 photo, taken a few years after the 1921 storm cleared out most of the piers and docks leading into the bay. Pier in foreground is the old fish dock railroad spur. Peninsula in background is the Harbor Acres area.

BATHING SUITS were becoming briefer and the crowds bigger in 1921. This is the beach below Roberts' Point on Siesta Key, compacted enough for the skinny-tired light-weight cars to drive down to the water's edge.

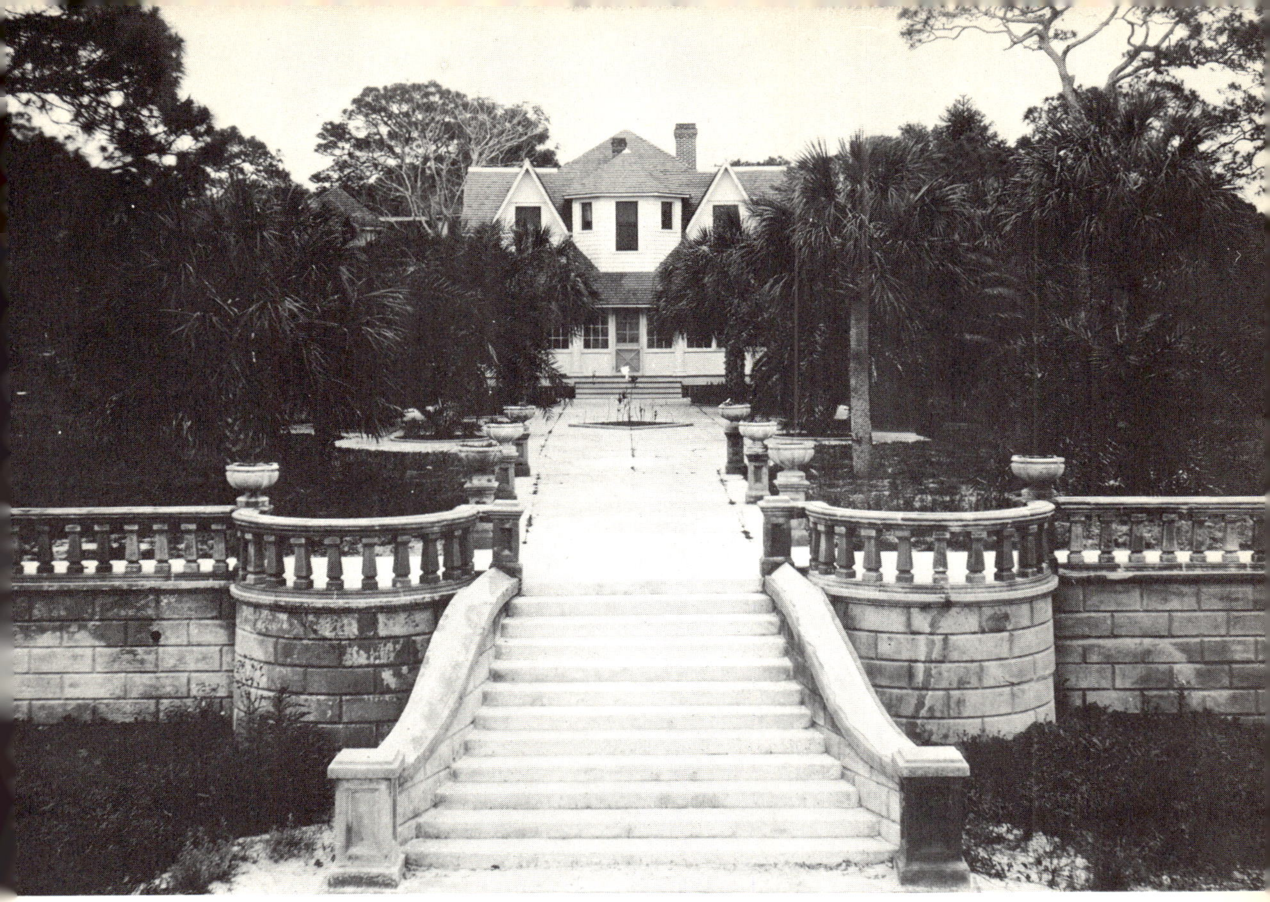

JOHN RINGLING'S FIRST HOME in Sarasota was this modest frame house (*above*). On his first trip to Sarasota in 1911 at the invitation of railroad executive Ralph Caples, Ringling was so impressed with the area that he purchased this house and its property, owned by Charles Thompson. Thompson, ironically, also was a circus man, having been manager of the Buffalo Bill Wild West Show. John and Mable Ringling spent winters in the home, but after a trip to Italy in 1923, Mrs. Ringling announced she wished to build a palatial mansion on the site. When construction was about to begin, their frame home was moved about 100 feet to the side. They continued to live in it during building of the Ca'd'Zan. Sadly out of repair, its awnings in tatters, it still sat on the property (*right*) near the mansion in 1948, long after the Ringlings had moved intc the mansion, and passed on.

MABLE BURTON RINGLING, described as "strikingly attractive," met John Ringling while she was a cashier at the World's Columbian Exposition in 1893 in Chicago. They were married and honeymooned in 1904, in his private railroad car. Mable made many plans for a happy life at Ca'd'Zan, but just three years after the completion of the home, she entered a New Jersey sanitarium for treatment of Addison's Disease and died on June 1, 1929, at the age of 54.

RESPLENDENT FROM LAND OR SEA, Ca'd'Zan was Mable Ringling's idea. She wanted a mansion modeled after the Doge's Palace in Venice, Italy, a city she and John Ringling called their favorite. Much of the exterior construction material—marble, tiles, mouldings—were shipped from Europe, as were the furnishings—tapestries, oil paintings, colored glass windows. But she also added fixtures she and John took a liking to in their national travels—the chandelier from the old New York Waldorf Astoria, the bar lounge from the Cicardi Winter Palace Restaurant in St. Louis. She even planned to duplicate the tower atop the first Madison Square Garden, but architect Dwight James Baum talked her out of it. As a final touch of authenticity, she imported a full size gondola and parked it on a small island near the home. A bad storm made short work of the small boat. Ca'd'Zan, willed to the people of Florida, cost approximately $1,250,000.

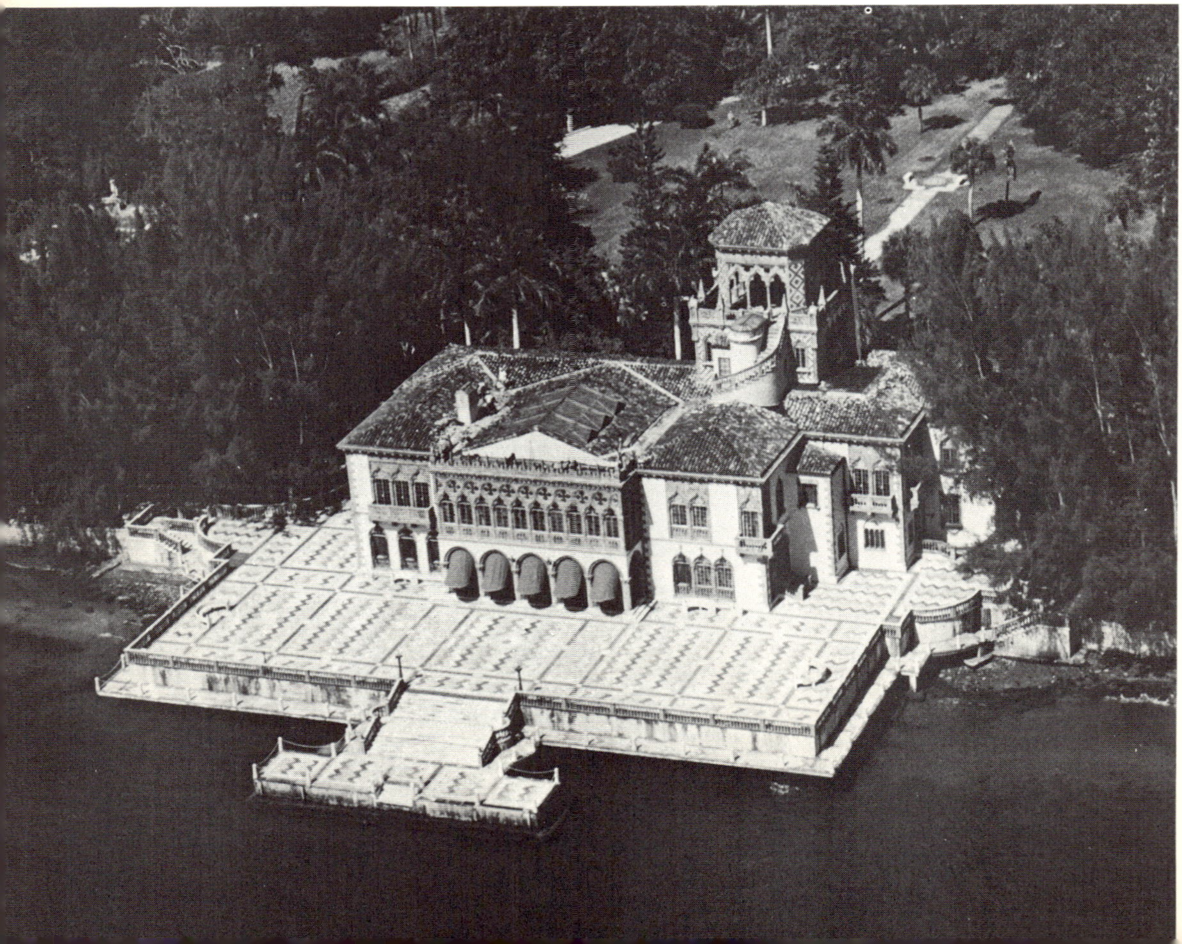

ORIGINALLY PLANNED as an outdoor courtyard, the Great Hall was finally designed as a 2½-story interior court. It measures 50 by 65 feet and some 30 rooms spread out from it. By redesigning it, the court became the main living room. It houses a $50,000 pipe organ that plays both manually and electronically.

GAME ROOM noted for a colorful ceiling decoration by the Hungarian artist Willy Pogany depicting John and Mable Ringling dressed in Venetian carnival costumes. The walls were lined with slot machines, and during Prohibition John Ringling always had an ample supply of liquor. He frequently "found" boats running illegal liquor right up at the dock at Ca'd'Zan.

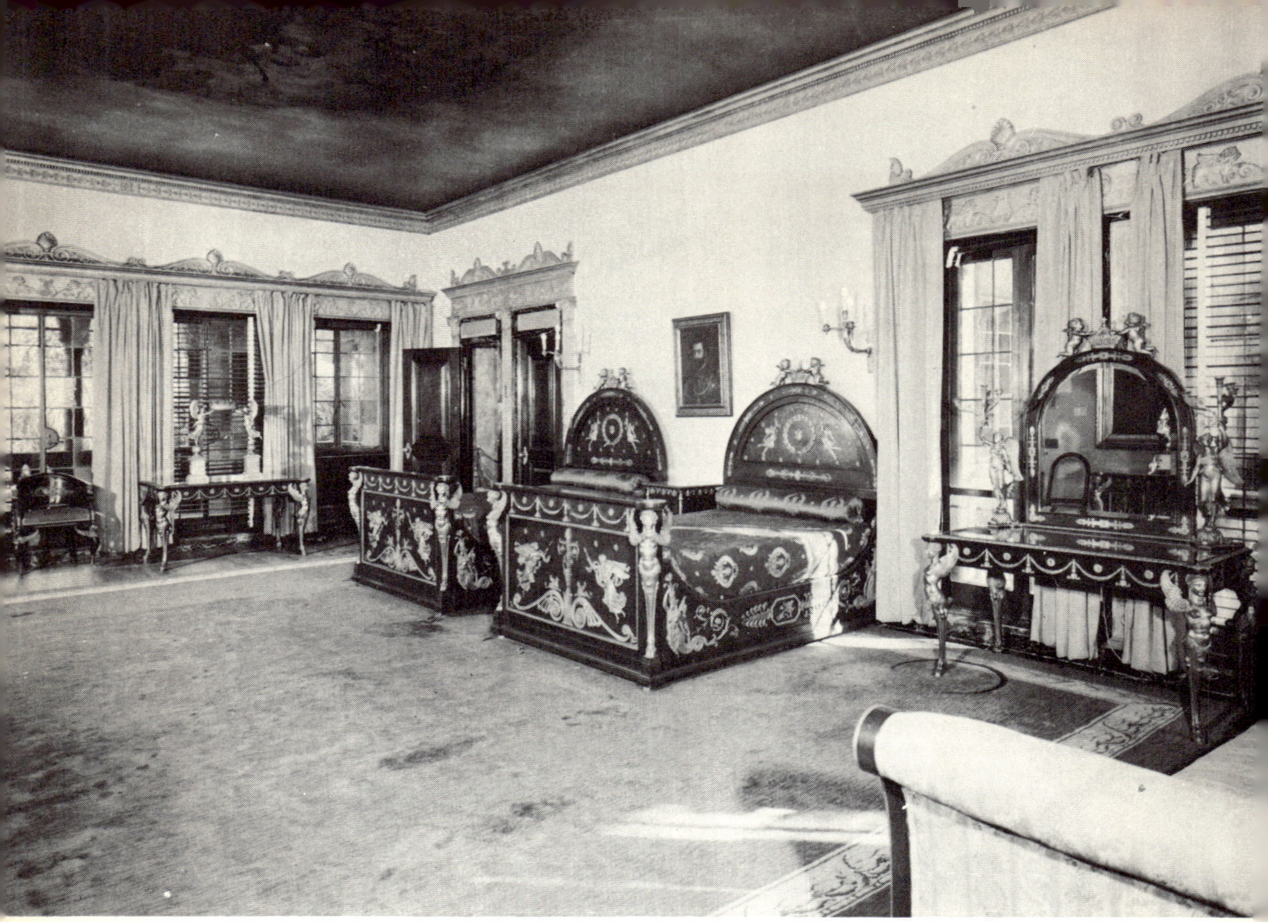

RINGLING'S MASTER BEDROOM (*above*) was decorated in French Empire style. The Barroom (*below*) had stained-glass windows, and the bar itself came from his favorite restaurant in St. Louis.

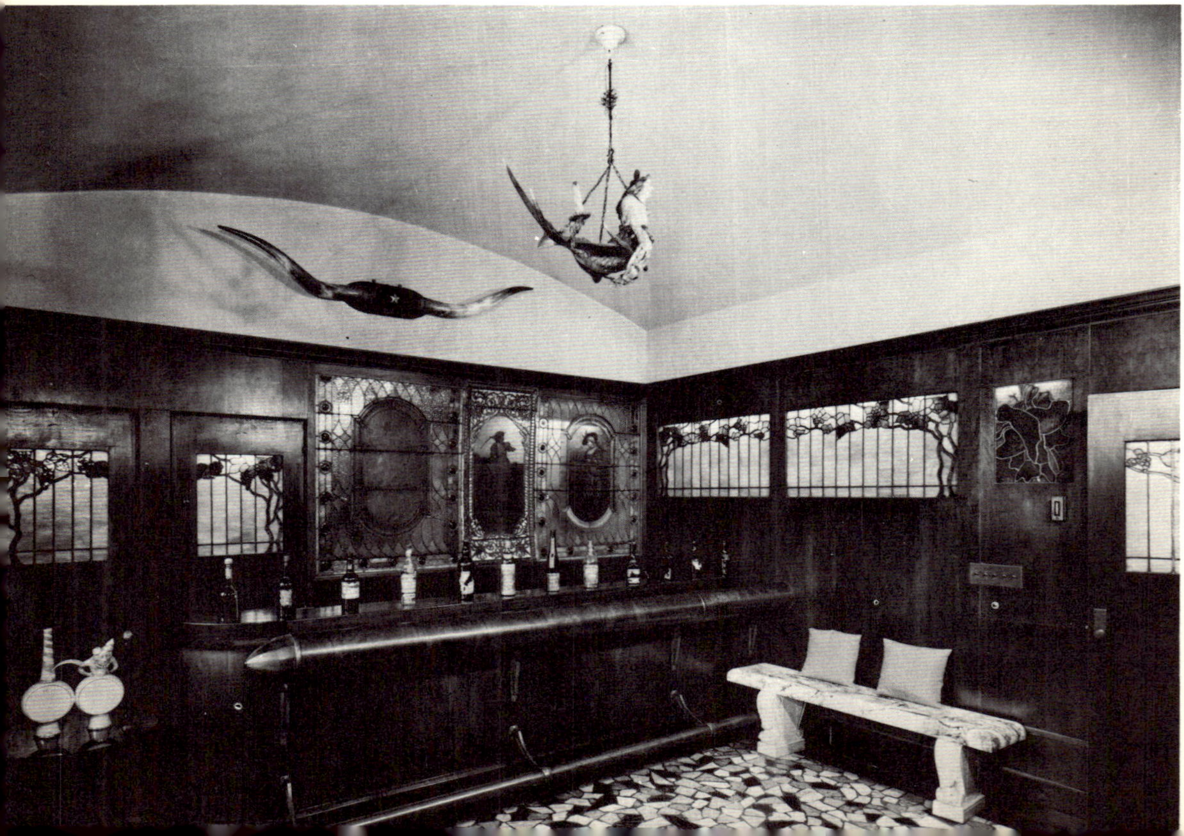

GEORGIAN MARBLE MANSION of Charles Ringling, built during the 1920s on property adjoining the estate and mansion of John Ringling. Charles Ringling died in 1926 but his wife, Edith, lived in the mansion until her death in 1953. It was built at a cost of $880,000, and now is owned and used by New College.

IN 1924 A WOODEN PRIMARY school was moved off this site on Golf Street to make way for this all-concrete Central School, costing $75,000. It housed all grades through junior high. In 1965 it was torn down to make way for the new Post Office building.

FEW SCHOOLS built back during the bustle of the 1920s still stand. Bay Haven School, put up in 1925 for $77,000, is one of the few. Although this picture was taken when completed, the structure's exterior has changed little. It is on West Tamiami Circle.

YELLOW CAB, the first in the city, was owned and operated in 1925 by Vincent Lowe. The city never did have a street car system, but kept experimenting with bus lines. Its first local bus, and it was just one, carried 18 passengers and traveled from Five Points to Siesta Key. It didn't survive, and a dependable line didn't come on the scene until 1939, under a city franchise.

FORTUNES WERE BEING MADE in real estate during 1924 and 1925, and the hysteria swelled the ranks of real estate salesmen. Here is the sales organization in 1925 of A. S. Skinner Co., reputed to be one of the largest selling organizations in the state at that time. That is the company's own airplane behind them. Testimonials were plentiful: "The Watrous Hotel a year ago was priced at $65,000; it sold last month for $225,000." "S. Davis Boylston, Sarasota druggist, netted $36,000 profit in two weeks on an initial investment of $500." "J. H. Lord declined $1,366,000 for a 99-year lease on the triangular lot at Five Points." Everyone was convinced the city would grow up and out, there was no stopping, so a new city charter was rushed through the Legislature extending the city limits up and down the coast, taking in islands and keys and the hinterland. Whereas the original town was only two square miles, it now, in 1925, was 69 square miles.

MANY A FINELY TURNED ANKLE appeared in this 1924 fashion show that had the onlookers lining stairs to get a look at what styles they could look forward to in the coming year. Bold patterns, caped wools, matching parasols, walking sticks, even a natty outfit suitable for the links (third from left) were fashion fares for Fall of 1924. The impeccable gentleman at right is Dr. Jack Halton, a physician in town since 1905. The show was held at the new Mira Mar Hotel.

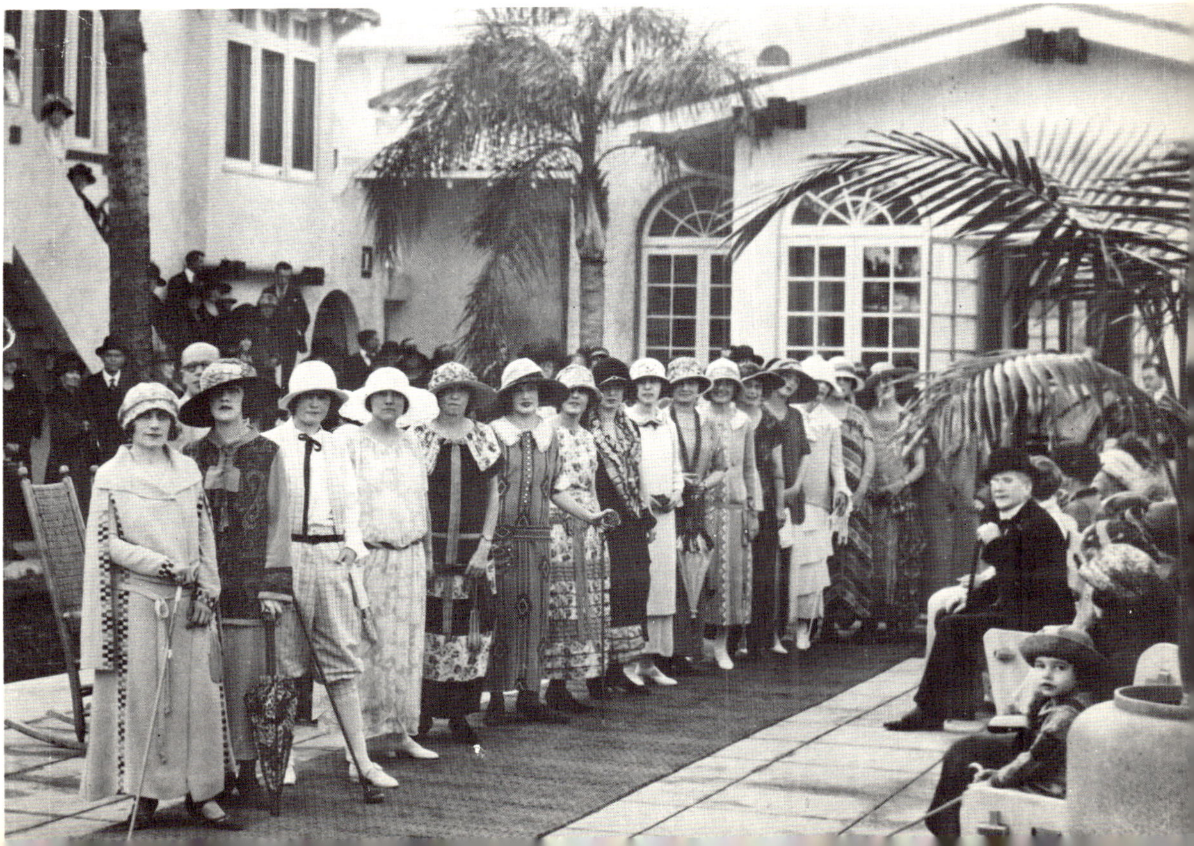

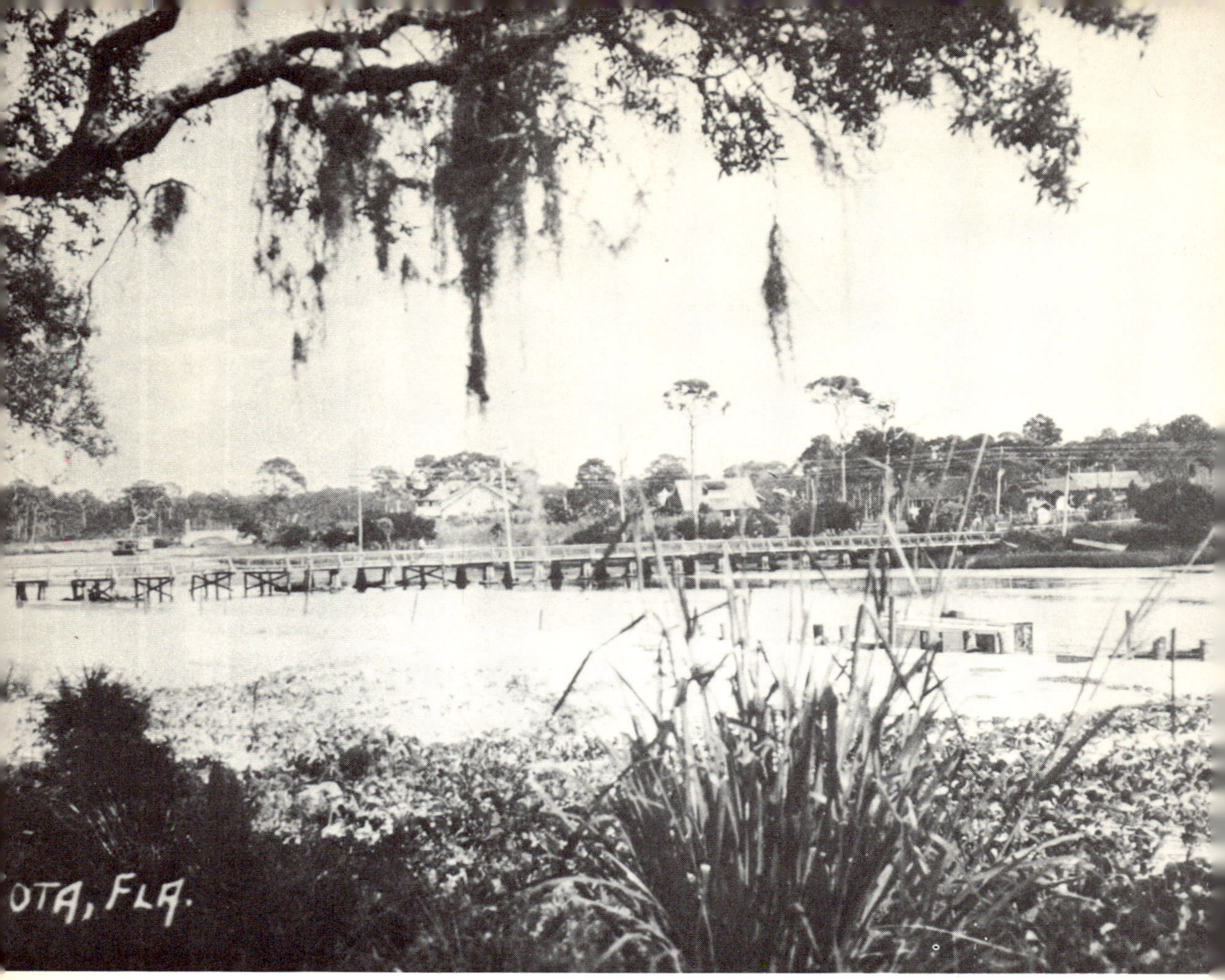

ORANGE AVENUE BRIDGE across Hudson Bayou in 1924. Between Hudson Bayou and Phillippi Creek settlers had moved in as early as the 1870s. By 1878 enough people homesteaded the area for a post office to be established. The community called itself Sara Sota.

ANOTHER "SKYSCRAPER" started upward, at Five Points, in 1924. It was the First Bank & Trust Co., headed by J. H. Lord. The bank lasted four years, going under during the bust in 1929. Depositors were paid 18½ cents on the dollar. Three days after it closed, it was reopened by Potter Palmer and carried his name. It remains the Palmer National Bank & Trust Co. today, a skyline landmark of the downtown.

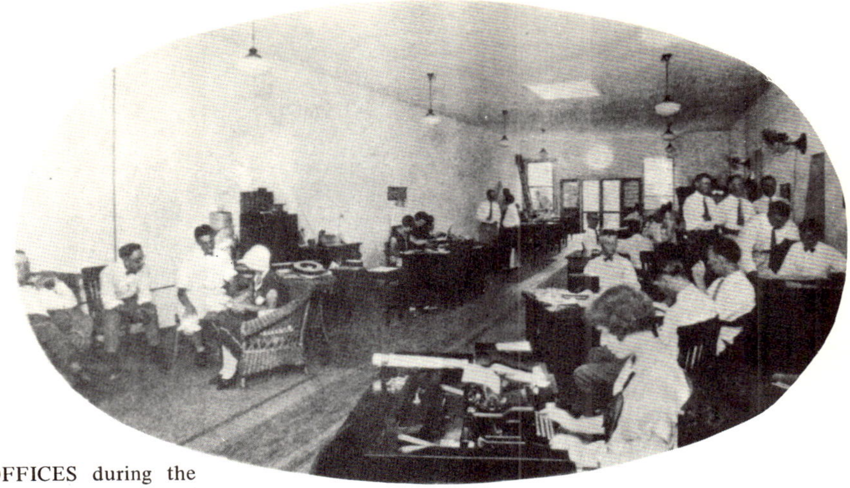

REAL ESTATE OFFICES during the hectic days of 1925 were always full of people looking for acreage buys leading to 'quick fortunes. This is inside the Davis-Reuter & Flory real estate office that year.

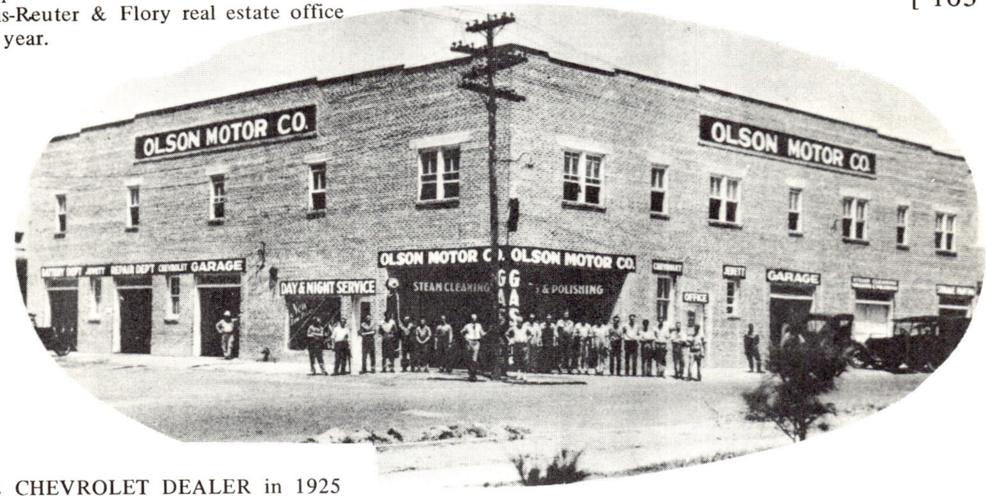

THE CHEVROLET DEALER in 1925 was the Olson Motor Co., at Orange and State. Occupying the building now is Mather Furniture.

FAVORITE PARTY SPOT on Siesta Key for many years was the Mira Mar Casino, built in 1925 as part of the Mira Mar Beach Subdivision project by Andrew McAnsh, Besides featuring "unexcelled cuisine," the casino advertised "matchless bathing on the smoothest, cleanest and safest beach in all America."

THIS RARE AERIAL PHOTO shows Sarasota in 1925 when the Belle Haven Inn was still standing and the Hotel Sarasota was completed. The Inn was torn down that year, a year of tremendous building activity in which real estate sales soared to $11,420,000 in October 1925. Nobody knew then

that this was the peak of the boom. The Mira Mar can be seen in the photo, two private bathhouses on piers, a pair of box cars loading up on the fish house spur dock, and the First Bank & Trust Company building, now Palmer Bank. The Bandshell in waterfront park was also new.

PINEAPPLE AND CENTRAL at Five Points in 1926 when the Commercial Court building was being built for offices further up Central (background). Building in foreground is an ice cream shop and to the left, adjoining it, is the Union Bus Station and Yellow Cab Co. At right is Lord's Arcade.

RINGLING CAUSEWAY UNDER CONSTRUCTION, a project built by John Ringling to provide access to his real estate holdings. Ringling in 1917 began buying up land, including Bird Key, St. Armand's Key, Coon Key, Otter Key, and several unnamed mangrove islands. In 1923 he brought in dredges to build up the mangrove islands and to fill in around Cedar Point (now Golden Gate Point), St. Armand's, Lido, and the southern end of Longboat Key, where he planned his luxurious Ritz-Carlton Hotel. He installed sewer and water mains and planted thousands of palms and Australian pines on his holdings. To get to them, he paid for the construction of the Ringling Causeway in 1925, pictured above. One year later it was opened to the public. Costing $750,000, Ringling presented the causeway to the city in 1927.

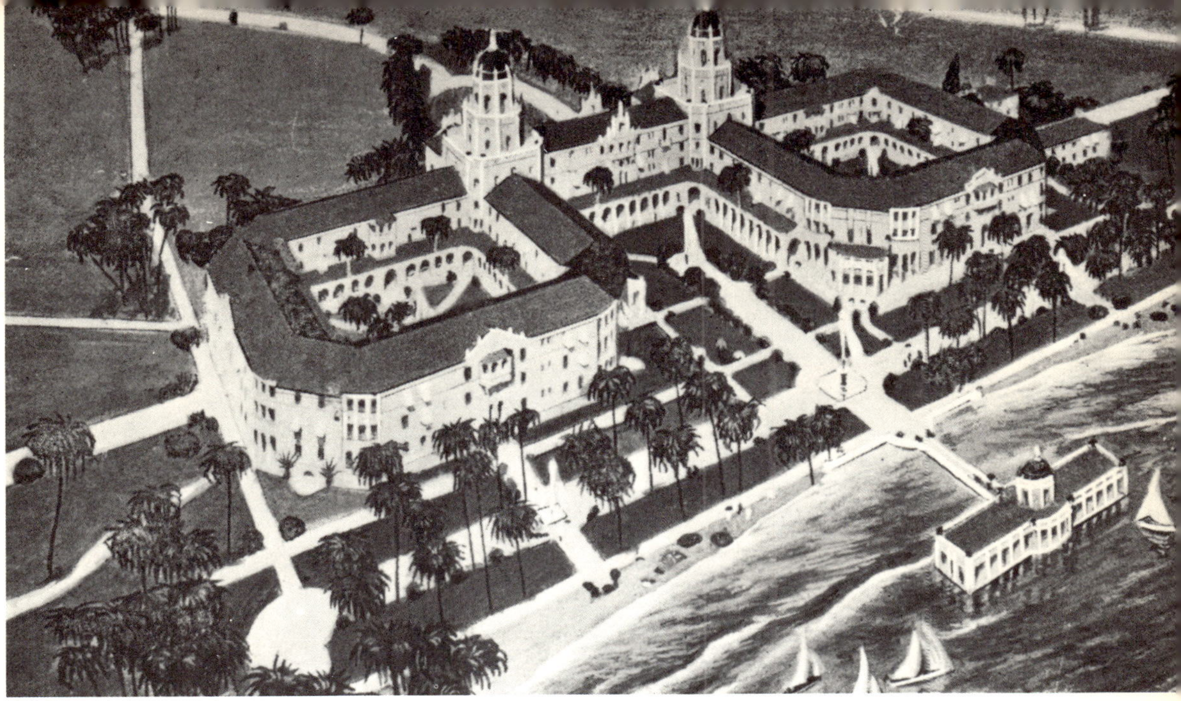

AN UNCOMPLETED DREAM of the booming 1920s was the Ritz-Carlton Hotel on Longboat Key. John Ringling wanted a deluxe hotel on the south end of the key. Above is the architect's rendering of what it would look like. Not any name would do, either, the story goes, with Ringling paying $5,000 a year for the right to use "Ritz-Carlton." Construction started in March 1926. More than $650,000 was poured into the project when the boom started to whimper and the stock market weakened. Work stopped, never to begin again. The shell of the dream (*below*) poked above the Australian pines on Longboat Key for nearly three decades before the property's new owners, Arvida Corporation, put a bulldozer to it in 1958.

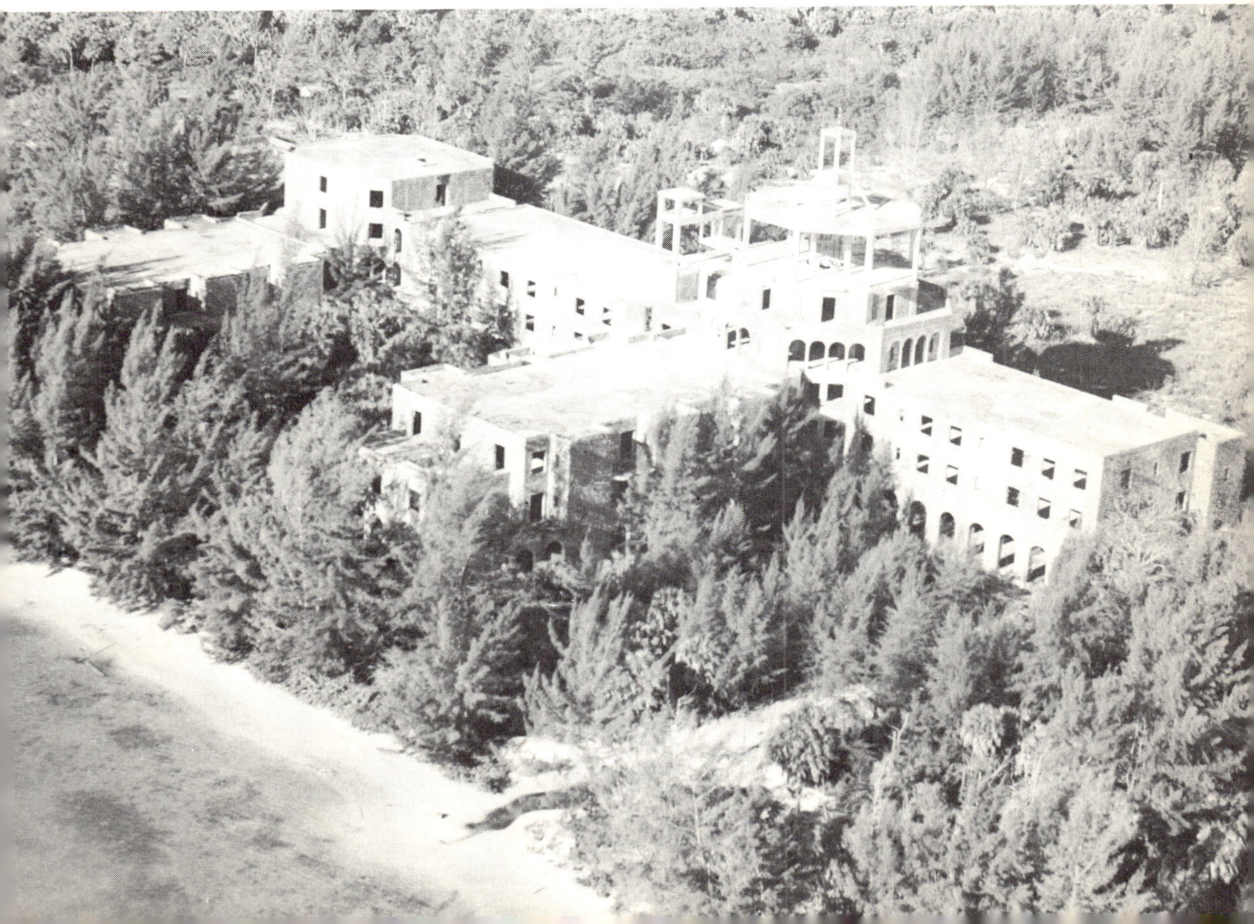

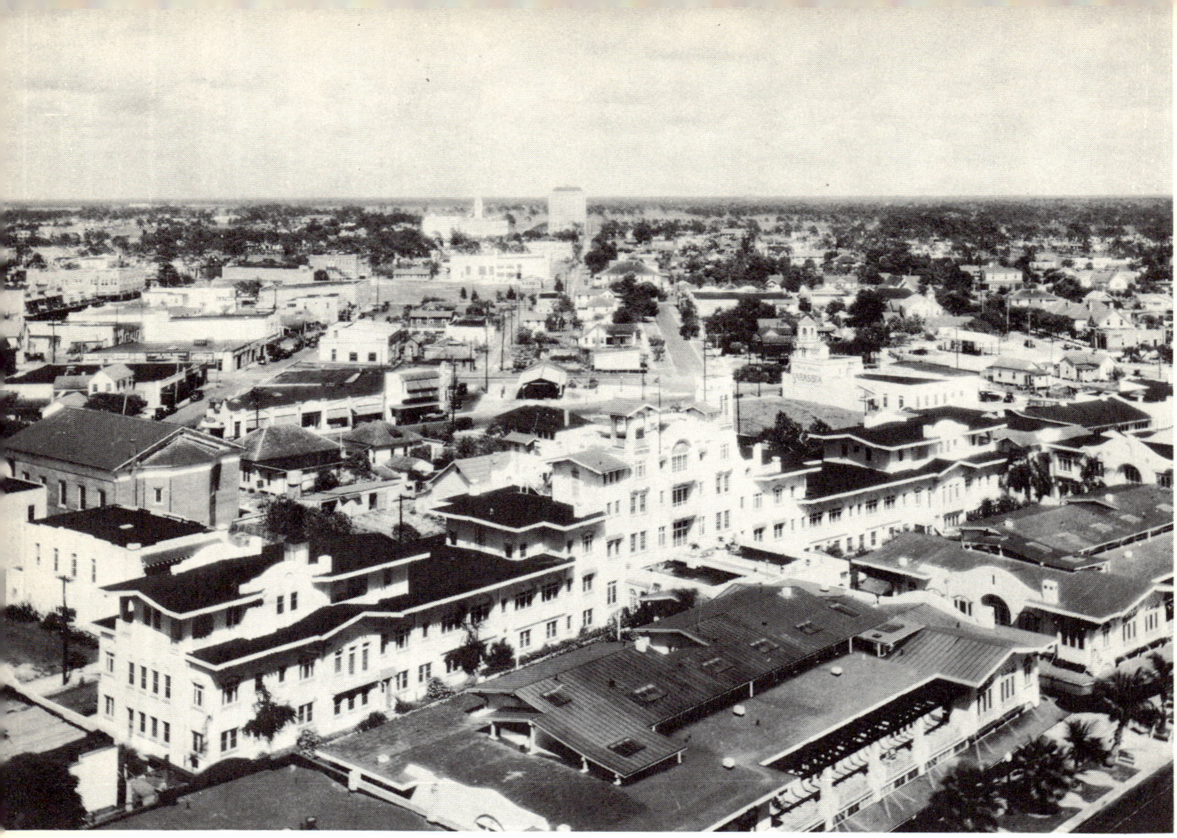

THE SPEEDIEST CONSTRUCTION JOB during the 1920s must be awarded the Mira Mar complex shown as it appeared in 1926 (looking east). A Scotsman with a flair for a good deal, Andrew McAnsh heard about the Potter Palmers' heavy investment in Sarasota and came from Chicago to investigate. He had been told Sarasota needed a good hotel so he made an offer–he would build a hotel, an apartment building, and a "nautatorium" downtown if the city gave him free light and water and would not levy any taxes against the buildings for 10 years. It was agreed. McAnsh promptly bought several large lots on Palm Avenue, ground was broken in October 1922, and 60 days later, after working around the clock under floodlights, the Mira Mar Hotel Apartments were finished. Six months later he began building the Mira Mar Hotel and the auditorium (*below*) rather than a "nautatorium" because that's what the city wanted; in six months they both were done. The next time McAnsh returned to Sarasota from a trip, he was given a siren-shrieking torch light parade.

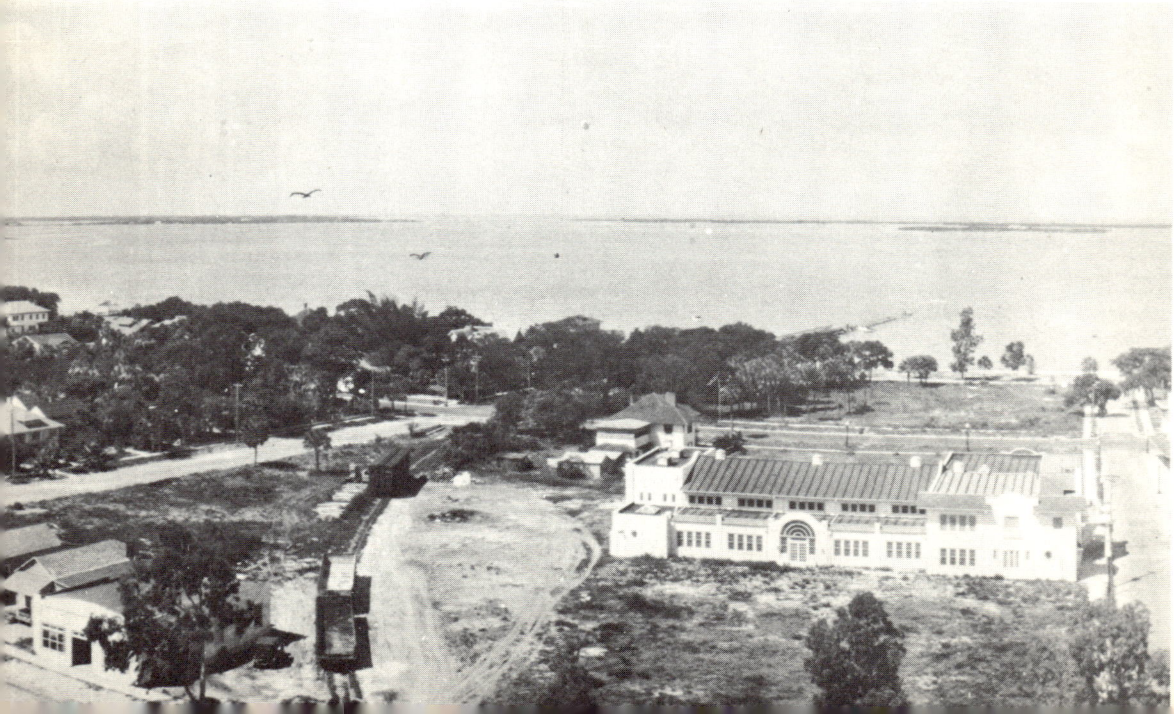

A 1926 SCENE OF SARASOTA'S MAIN STREET looking east toward the Lemon Avenue intersection. A young city with no traffic problems, the train (left center) crossed this main artery many times daily. The building with the Coca Cola sign was the Ouida Hotel, later called the De Soto Hotel, still standing today beside Norton's Camera Shop. A building on the south side of the street advertises Sarasota Theater's upcoming movie, a Zane Grey western, "The Thundering Herd."

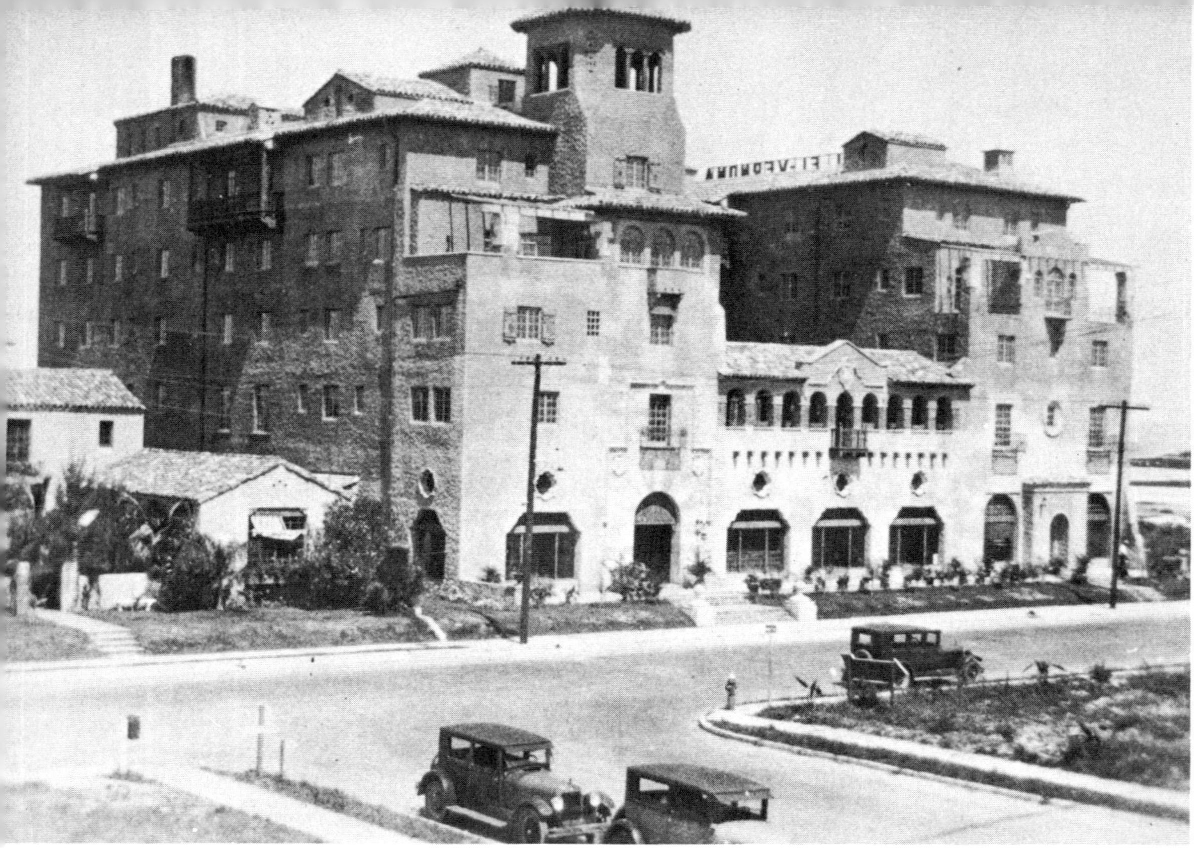

FABULOUS STORIES still are told of events in this incomparable hotel—the El Vernona. Designed by Dwight James Baum (who did the Ringling Mansion and the courthouse), the hotel was described by architects as "the most perfect example of Spanish architecture in Florida." Owen Burns, who made a fortune in Midwest banking and moved to Sarasota for the fishing, built the El Vernona in 1926 and named it after his wife. Meanwhile, on Longboat Key, John Ringling was building his Ritz-Carlton, but work soon was to stop because the economic doldrums were setting in. When Ringling's project stopped, he bought the El Vernona and renamed it the John Ringling Hotel. Under his ownership, celebrities wandered in and out, circus acts were staged, and a seven-foot-tall giant, decked out in a gold uniform with big brass buttons, was stationed out front as the doorman. Nearly everything fashionable that went on in town was held at the hotel, where six chefs in the kitchen served dinner on golden plates that were counted every night. The hotel never was open more than a few months during the season. Arvida Corporation eventually acquired it from the Ringling estate, and it was closed for nearly eight years. It reopened in 1964 as the Ringling Towers under the ownership of H. W. Robinson with the 150 rooms converted into apartments.

IN THE "BACKYARD" at the circus is John Ringling, the circus king, as he appeared in 1926. With him is Pat Valdo (center), assistant to equestrian director Fred Bradna (right).

REMEMBERED AS THE HOME of Karl Bickel, the president of United Press who retired to Sarasota in 1935, this Spanish building when first built in the 1920s served as administrative offices for the Ringling enterprises. It is adjacent to the Ringling Towers on the Tamiami Trail. Bickel purchased it in 1933.

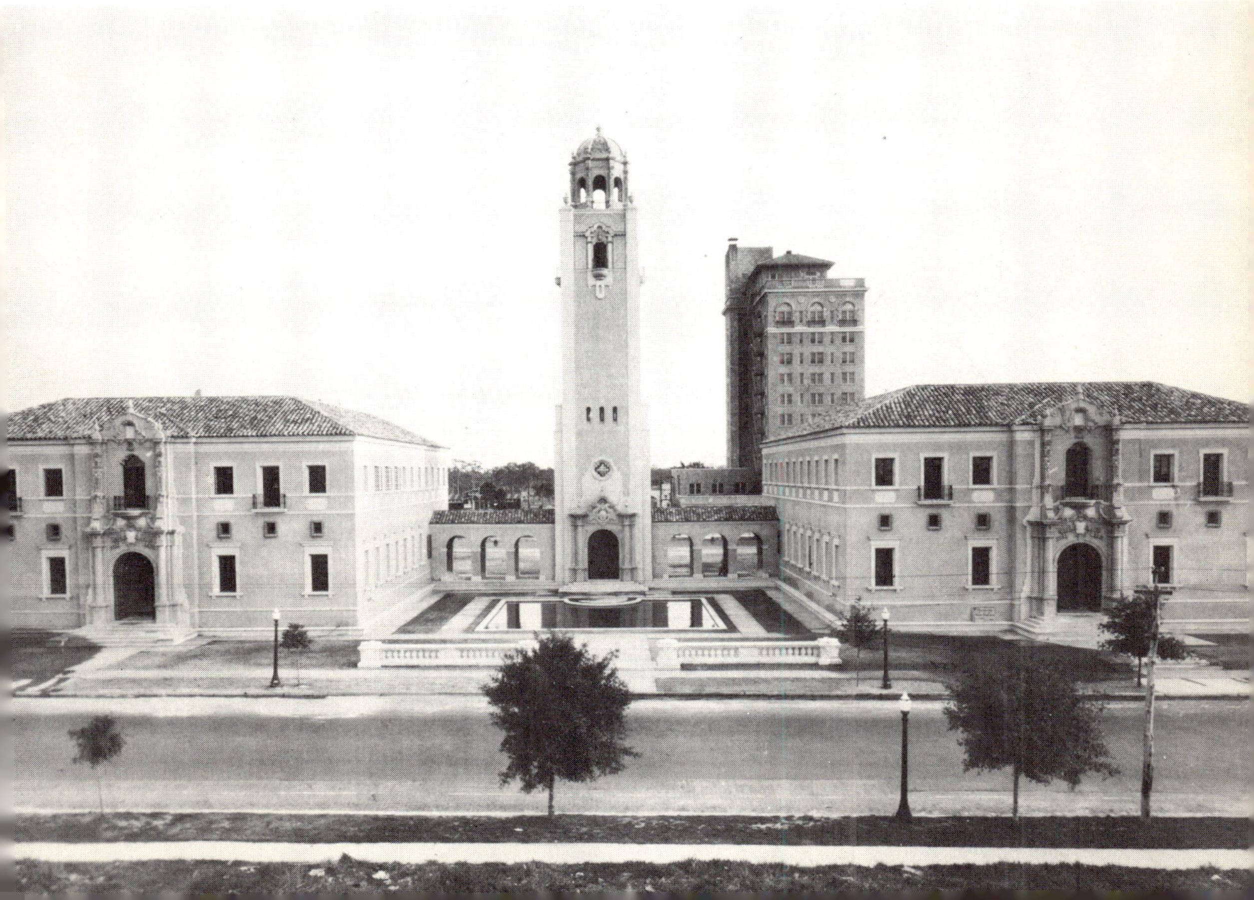

ALWAYS A PART OF MANATEE COUNTY, Sarasota felt it never got back its own tax dollars in area improvements. Residents complained about lack of schools and roads. Finally, they decided to secede and form their own county. After a year of political maneuvering to overcome Manatee's objections, leading citizens in Sarasota succeeded in getting the Legislature to pass the proposal. The year was 1921. A courthouse was needed, and Dwight James Baum, the architect involved later in designing the Ringling Mansion and Ringling Hotel, was assigned. Meanwhile, a temporary courthouse was set up in the Arcade building at the pier. On May 13, 1926, the courthouse cornerstone was laid at Main and Washington. Finished in February 1927, and paid for by a $500,000 bond issue, the courthouse was widely acclaimed as one of the most artistic public buildings in the country. This photo was taken that year. The tall building in the background is Sarasota Terrace.

HOME of the *Sarasota Times* in 1926, under the ownership of L. D. Reagin. Reagin bought the *Times* two years earlier, and moved into this new building on 1st Street just off the Tamiami Trail. The *Times* went into receivership in 1929, but the building attracted a variety of tenants, including artist Syd Solomon, architect Victor Lundy, even a company that made guava jelly. In considerable disrepair yet appealing, the building still houses offices and studios for professional and artistic people.

ROTARY WENT TO LUNCH in 1927 at the Winter Quarters of the Ringling Circus. The club received its charter in 1926.

THE EDWARDS THEATER shortly after its grand opening in 1926. Some of the nation's top entertainment came to the theater on North Pineapple, including humorist Will Rogers and the Chicago Grand Opera. The $350,000 theater opened with the movie "Skinner's Dress Suit" starring Reginald Denny and Laura La Plant. Furnished with an orchestral pipe organ, the theater management brought in a New York organist for opening nights. A. B. Edwards, who built the theater, remembered he "played entirely too loud . . . he must have thought we were all deaf." Will Rogers appeared at the Edwards Theater a few nights after it opened. He was a frequent guest of the John Ringlings. During his performance on stage, the Ringlings and their guests arrived late, and Rogers quipped, "The country folks coming in must have had Ford trouble on the way." Edwards Theater later was sold and renamed the Florida Theater, which Mr. Edwards recalled as "the most disappointing memory of the building." It remains the Florida Theater today.

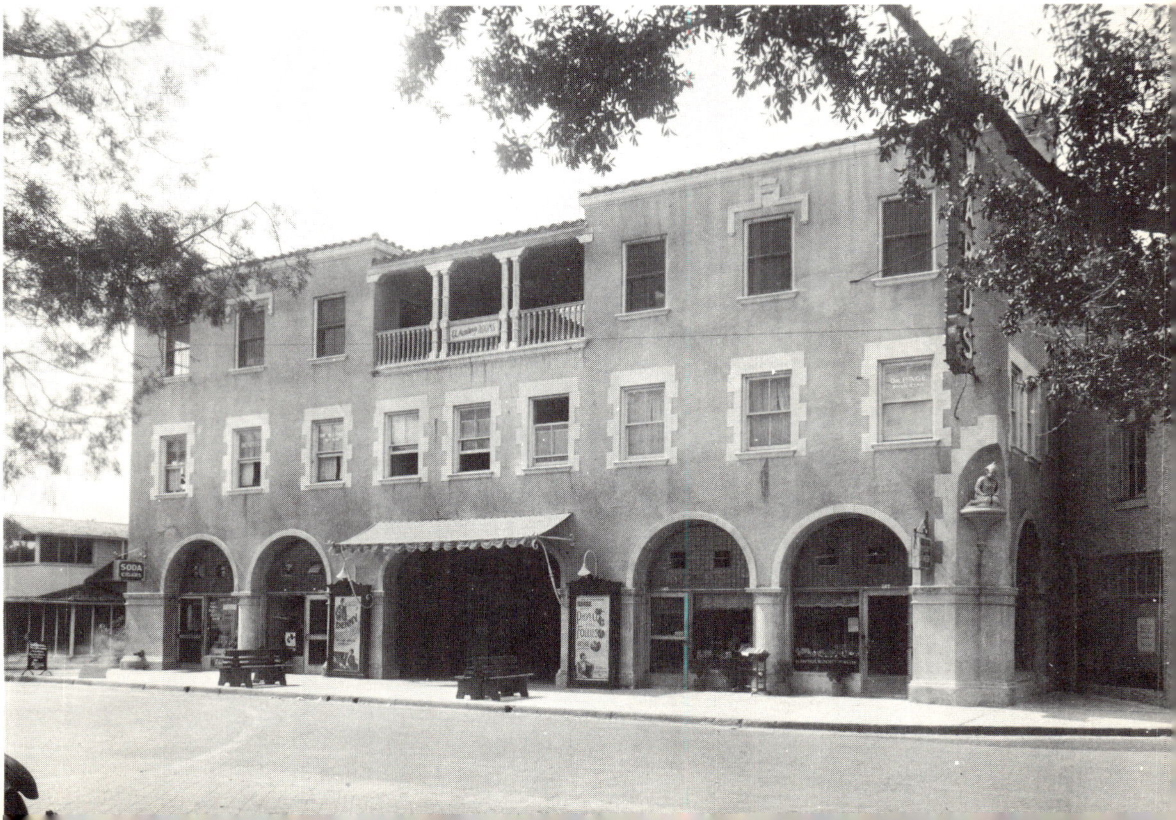

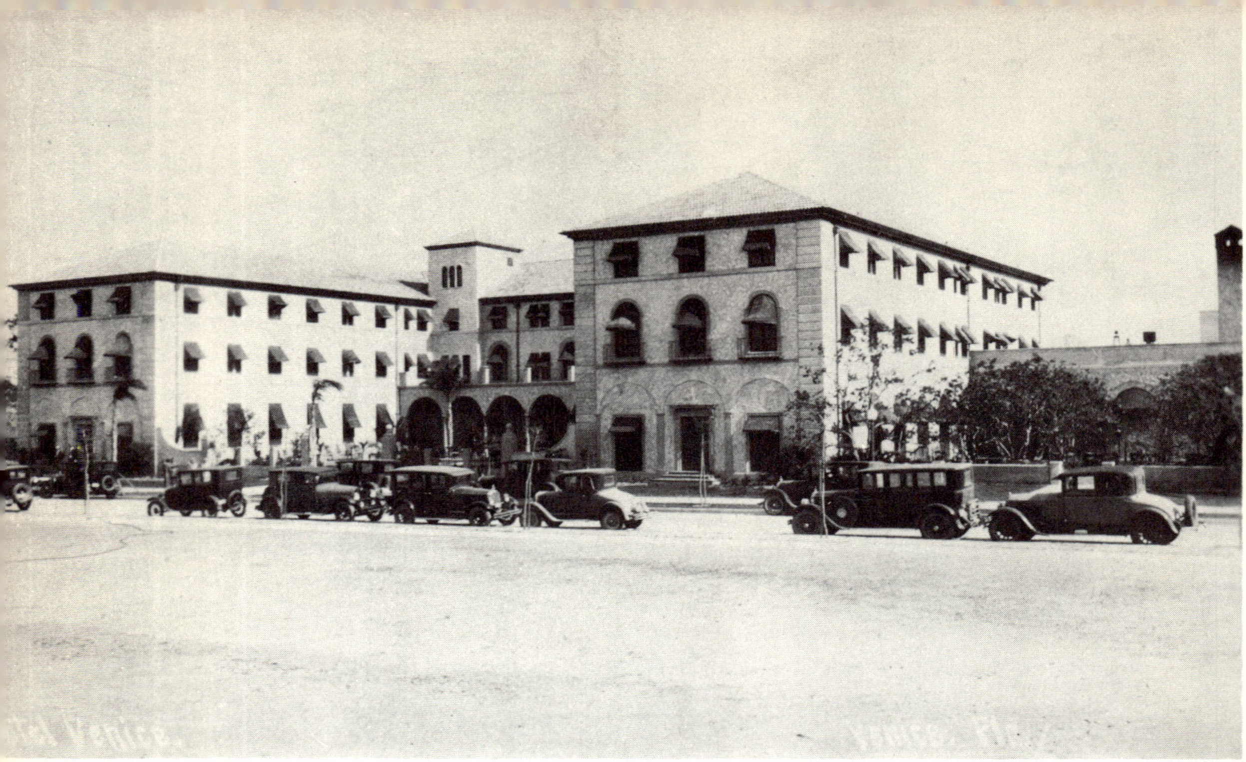

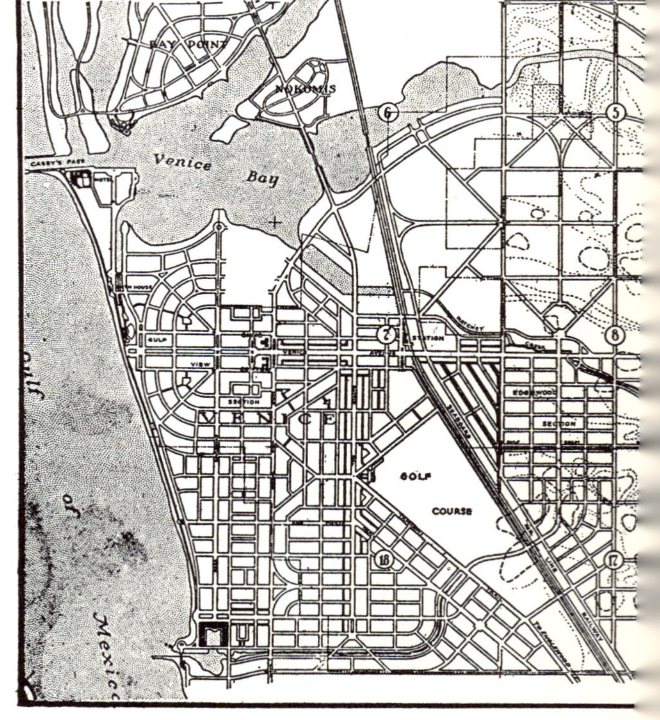

CITY OF VENICE as planned by the Brotherhood of Locomotive Engineers and city planner John Nolan in 1927. The map points out the emphasis put on farming. Intending to create the most stable city possible, the BLE planned east of the city an agricultural empire "not only to put a solid foundation upon the city but to afford to thousands of ordinary men a chance to achieve independence with health and comfort."

HOTEL VENICE (*opposite page, top*) and the SAN MARCO HOTEL (*above*), the beginnings of Venice's dream of becoming the state's most model and modern city. The two hotels, shown upon completion in 1927, never fulfilled their role of the focal points of a mushrooming city. Instead, the economic slide that began in late 1926 and eventually ruined plans that the Brotherhood of Locomotive Engineers had for Venice, emptied the two hotels. Five years later both were taken over by the Kentucky Military Institute, which wintered in Venice for 38 years. When KMI left in 1970, the two hotels were sold to a condominium developer.

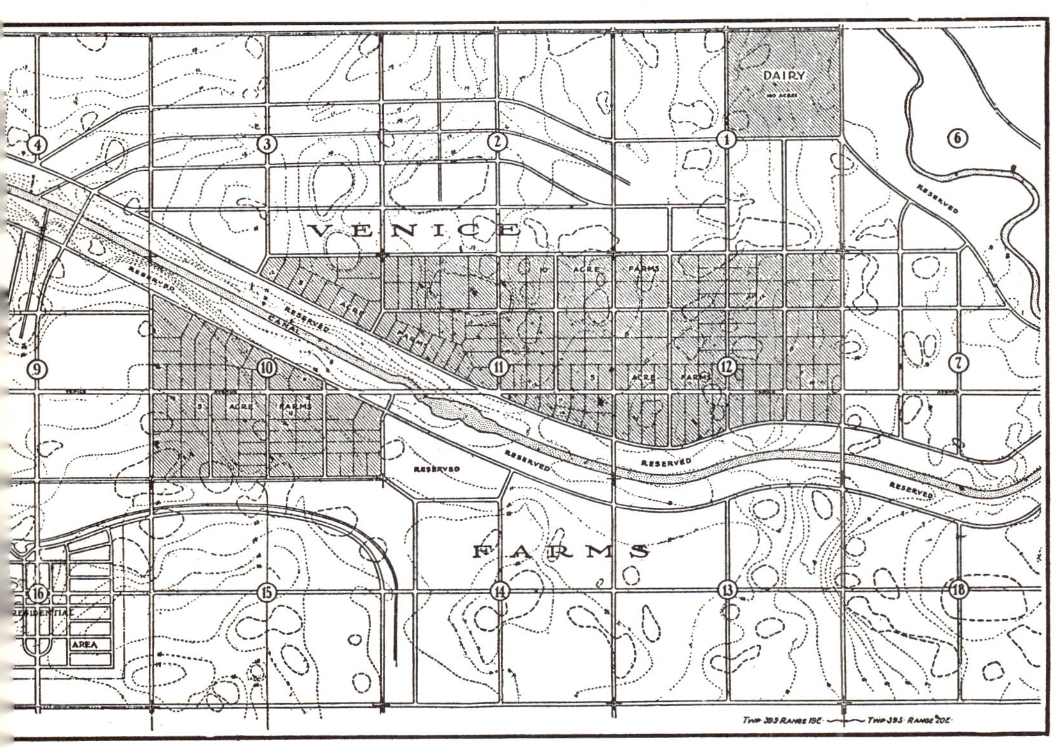

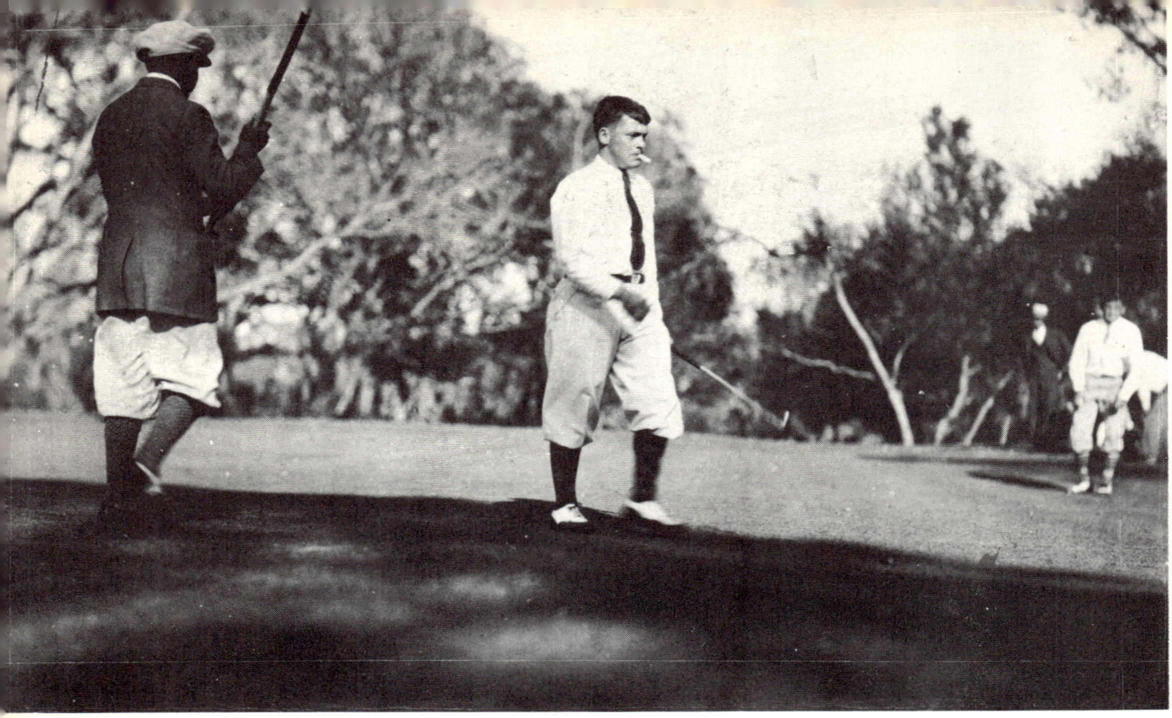

BOBBY JONES comes off the 15th green in 1927 during the formal opening of the golf course named in his honor. The city's old golf course was purchased by Charles Ringling, who made plans to build the courthouse subdivision and Sarasota Terrace Hotel in the area. Left without a course, the city purchased 290 acres about 2½ miles northeast of the courthouse for an 18-hole course. Star attraction at the dedication was Bobby Jones, and 1,500 turned out to watch him shoot the course in 73. The preceding evening Jones and the city's leading citizens gathered for a party at the Mira Mar Hotel, at which the decision was made to name the course the Bobby Jones Municipal Golf Course to give it "prestige."

EVENT OF THE SEASON in Sarasota was, and still is, the Coronation Ball held during the city's annual pageant. Years ago it was called the Sara de Soto Pageant, now changed to King Neptune Frolics. Pausing for the photographer at the 1928 Coronation Ball were, from left, Mrs. Frances Booth, J. W. Burns, Mrs. A. E. Cummer, John Ringling, Frances Edwards (chosen queen that year), and Samuel Gumpertz, general manager of the Ringling circus. Frances Edwards recalls that the Ball "caught me without a gown just for that specific occasion. The Ball had a Spanish theme, so I had to come up with something. My mother, a very clever person, took a dress I already had, sewed on rhinestones and fashioned a silky shawl to the dress. There I was and I won the title."

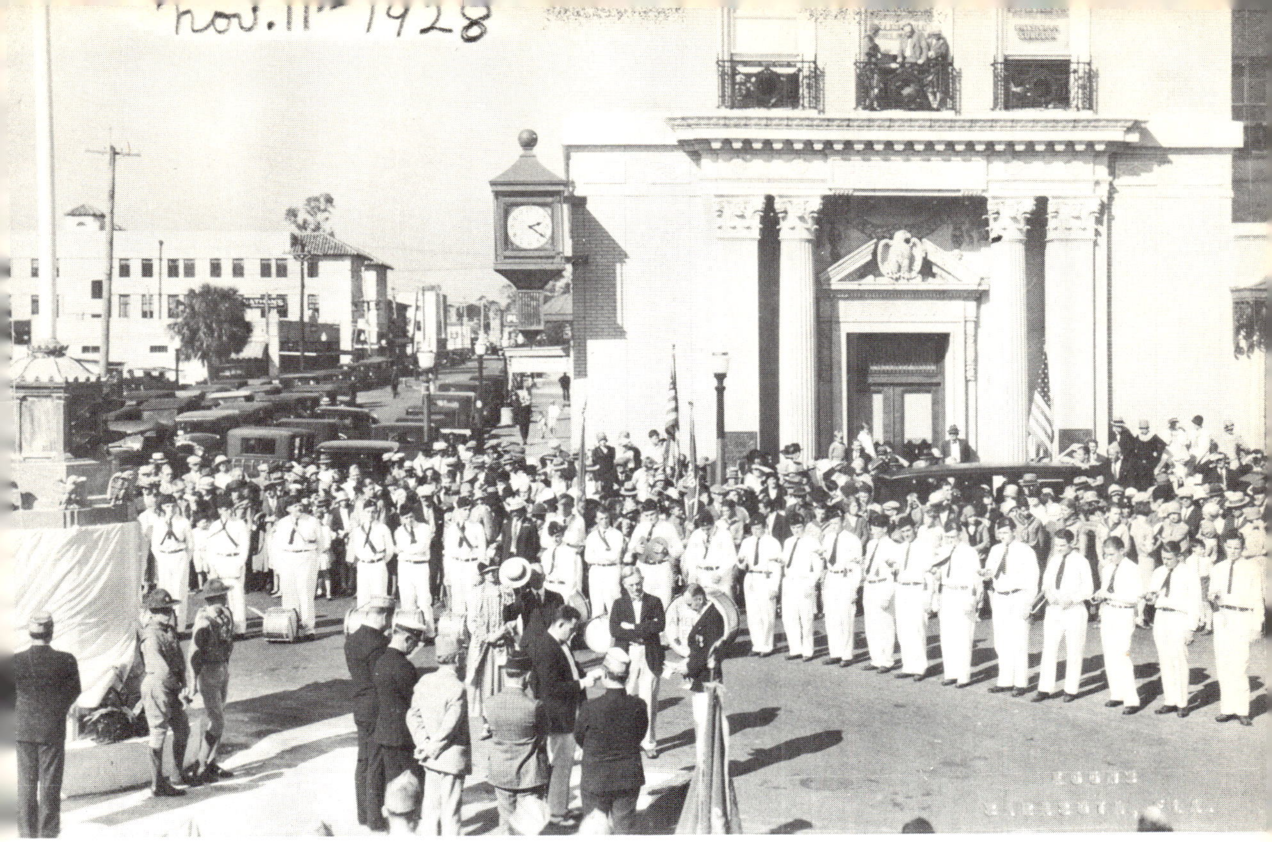

Nov. 11 1928

MONUMENT HONORING WORLD WAR I veterans, gift of the American Legion, Sarasota Bay Post 30, was erected in the intersection of Five Points on November 11, 1928.

SANTA CLAUS came to the Elks Club at Golf and Links Avenue in 1929. The building was once the clubhouse for Col. J. Hamilton Gillespie's golf course.

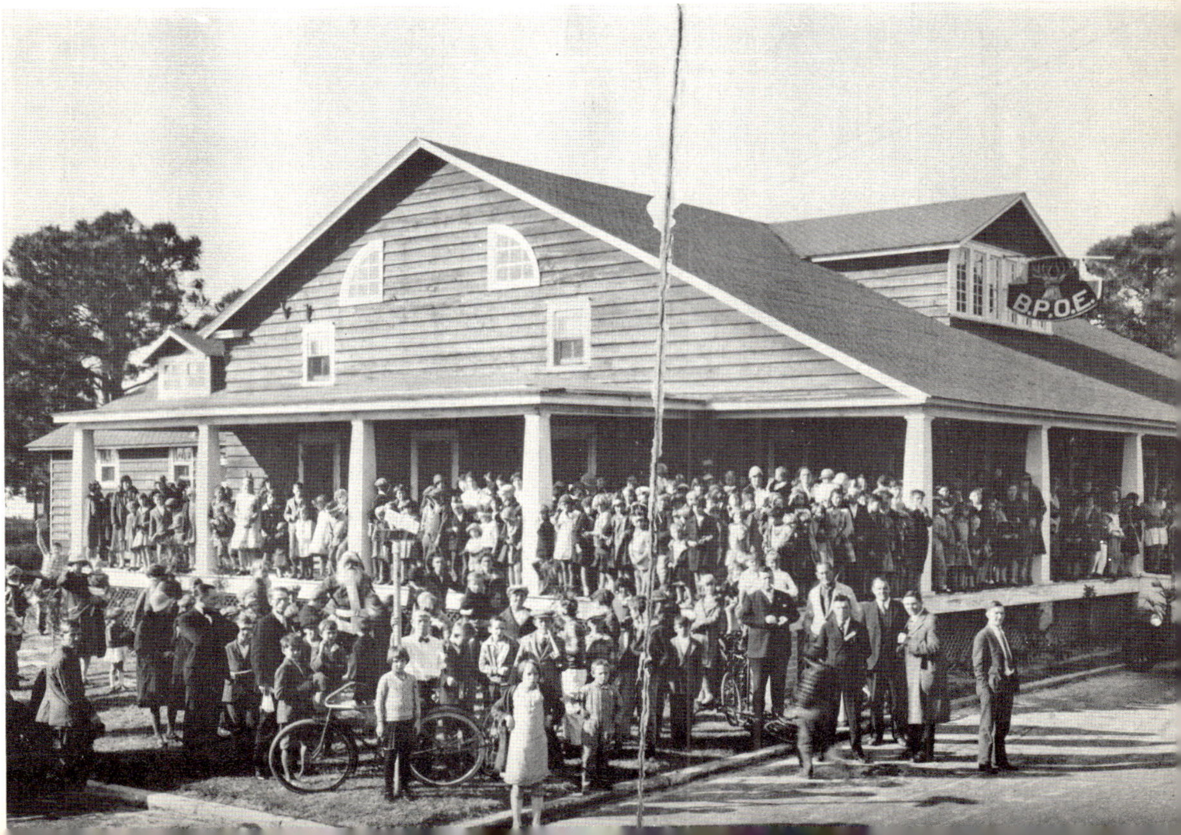

RINGLING'S YACHT, the *Zalophus*, moored at the pier in front of the El Vernona Apartments on Sarasota Bay in 1929. The *Zalophus*, meaning "sea lion," met disaster in 1930 when it motored out into the Bay on a pleasure cruise to Boca Grande. Aboard was the mayor of New York City, Jimmy Walker. A bad storm came up, and at 3 a.m. the *Zalophus* rammed a sandbar and began to list. No one was injured and the passengers were taken off. It remained on the sandbar, deteriorating, until towed off later to Hog's Creek. Captain Roan always joked about the incident, answering questions with "we struck a jelly fish." Ringling later bought a cruiser, *Zalophus II*, in which he was motored around the Bay while recovering from a heart attack in 1932.

"I WANT A MUSEUM built to put my art collection into." That remark, made by John Ringling to architect John H. Phillips, led to one of the finest art museums in the country. Phillips was visiting in Sarasota, and upon meeting the Ringlings he mentioned he had helped design the Metropolitan Museum of Art in New York City. That information prompted Ringling's remark, and two months later he sent Ringling plans he had sketched and a small cardboard model. Ringling liked it and ordered work to begin in the summer of 1927. Original wall foundations were brought from Italy, columns 1,000 years old shipped from Greece, and hundreds of antique arches, doorways, and statues purchased from historical structures in Europe. Built around a courtyard 150 by 350 feet, it cost $2,500,000, and houses one of the world's finest collections of Baroque art, purchased by Ringling on trips to Europe. In January 1930 the Ringling Museum of Art was dedicated and subsequently opened to the public.

Following page: UPON HIS DEATH, John Ringling willed the Museum, shown here after its completion, to the people of Florida.

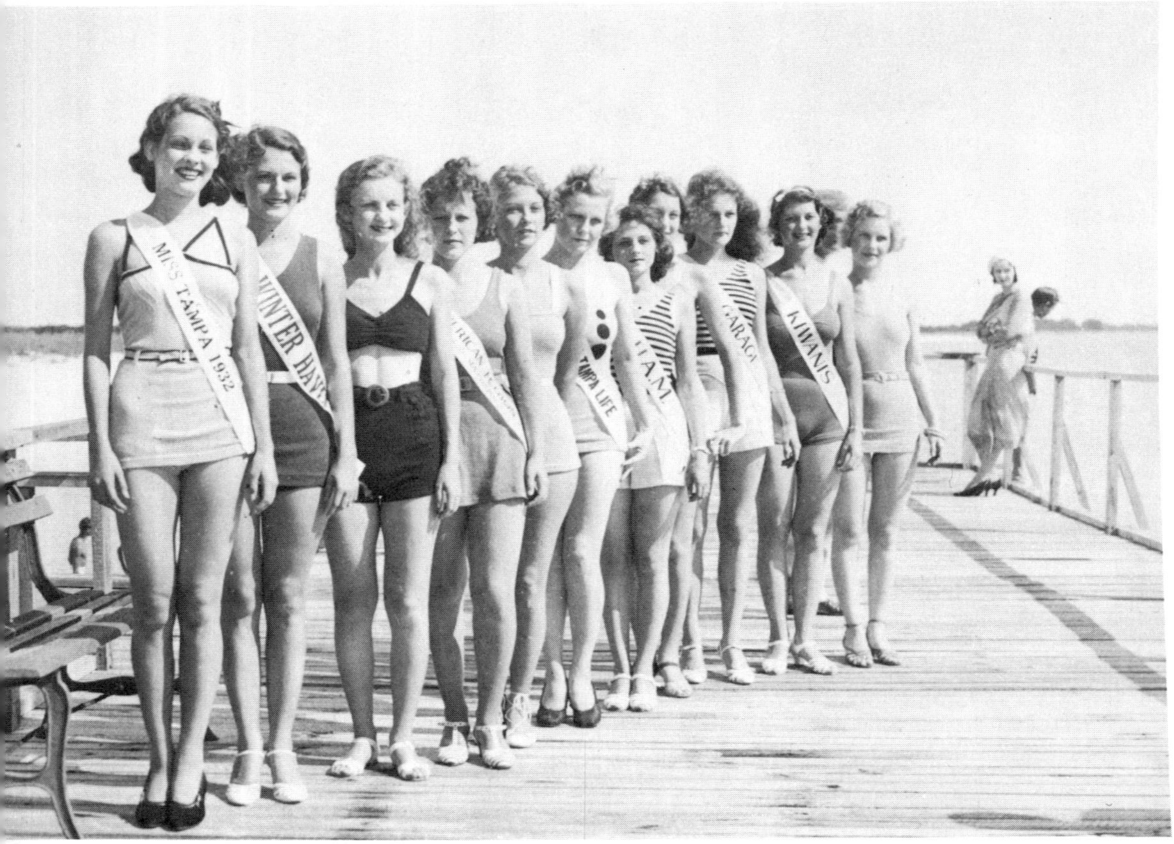

BEAUTY CONTEST in 1932 attracted the prettiest from surrounding cities and organizations. In 1956, and several years thereafter, Sarasota was the home of the Miss Florida Pageant.

THE 1931 MISS SARA DE SOTO, Mary Alice Welch, sits for a publicity shot in a brocade costume richly festooned with ropes of sequins.

Sarasota in the 1930s

THREE MAJOR APARTMENT complexes pictured here in the 1930s still grace the northwest side of downtown. In center foreground are the Frances-Carlton Apartments, built in 1924 by C. O. Teate Sr. and named after his wife and son. Ringling Hotel at left is now an apartment building, and was owned by the same man who built the apartment building at top right, the El Vernona Apartments, now known as the Belle Haven.

A HEAVY OVERNIGHT RAIN inundated the Sarasota Mobile Home Park in 1931. A chain gang from the county jail was brought in the next morning to dig drainage ditches.

SARASOTA MOBILE HOME PARK and Payne Park baseball diamond a few years after the city lured the national convention of Tin Can Tourists to the trailer park. The tourists had been convening in Arcadia, but because the Sarasota economy was lagging and the Tin Can Tourists were known to spend a great deal of money, a successful pitch was made to bring the trailer tourists to Sarasota. Every year, until 1937, they trailered in from around the country for their convention, swelling the park with nearly 2,000 trailers. Several versions of why they were called "Tin Can" tourists have circulated; one attributes the name to the tourists eating out of tin cans, while another says it was because their trailers looked as cheap as tin cans. Still another explanation is the tourists put a tin can over their car's radiator cap to identify themselves on the road to other club members.

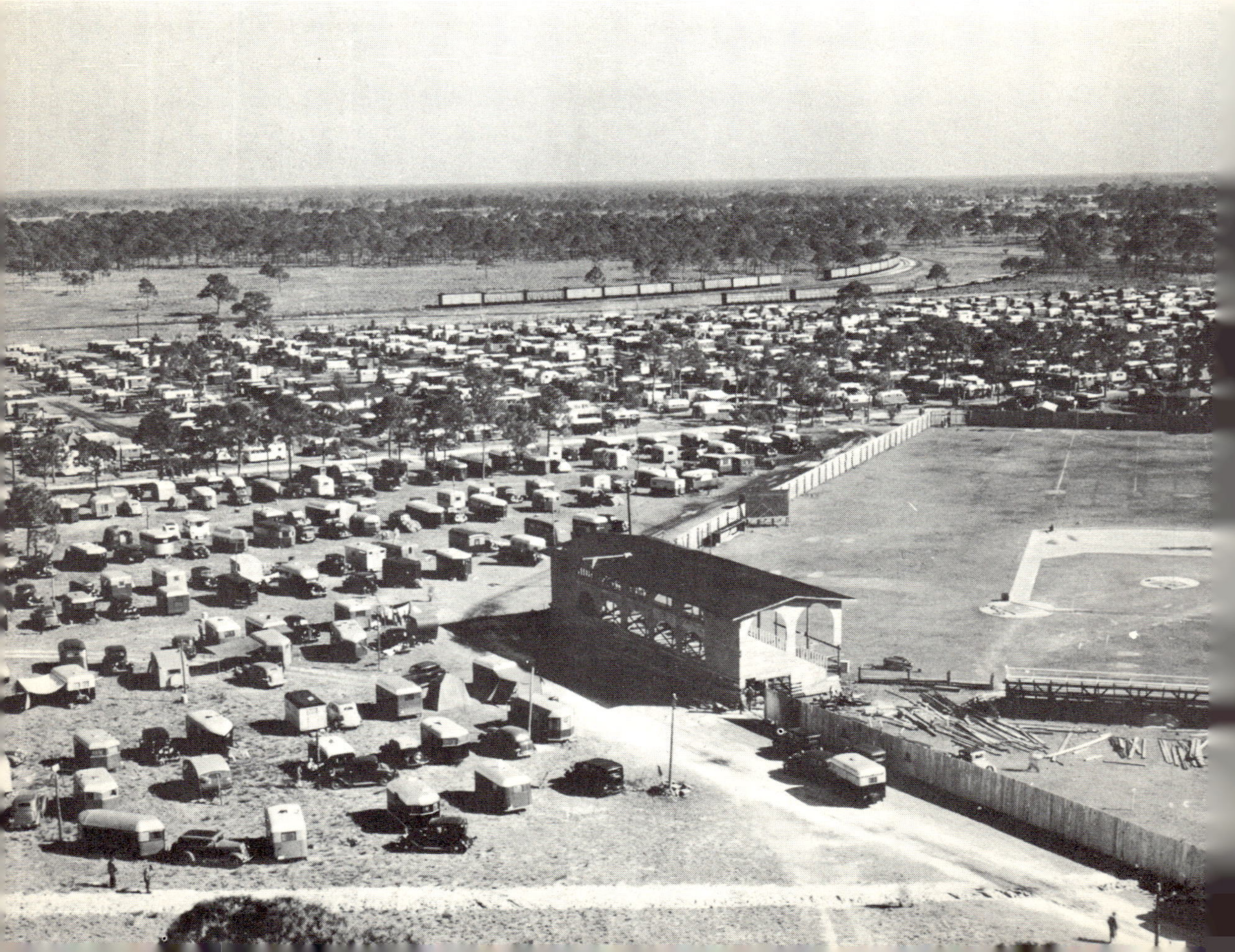

TO SPUR DEVELOPMENT of the properties owned by John Ringling on Lido, St. Armand's and Longboat Key in the late 1920s, a bathing pavilion was built in 1926 on Lido Beach by Ringling and his close friend and associate, Samuel Gumpertz. Shown is the pier in front of the pavilion in 1935.

SINCE 1878, SARASOTA POST OFFICES have been housed in half a dozen or more buildings. No special structure was ever erected until 1934 when the Post Office moved to this building at Golf and Orange Avenue which cost $110,000. It is now the Federal Building. There is a new Post Office on Ringling Boulevard.

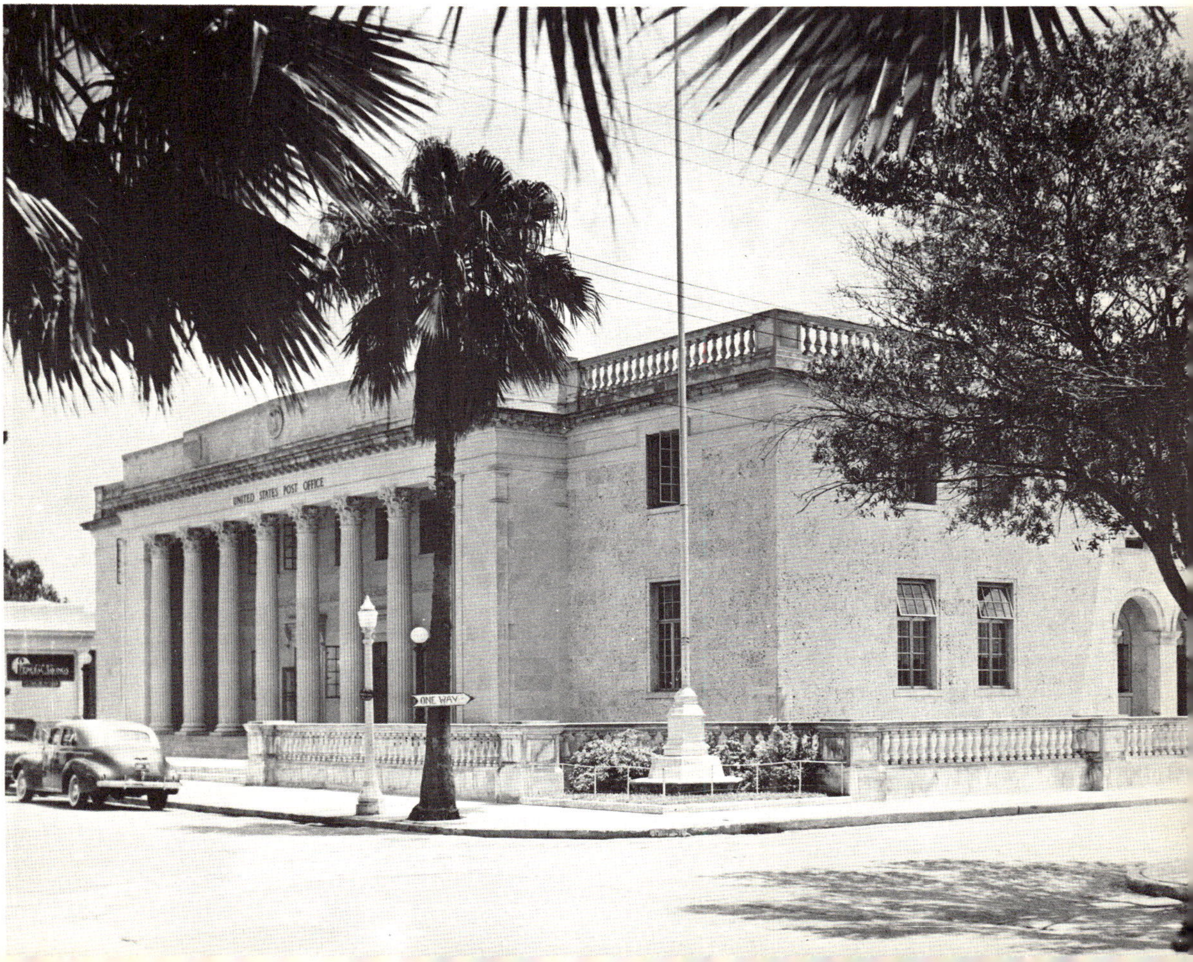

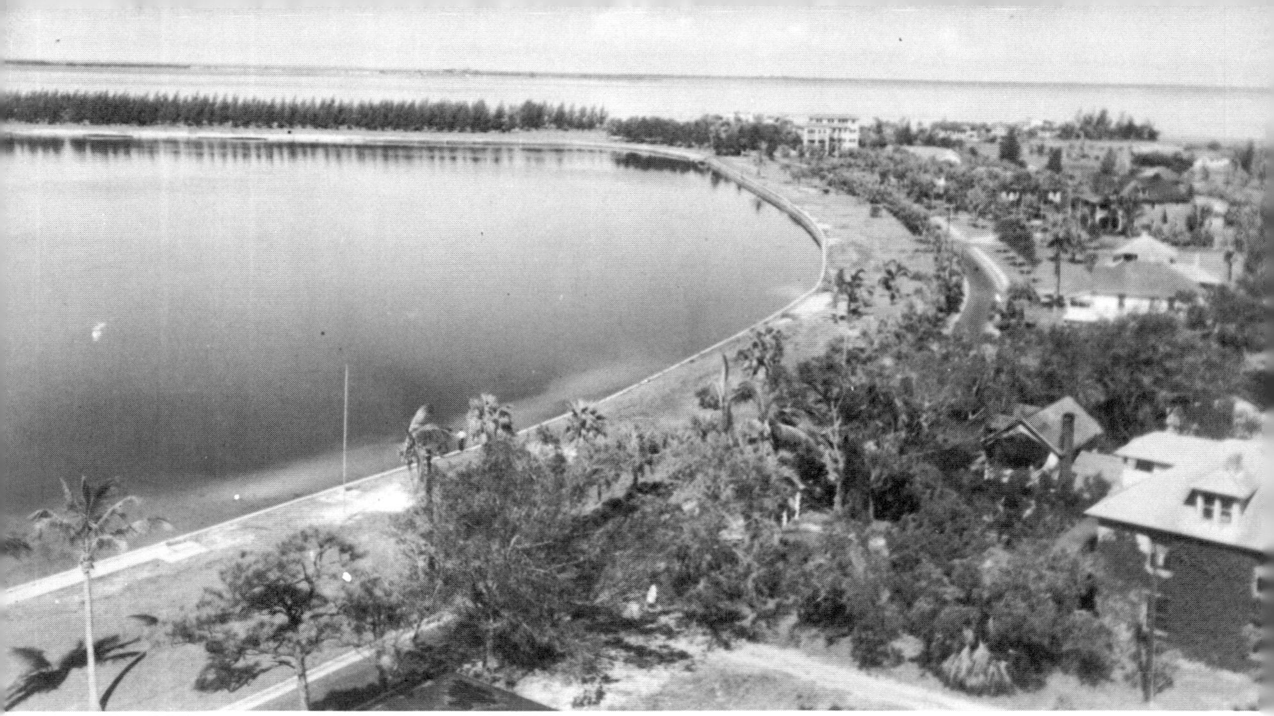

BUILDING ACTIVITY CEASED, the fishing industry waned, and merchants' profits ended at the depth of the Depression in Sarasota. These inactive years seem illustrated by the tranquil scene above in 1935. Winter tourists were scarce. Even the Ringling Causeway ceased carrying traffic, the wooden planks having rotted with no funds available to fix them. One of the few buildings in this picture that still stands today is the house in lower right. It was former mayor Harry Higel's home, on Gulf Stream Avenue just north of lower Main Street. Survival is attributed to the concrete blocks used for the house; they were made in the city's first concrete plant set up by J. Louis Houle back in 1905. The few business and residential buildings still standing are mostly of Houle's blocks. Tall building at center top is the Sunset Apartments, formerly the Sarasota Yacht and Automobile Club. Island in distance is Longboat Key.

FOR FOUR YEARS the city had both a *Sarasota Herald* and a *Sarasota Tribune*. The former was organized in October 1925 by David B. Lindsay, E. E. Naugle and Paul Poynter (father of the present publisher of the *St. Petersburg Times*). Poynter and Naugle soon afterwards sold their interest in the *Herald* to Lindsay. Meanwhile, in 1934, the *Tribune* was organized, with B. W. Powell as publisher. It was situated in this building on South Pineapple. In 1938, the *Tribune* was sold to Lindsay.

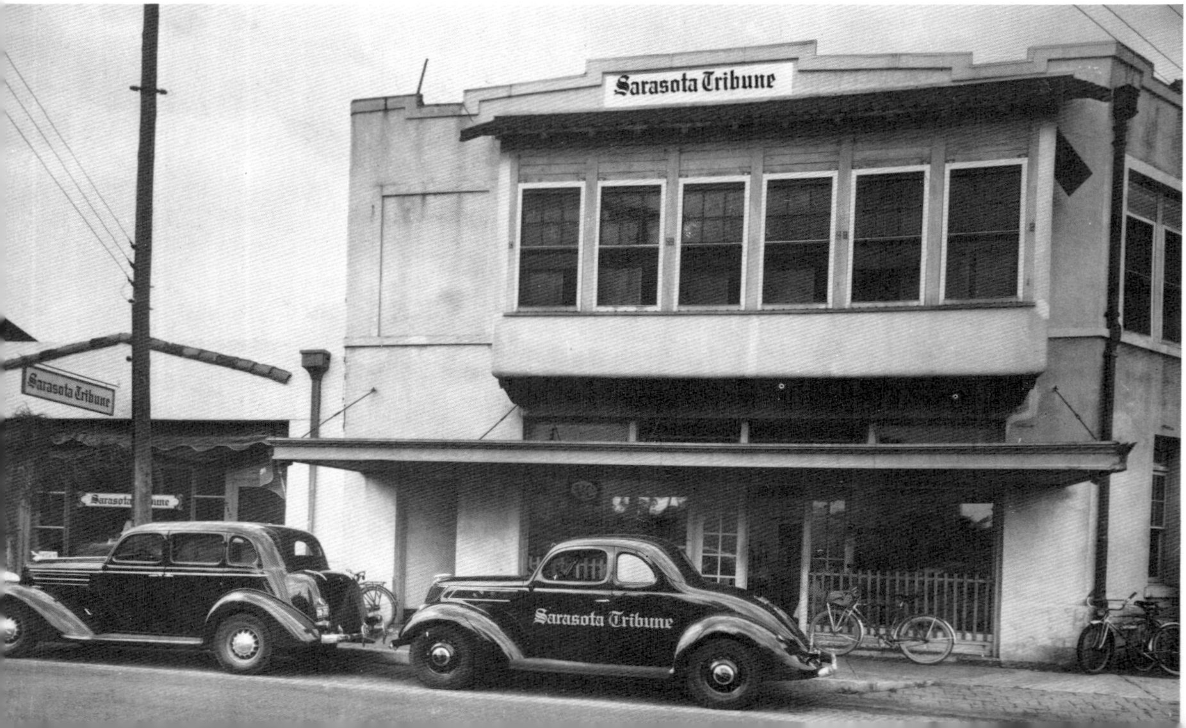

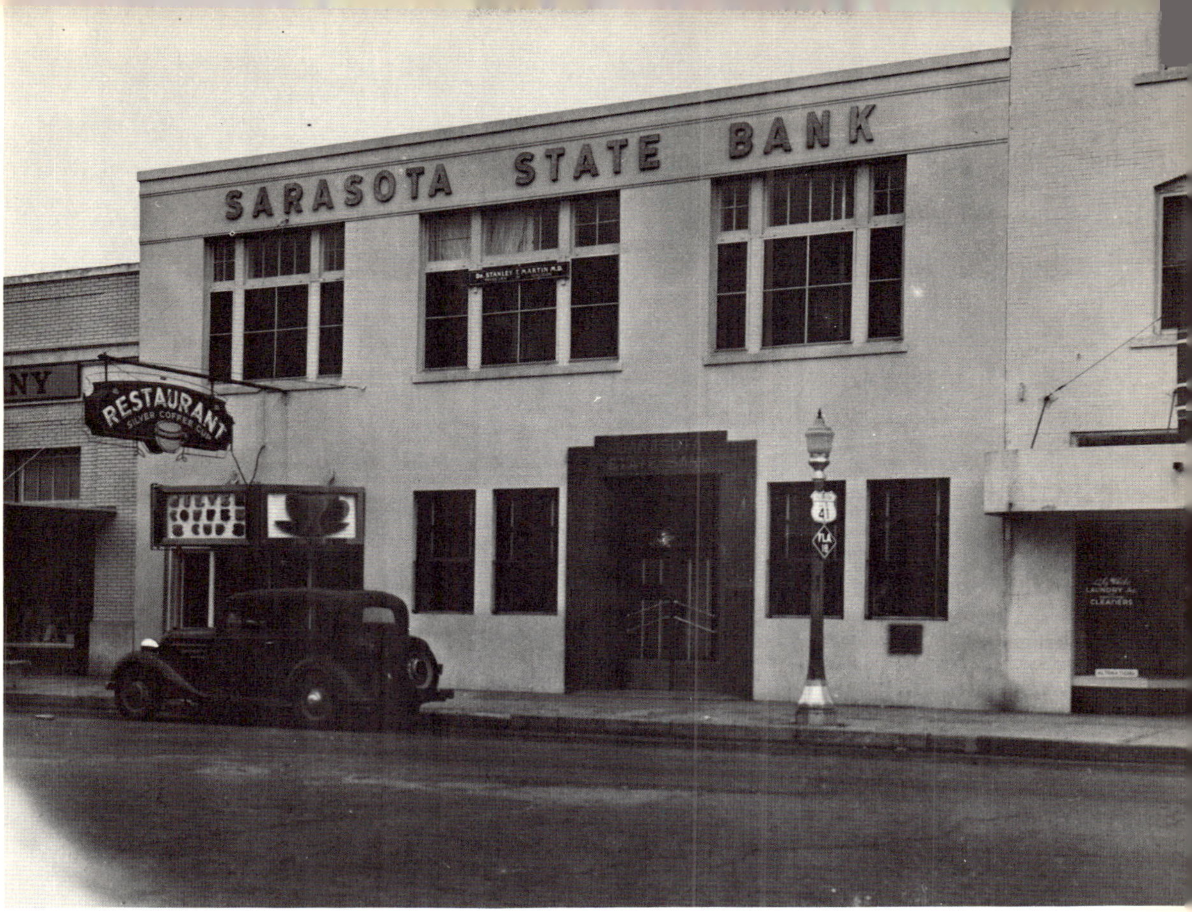

SARASOTA STATE BANK's humble beginning was in this building in 1939, when it opened with total assets of $240,000. Reorganized into the Sarasota Bank & Trust Co. in 1951, the firm now is housed in a beautiful new 11-story structure at Orange and Main Streets; its assets have gone up, too, now totaling $137,000,000 with trust assets over $225,000,000.

CONCERTS DURING THE WINTER SEASON always have been a Sunday afternoon attraction at the city's mobile home park. This is a photo of a rehearsal of the Trailer Park Concert Band in 1937. Today's park band has 45 members, all park residents. Their average age is 78.

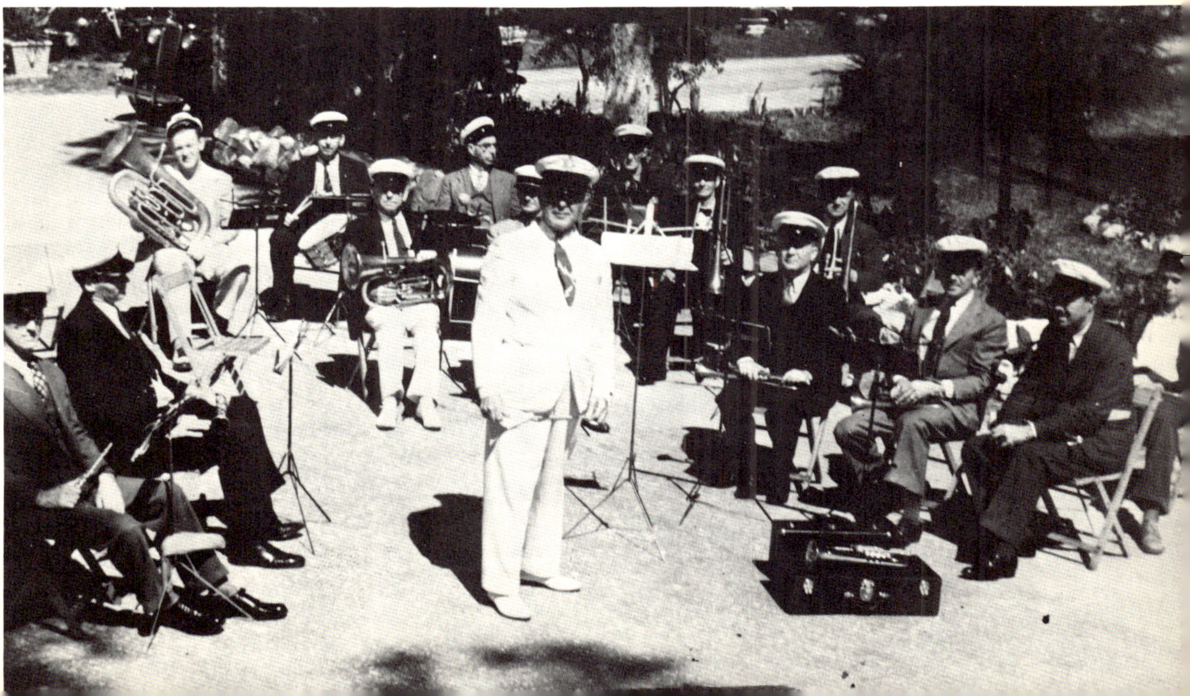

PANORAMIC VIEW IN 1937 of Sarasota looking toward the islands and the Gulf of Mexico. Although the Ringling Causeway to the islands had been built more than 10 years earlier, the beaches remained relatively undeveloped because of the Depression. The stand of pines from which the bridge

starts is Golden Gate Point. Bird Key, the first island, was inhabited only by the Ida Ringling North family. The Lido Beach Casino was still a year away from construction. Siesta Key is to upper left.

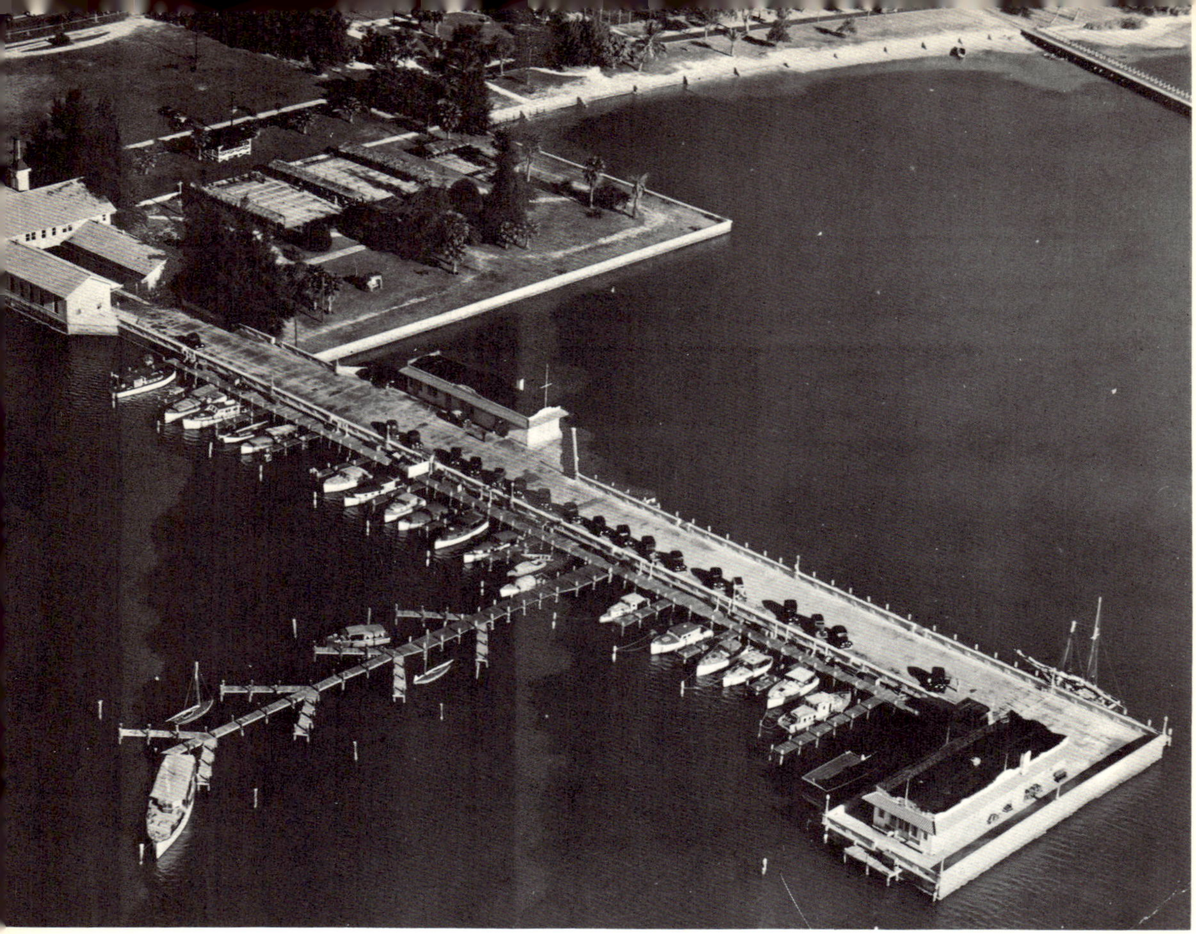

VAST CHANGE from the city pier prior to World War I, when it supported fish houses and machine shops, is the pier in 1937, shown above. When the 1921 storm washed out the old pier, the city ordained the pier would be used solely for recreation. The building in center of pier is Chamber of Commerce. At left is City Hall.

THE WPA'S STAMP on the city was the 37-acre Bayfront park project on the Tamiami Trail. Mayor E. A. Smith in 1935 proposed the idea of a municipal park on what was the last large waterfront tract in the city still available for development. The tract could be obtained for back taxes of about $15,000, owed on the land by the defunct Sarasota Bay Hotel Co. The city bought the tax certificates, then succeeded in getting Federal funds to build the park. A WPA project, clearing and construction started in 1937. A year later the city had its Municipal Auditorium, lawn bowling, shuffleboard courts and a park beautified by the Garden Club. The photo was taken in 1938 after it was opened for its first event, the Sara de Soto celebration.

THE BUST THAT SET IN in 1926 led to the Orange Blossom Hotel at Palm and Main. The building started out as a bank—the American National Bank—in early 1926. It was erected by the building company that owned and razed the landmark Belle Haven Inn, which was on the site. In May 1928, the bank's vice president announced: "Due to our inability to realize on past due paper, coupled with a number of heavy withdrawals recently, we are unable to continue without probable serious losses." Depositors had $462,000 in the bank, but received back only 18¼ cents on the dollar. For several years the building stood vacant. In 1937 it was converted into the Orange Blossom Hotel. But in 1965 it, too, was closed, and again it was vacated, not to be occupied again until 1967 when it reopened as the Orange Blossom Club Apartments.

FAMOUS FOURSOME playing golf in 1937 at the Bobby Jones Municipal Golf Course. From left, Dizzy Dean, Babe Ruth, Paul Waner, and Lloyd Brown, all Major Leaguers in and near their prime. Sarasota was the Spring training home of the Boston Red Sox at that time.

THE STRONG INFLUENCE of Karl Bickel spread out over dozens of community projects. Resident of Sarasota since 1935, the former United Press president often called special luncheon meetings to inaugurate or accelerate such programs as beautification of the city, construction of the Lido Beach Casino, preservation of Florida and Sarasota history, and advancement of the Ringling Museum of Art. This particular meeting, in the Ringling Hotel in 1938, was attended mainly by publishers of area newspapers. Bickel is at head of table: at his left is Mayor E. A. Smith.

A $16,000,000 INVESTMENT that turned into a ghost town. This is Venice in the 1930s, a perfect example of bad timing. The Brotherhood of Locomotive Engineers in September 1925 purchased 30,000 acres to create the town of Venice and poured millions into development and sales; unfortunately, the boom peaked in October that year, then started downward. Four years later the grandiose plan folded, nearly bankrupting the brotherhood. The dream was gigantic, with sales brochures stating "for the first time on record, a city has been built from the very foundation stone according to carefully prepared and logically executed plans." John Nolen, a well-known city planner

from Massachusetts, was brought in to lay out the city. A special architectural department was established to see that the "Northern Italian" style of architecture was carried out in all buildings. The BLE included an extensive farming operation, calling for 25,000 acres known as the Venice Farms to become a self-sustained agricultural unit. At its peak, in the late 1920s, Venice boasted 4,000 residents. The view above is looking north. The cluster of buildings at upper right are the old Hotel Venice and San Marco Hotel, used at the time of this photo by the Kentucky Military Institute. A rejuvenated Venice now contains nearly 10,000 people.

LIDO BEACH CASINO under construction in 1939. A WPA project costing $250,000, the city in 1938 bought 1,300 feet of beach frontage from the Ringling estate in a tax settlement for the Casino site. The city at first leased it to a private operator but this experiment failed and its operation was turned over to the city recreation director. The complex included six large buildings, among them two restaurants, a large dress pavilion, stores and shops, 39 beach and pool cabanas, plus one of the West Coast's finest beaches. The pool often was used for swimming meets. By 1968 it needed major repairs. Rather than renovate it, the city tore it down and built a new one.

Facing page: THE PRESENT PUBLIC LIBRARY in the civic center park was a donation to the city by John Chidsey, a winter visitor from Connecticut. Cost was $18,500. This photo was taken upon completion in 1941. In prior years, the library was in the Woman's Club (from 1914 to 1940). Plans are for a new and larger library on the park grounds. Mrs. Betty W. Service has been librarian since 1927.

Sarasota since 1940

BOWLING ON THE GREEN, one of the recreational facilities included in the civic center park during its construction by the WPA in 1938.

FISHERMAN ON THE RINGLING CAUSEWAY became more numerous during the season than the automobiles traveling over it to get to the relatively undeveloped areas of Lido, St. Armand's, and Longboat Key. The wood-planked bridge, built in 1925, served as the link to the Gulf beaches until torn down in the 1960s and replaced by a twin concrete causeway.

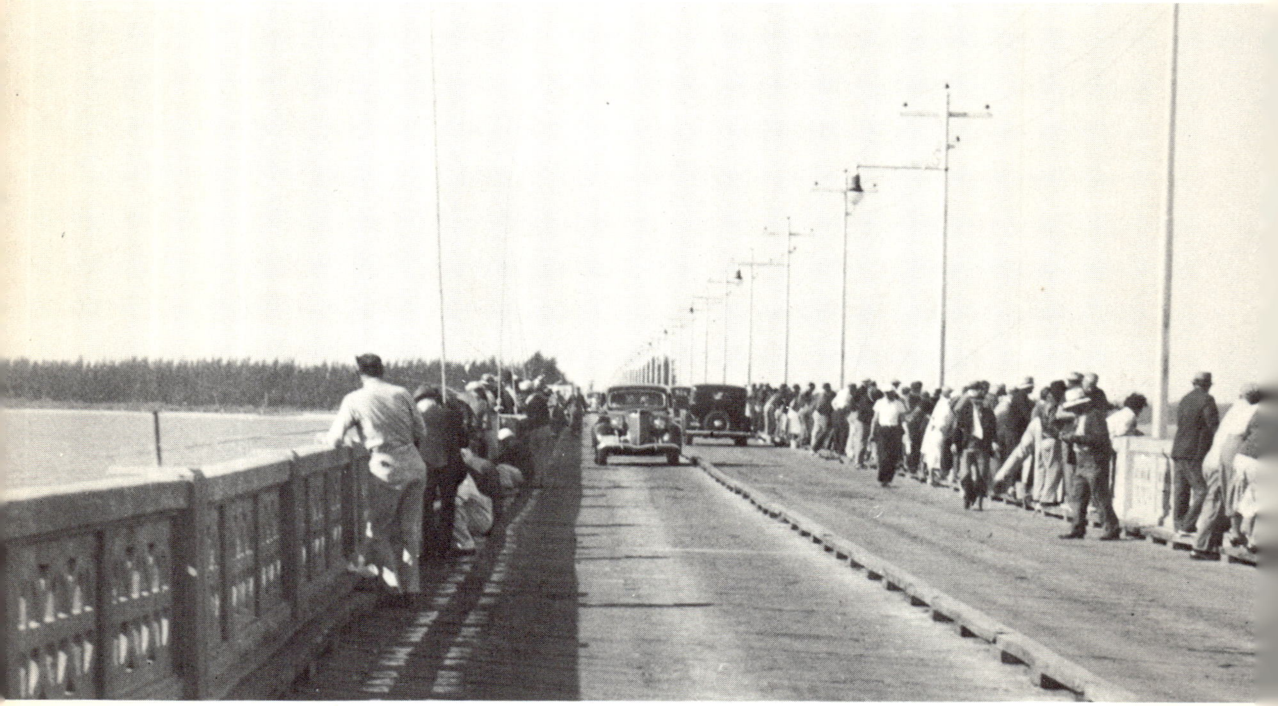

Preceding page: LOOKING NORTH ALONG SARASOTA BAY in the 1940s, this view shows the recently completed park for the Municipal Auditorium and the new Public Library built in 1941. Payne Terminal is near top of picture. The apartment building in lower right is the El Vernona, built by Owen Burns and still standing but now named the Belle Haven. Van Wezel Hall site is near clump of trees in center of photo.

SNAPPY SARASOTA HIGH SCHOOL BAND on Armistice Day 1941. Leading the Sailor band is Drum Majorette Harriet Sturgis. Band Master was V. D. Sturgis.

JUST THREE WEEKS BEFORE PEARL HARBOR, the local unit of the Florida State Guard stands at parade rest during Armistice Day ceremonies downtown. The state guard was organized to replace the National Guard unit, which had been called into active duty.

MODEST BEGINNING of the Salvation Army in 1927 was a small room on Main Street, after which it moved from place to place until it built its own Citadel (*above*) on South Pineapple in 1941. Expanded work by the Army now has it operating out of buildings on South Tuttle and on 4th Street.

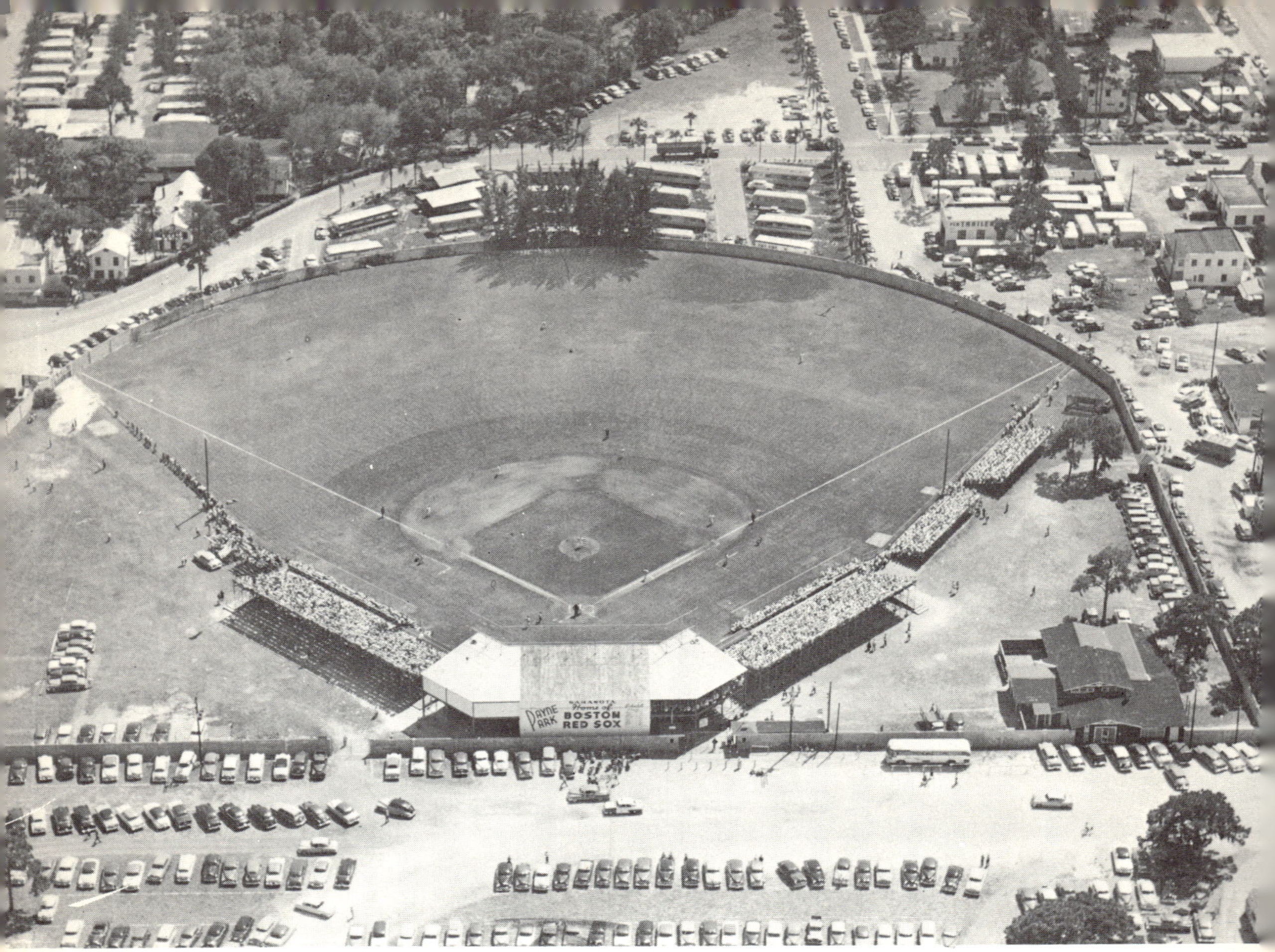

PAYNE PARK, the Spring Training headquarters for three Major League baseball teams—the New York Giants, followed by the Boston Red Sox (when this photo was taken), and the Chicago White Sox today.

A CAPTURED DELICACY, one hefty sea turtle, landed in 1942. Turtle meat was a favorite with so many people. Not just the meat was enjoyed, but the eggs. "Leathery and full of thick yellow yolk," one pioneer recalls, "they made the lightest cake you ever tasted."

A MINIATURE SUBMARINE put on display on Main Street during World War II. Sixty-seven men and one woman from Sarasota County gave their lives during the war.

156 ACRES OF WINTER QUARTERS–an expensive complex of buildings for animals and workers, of railroad tracks and cars, and a huge parking lot to accommodate the thousands that visited the circus in the off-season. Tall building housed administrative offices. John Ringling's announcement on March 23, 1927, that he was moving the circus Winter Quarters from Bridgeport, Connecticut, to Sarasota was a financial shot in the arm to the city. The turbulent boom days of 1925 had passed, and the economy was dragging. Predictions that Ringling would pour large sums into the area for the quarters were accurate. Close to a million was spent at the Quarters on buildings and labor. In addition, high salaried circus performers made Sarasota their home, and publicity brought thousands of tourists to the new attraction.

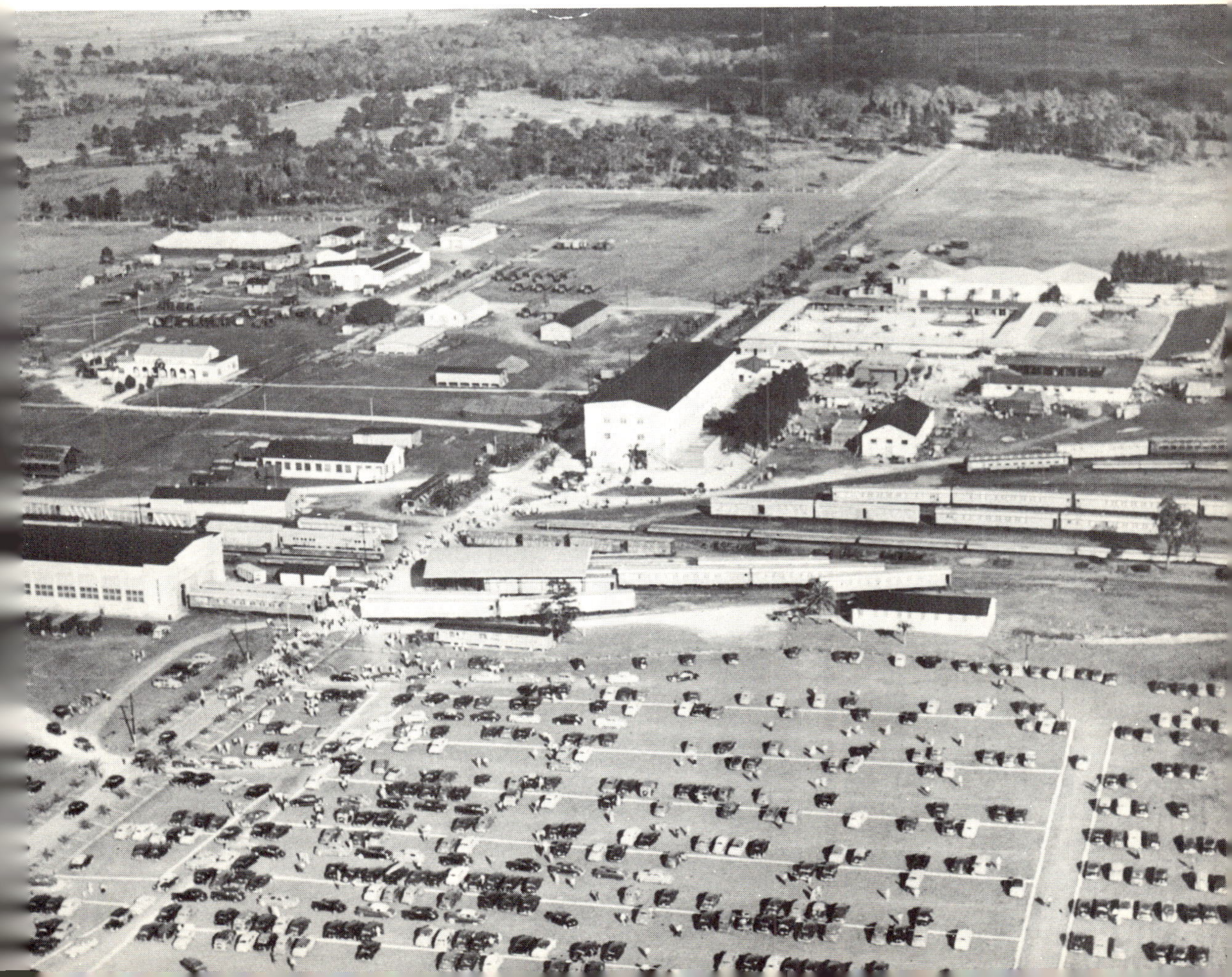

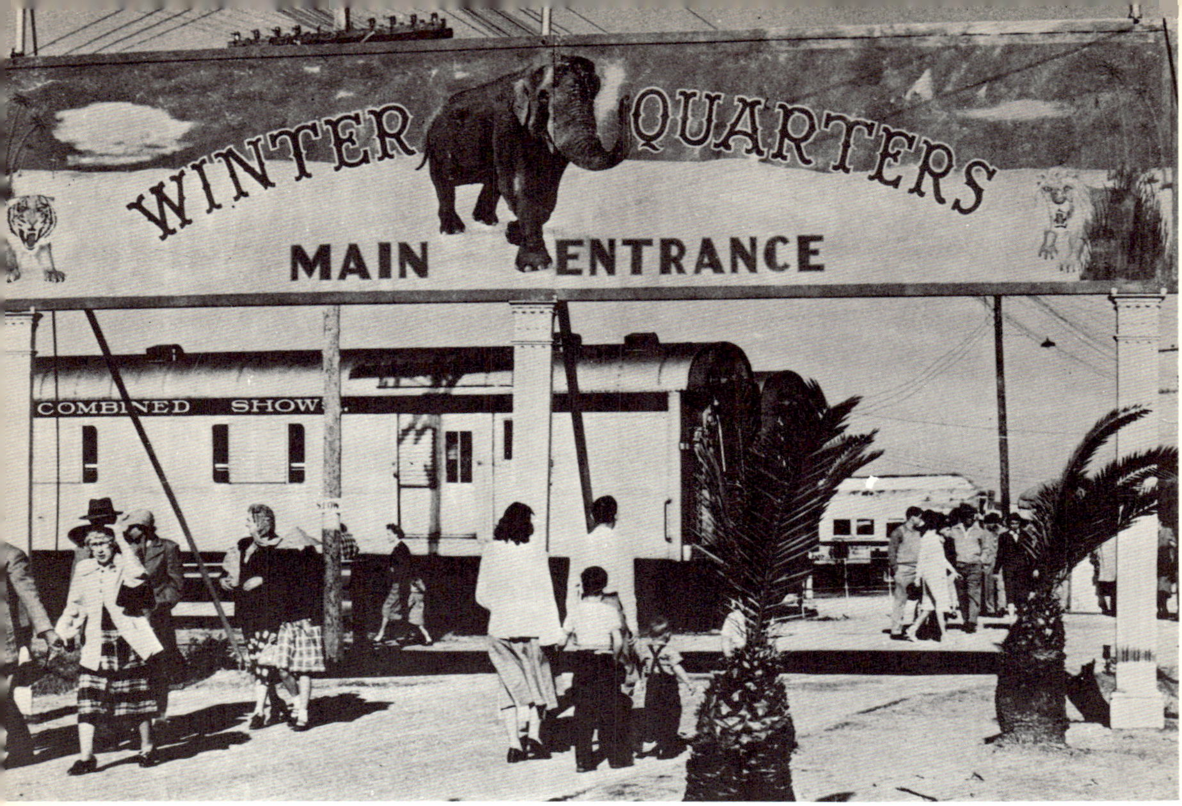

WINTER QUARTERS of the circus took over the old fairgrounds out on Fruitville Road (*above*) in 1927 and remained there for 33 years. The circus then moved to Venice, in 1960, and now winters there. The herd of elephants (*below*) at the quarters numbered as high as 40, and always were a main attraction, as shown in this 1945 photo. Circus officials often brought the elephants into downtown for parades or special events.

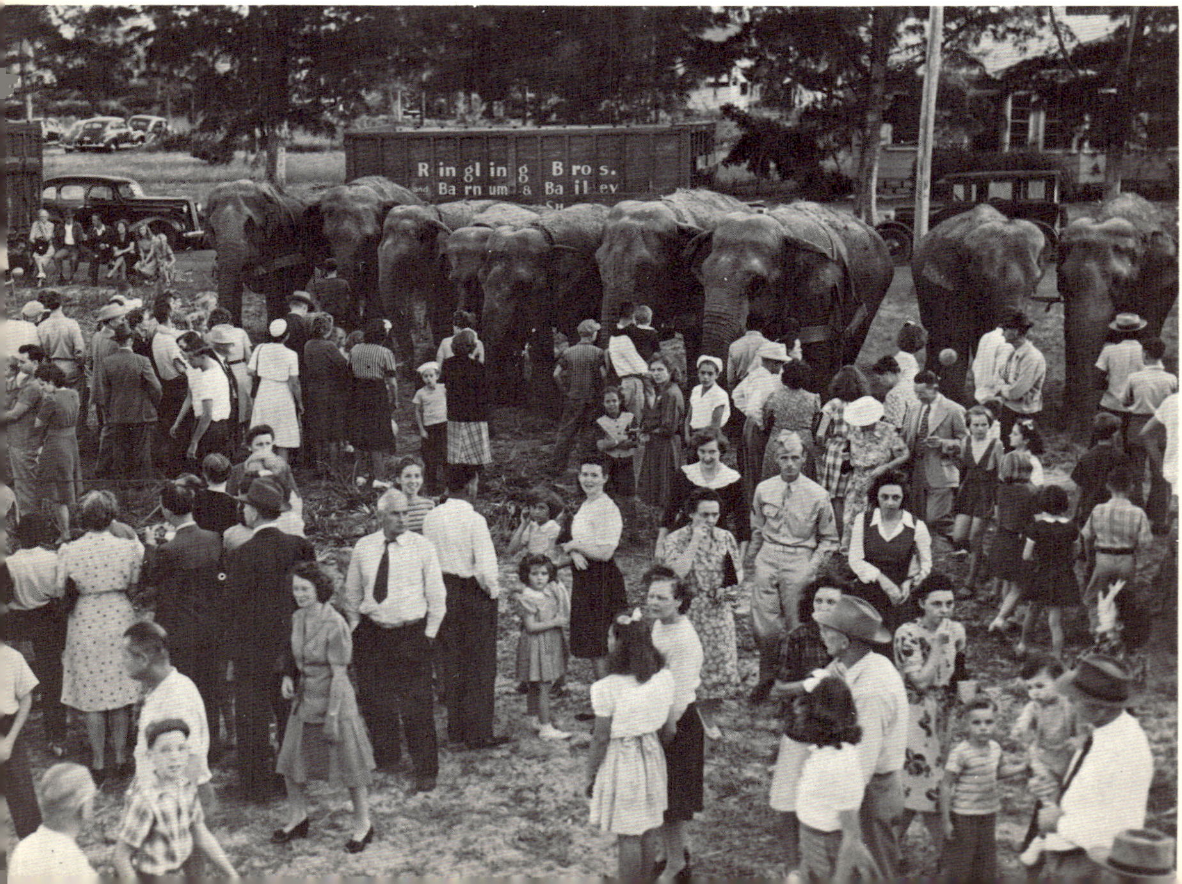

AMERICAN LEGION COLISEUM was popular with boxing fans in the 1930s and 1940s. Post 30 sponsored the matches, first in its small clubhouse at Golf and Washington; when the crowds got too big for the building, the Post took over the above structure, which was intended to become the city's Studebaker agency building. The end of the boom kept the car dealer from completing the building, so the Legion bought it. It is now a restaurant, the Legion having moved to 6th Street.

TRAIN STATION of the Seaboard Air Line at Main and Lemon, during World War II. Because of the many servicemen at the Air Force bases in Sarasota and Venice, the depot was at its busiest during the war.

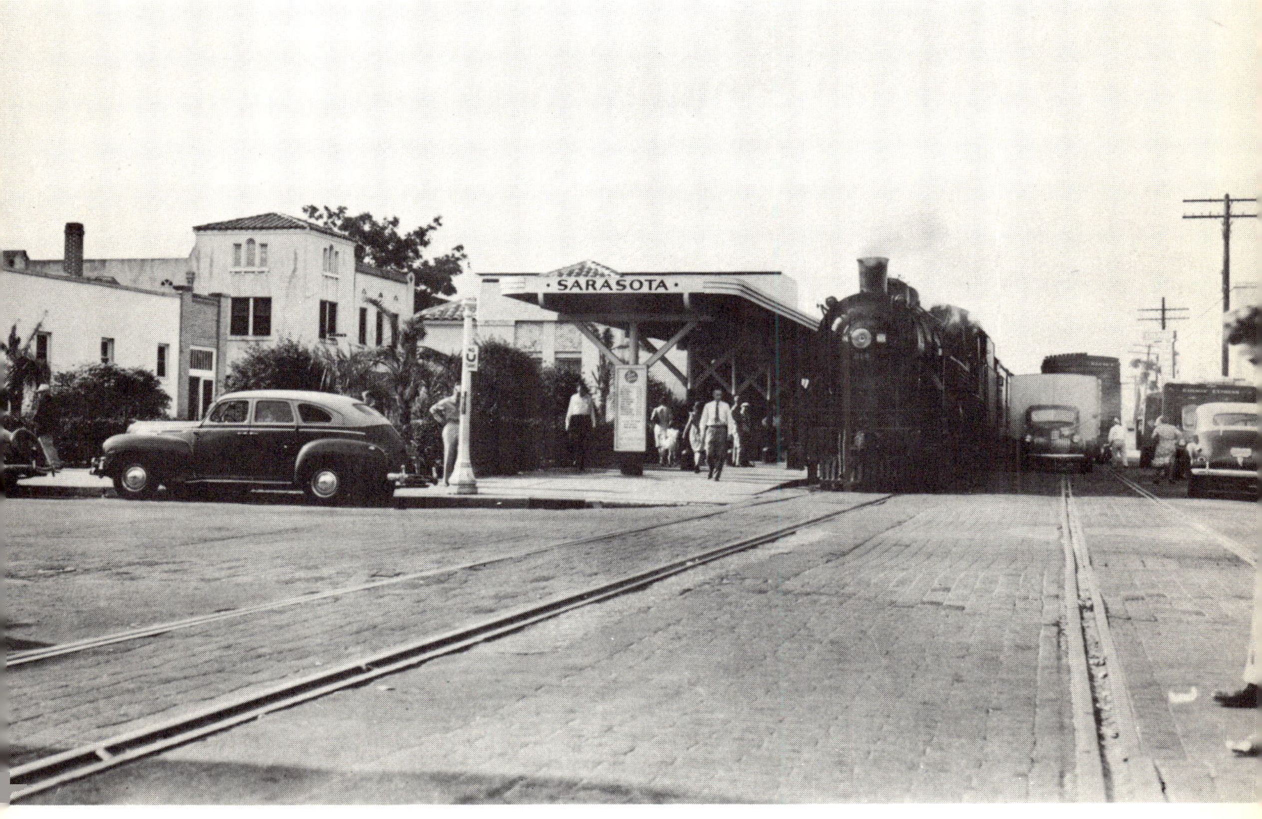

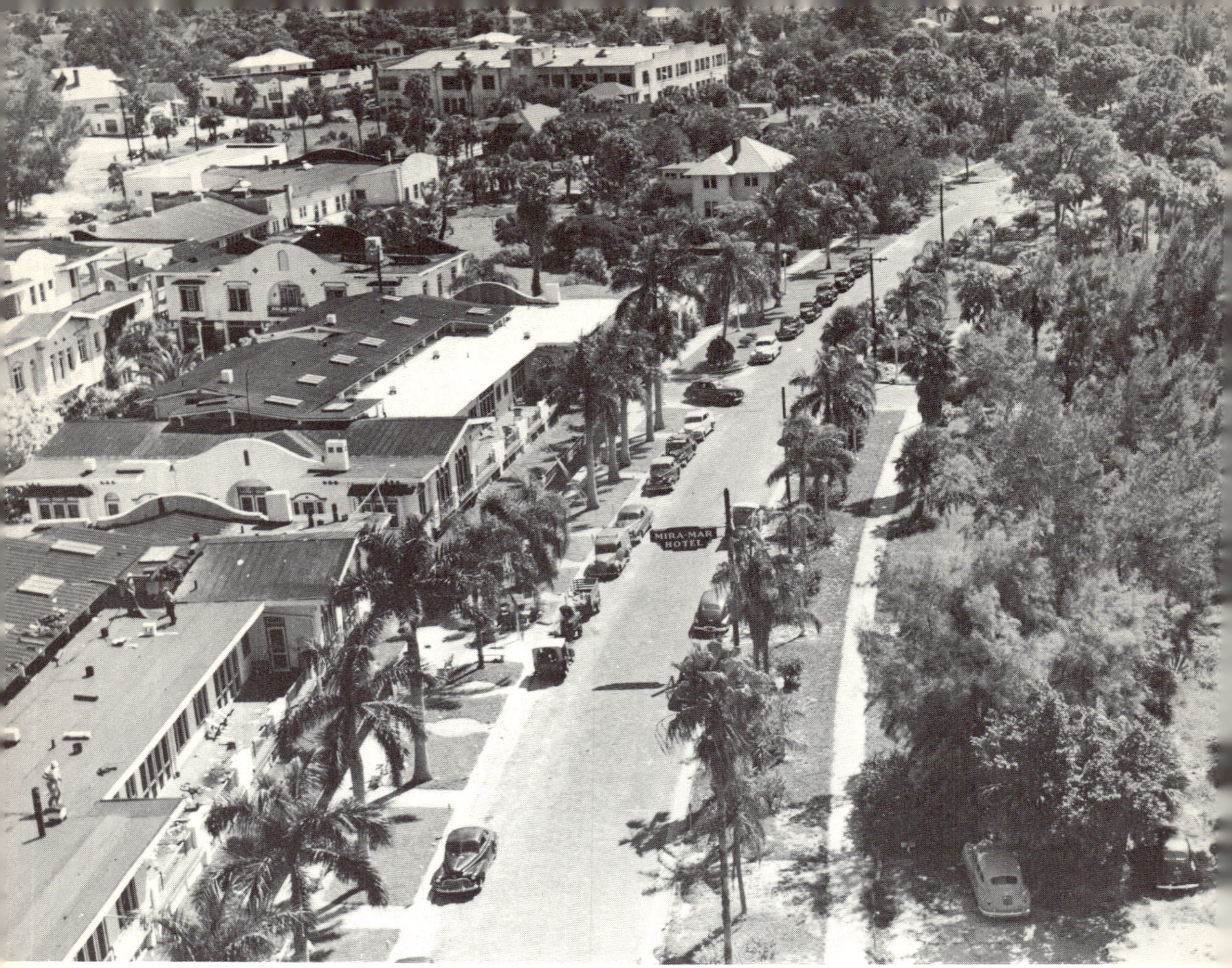

PALM AVENUE after World War II, with the Mira Mar Hotel at left. Property across street is now lined with offices.

A FIXTURE AT LITTLE FIVE POINTS for more than 30 years was the *Sarasota Herald*, which in 1938 became the *Sarasota Herald-Tribune*. Its first issue appeared in 1925, under the editorship of George D. Lindsay. The *Herald-Tribune* has since built a new plant and offices on the South Tamiami Trail, leaving the building shown above to become the site of the Woman's Exchange in 1944.

THE SARASOTA TERRACE, a boom-time hotel, was part of Charles Ringling's venture into real estate. He purchased the old Gillespie golf course and put up several office buildings. The Sarasota Terrace at Ringling Boulevard and South Tamiami Trail was part of the development and opened in June 1926. It was one of half a dozen skyscrapers that pierced the Sarasota skyline in 1925 and 1926. Also rising during those two years were the Hotel Sarasota (now vacant), the El Vernona (now the Ringling Towers), the First Bank & Trust Company (now the Palmer Bank), and the American National Bank (now the Orange Blossom). In 1972, the county took over the Sarasota Terrace for additional office space.

SHELTERED BY THE KEYS but still large enough to pick up the breezes, Sarasota Bay always has been fine sailing water. This is a Snipe Class race in the late 1940s.

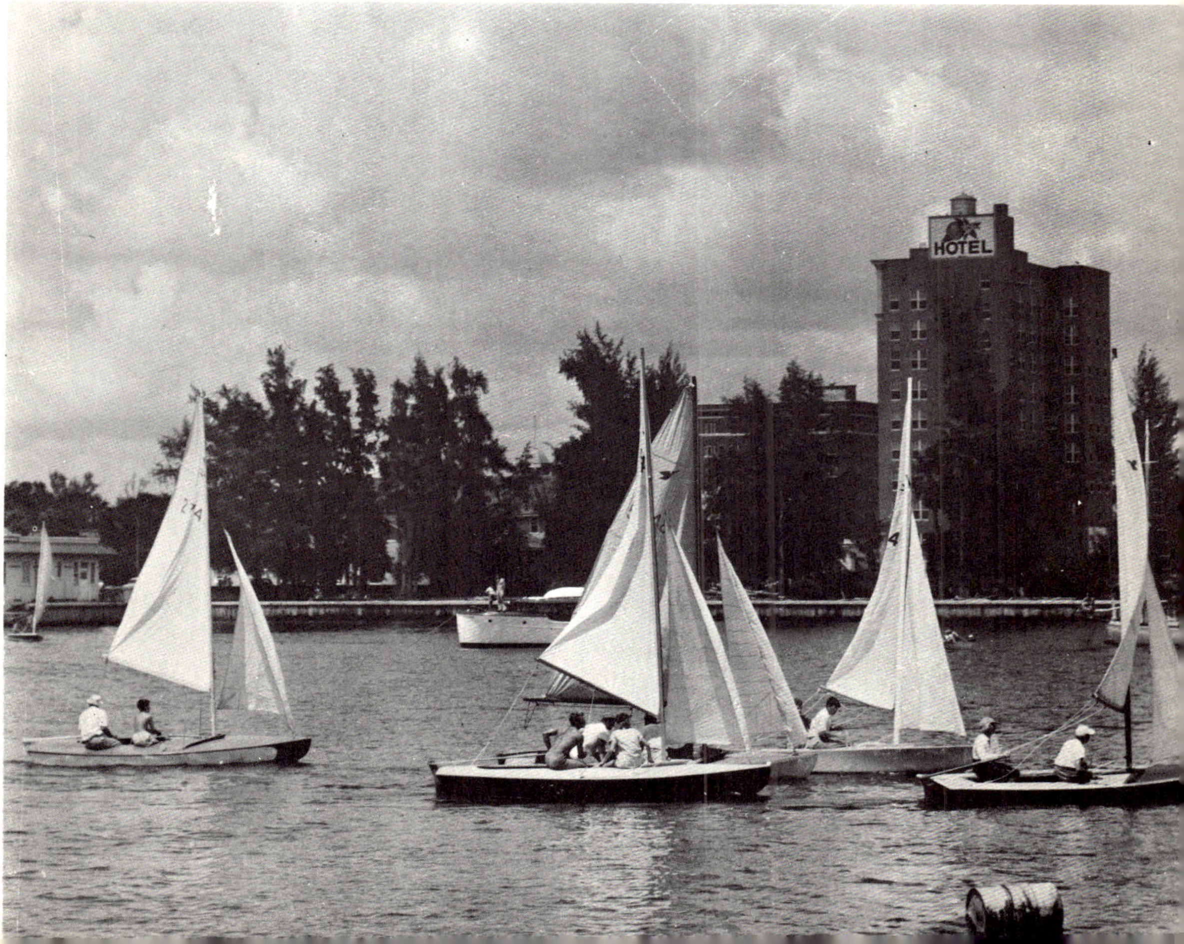

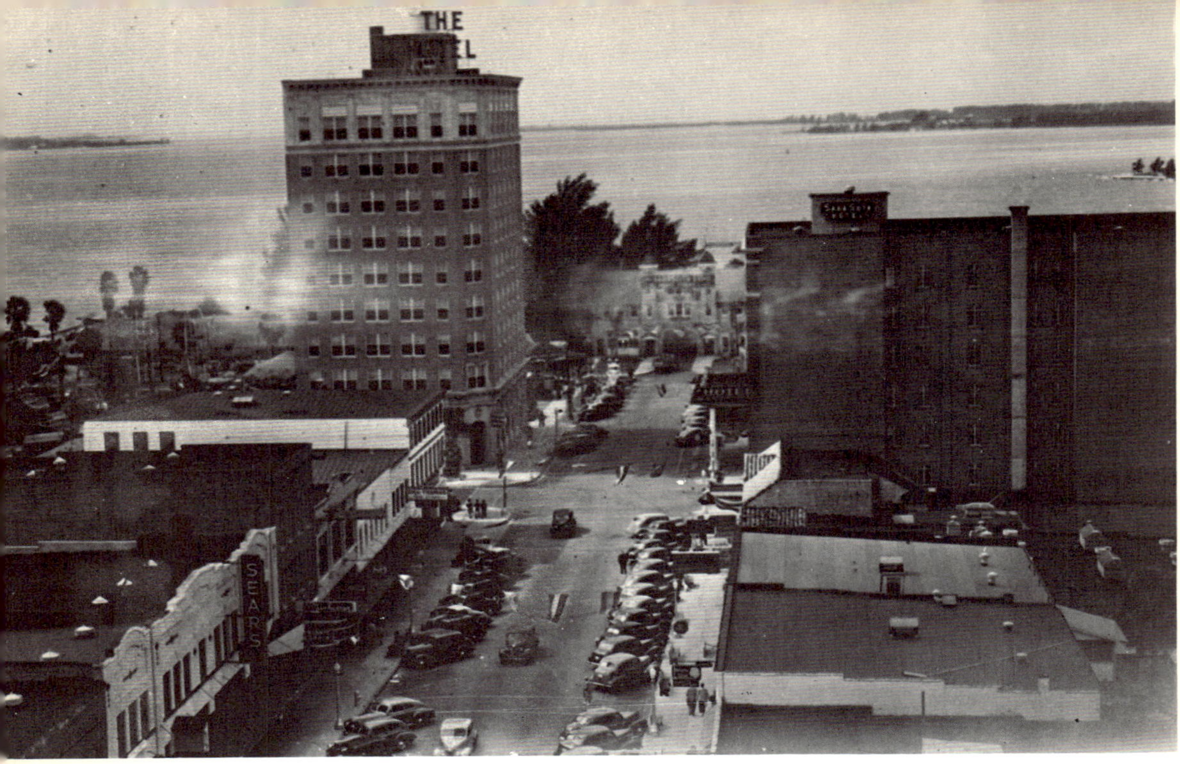

DOWNTOWN WAS THE HUB of city in the late 1940s and remained so until the housing boom took off in the mid-1950s with its emphasis on subdivisions and shopping centers. With World War II over, and winter visitors again coming to Sarasota, it became obvious to city officials they had to prepare for another spurt of growth. One decision included changing the city charter, providing for a city manager. Another was planning for a new waterfront area, which included filling in Sarasota Bay far beyond Gulf Stream Avenue. Still another was working with Arvida Corporation, the Arthur Vining Davis firm that purchased much of John Ringling's real estate for development, particularly the offshore keys. The views shown are lower Main Street, from Five Points toward the pier (*above*) and Main Street, looking east (*below*).

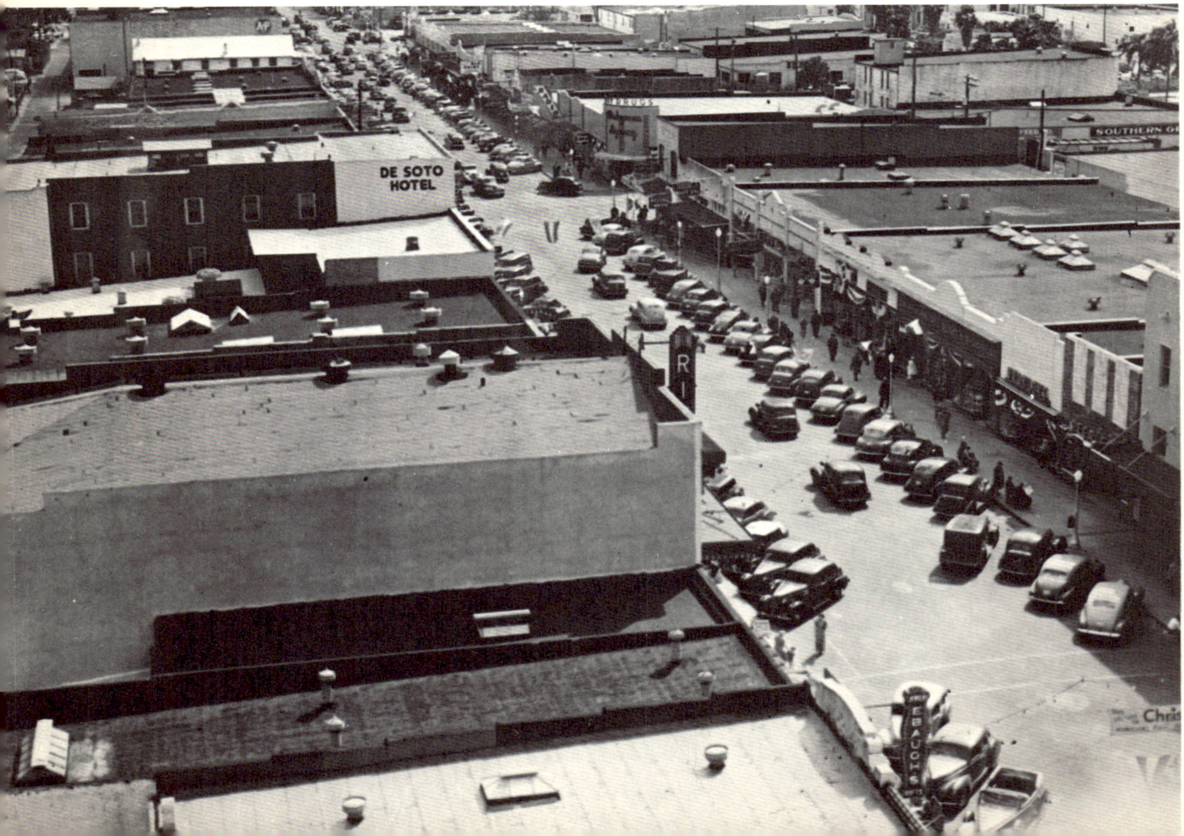

A SMALL CITY by most standards today was Sarasota in the late 1940s when this photo was taken. The population figure was almost 20,000, and most offices and homes huddled around the downtown core. Little development is seen east of the courthouse (at top) and to the south (right). Even the property along the waterfront remained undeveloped.

SIESTA KEY, in 1950, when it was described in National Geographic magazine as one of the four most beautiful beaches in the world. The view is from Point of Rocks (foreground) northward around Crescent Beach. Several attempts were made by Harry Higel to develop Siesta Key, the first in 1907; in one case, no bridge from the mainland thwarted interest, and later, just before the first span was built in 1917, the Higelhurst Hotel that he had put up on the north end of the key in anticipation of business burned to the ground. The 1917 bridge was the first connection between the mainland and any of Sarasota's fine Gulf beaches. It finally was replaced by a more modern span in 1927. Siesta Key's popularity sprung to some extent from Sarasota businessmen. I. G. Archibald built a pavilion and several cottages at the beach in 1920 and the businessmen made it their weekend resort.

BACK FROM THE WAR, baseball star Ted Williams unloads his car and prepares for the Boston Red Sox Spring training season in Sarasota. With him is his first wife, Doris Soule.

NO BEARDS, NO MUSTACHES, NO LONG HAIR in the ranks of this Sarasota High School football team of 1952. They were the champs of the Southern Division of the South Florida Conference.

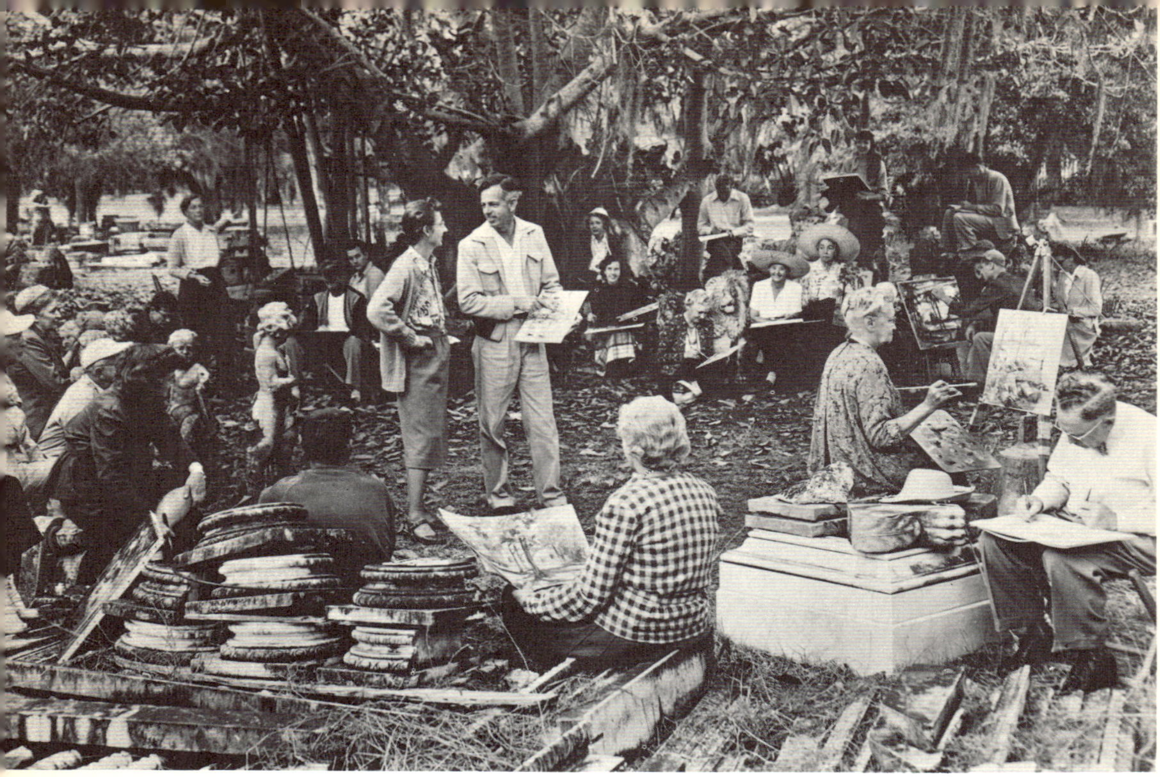

TO MANY PEOPLE, artists and Sarasota are synonymous, perhaps because tourists often see such scenes as this, the Amagansett Art School in an outdoor class in the 1950s. Instructor is Hilton Leech (in center) with his wife, Dorothy. The class was a lesson in outdoor landscape painting, on the grounds of the Ringling Mansion.

ARTISTS AND WRITERS get along famously in Sarasota. Some of the most well-known names picked this spot after World War II to write or paint. Here are a few who came in the early 1950s and stayed: John D. MacDonald (*above*), MacKinlay Kantor (*left*). *Facing page, clockwise*: Syd Solomon, Ben Stahl, Irving Bendig, Richard Glendinning, and Thorton Utz.

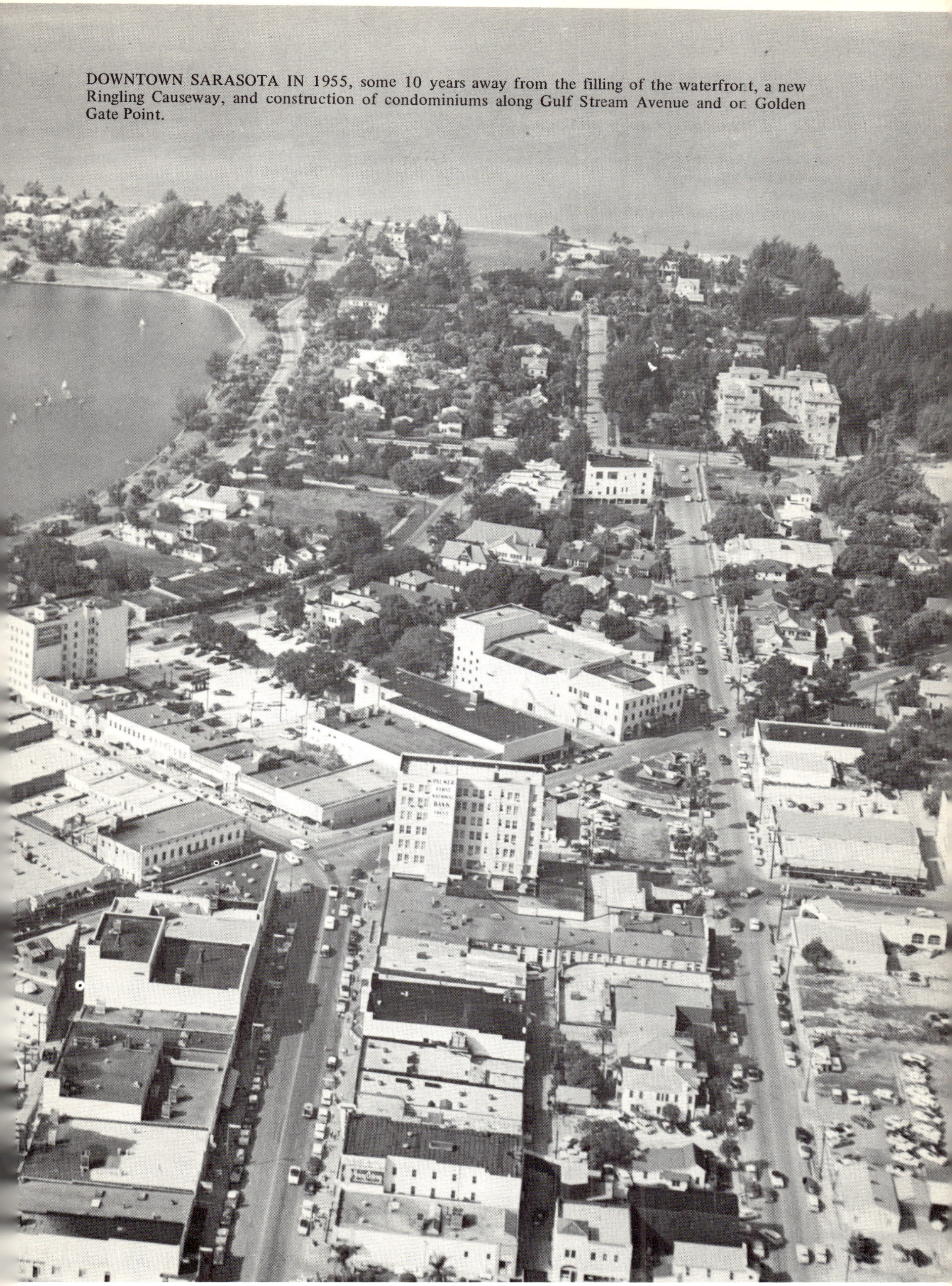

DOWNTOWN SARASOTA IN 1955, some 10 years away from the filling of the waterfront, a new Ringling Causeway, and construction of condominiums along Gulf Stream Avenue and on Golden Gate Point.

LIDO BEACH looking northward in 1954. High-rises were unheard of, and not many folks were interested in living on the Bay side. To the north, Longboat Key (at top) remained comparatively uninhabited, even though a bridge connecting Lido and Longboat Keys spanned New Pass as far back as 1929. Development of Longboat Key was retarded when a bridge on the north end of the key, connecting Longboat with Anna Maria Island near Bradenton, washed out during a 1932 storm and was not replaced for some 30 years.

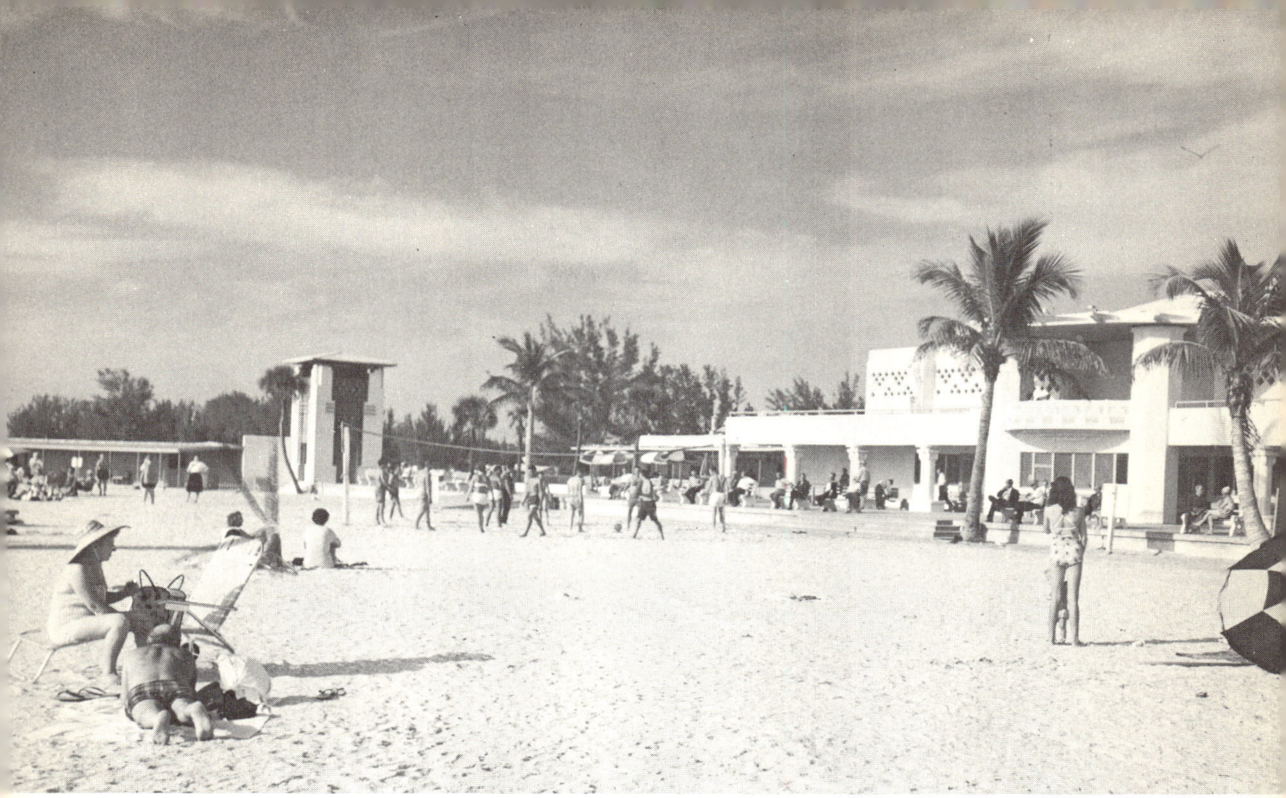

FOR EVERY WINTER TOURIST a day at the city-owned Lido Beach on the Gulf of Mexico was a must. This photo in the 1950s shows the old casino built in WPA days.

ON A CLEAR DAY IN 1955, this aerial view from the Gulf of Mexico toward Lido Beach Casino (foreground) reveals the slowly developing beach property. Bird Key (top right) remains unfilled and without residents. At left, St. Armand's Key has yet to be "discovered."

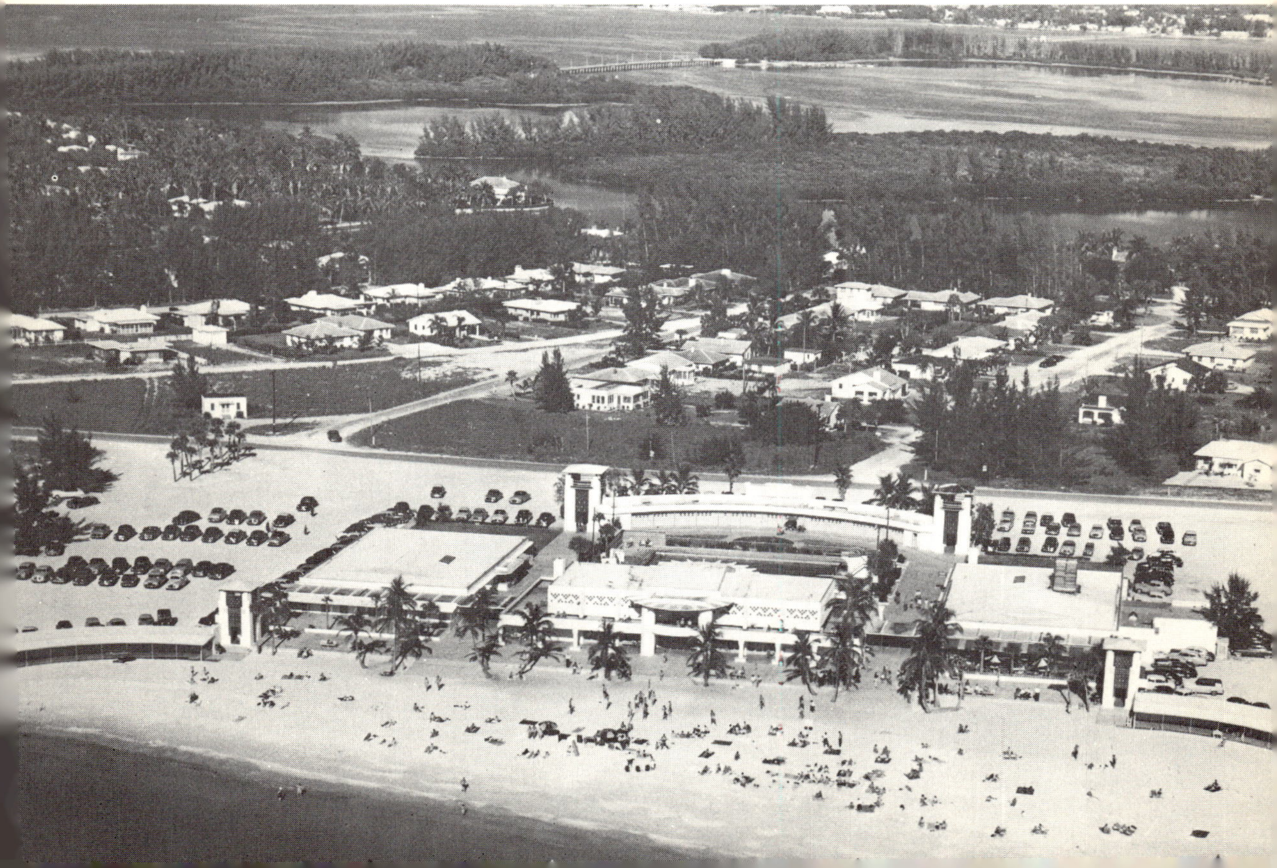

MANASOTA KEY in the mid-1950s. Span at right is the Charlotte Beach bridge.

HIGHLY DECORATED circus wagons like this Two Hemispheres band wagon were carved wood, topped with gold leaf, and pulled by horses. One such wagon, the "Five Graces," led the circus parades and was drawn by a team of 40 matched horses. The Baroque-style hand carving made these parade wagons duplicates of the seventeenth century wagons used in Europe for pageants. The above wagon, photographed in 1955, is being removed from a flat car at the Winter Quarters for display in the Circus Hall of Fame.

PRIZED CIRCUS TICKETS were earned by hundreds of Sarasota youngsters putting up the "Big Top." Guided by circus tent men in a time-honored procedure, the youngsters in this 1953 photo are "shaking out" the heavy tent canvas.

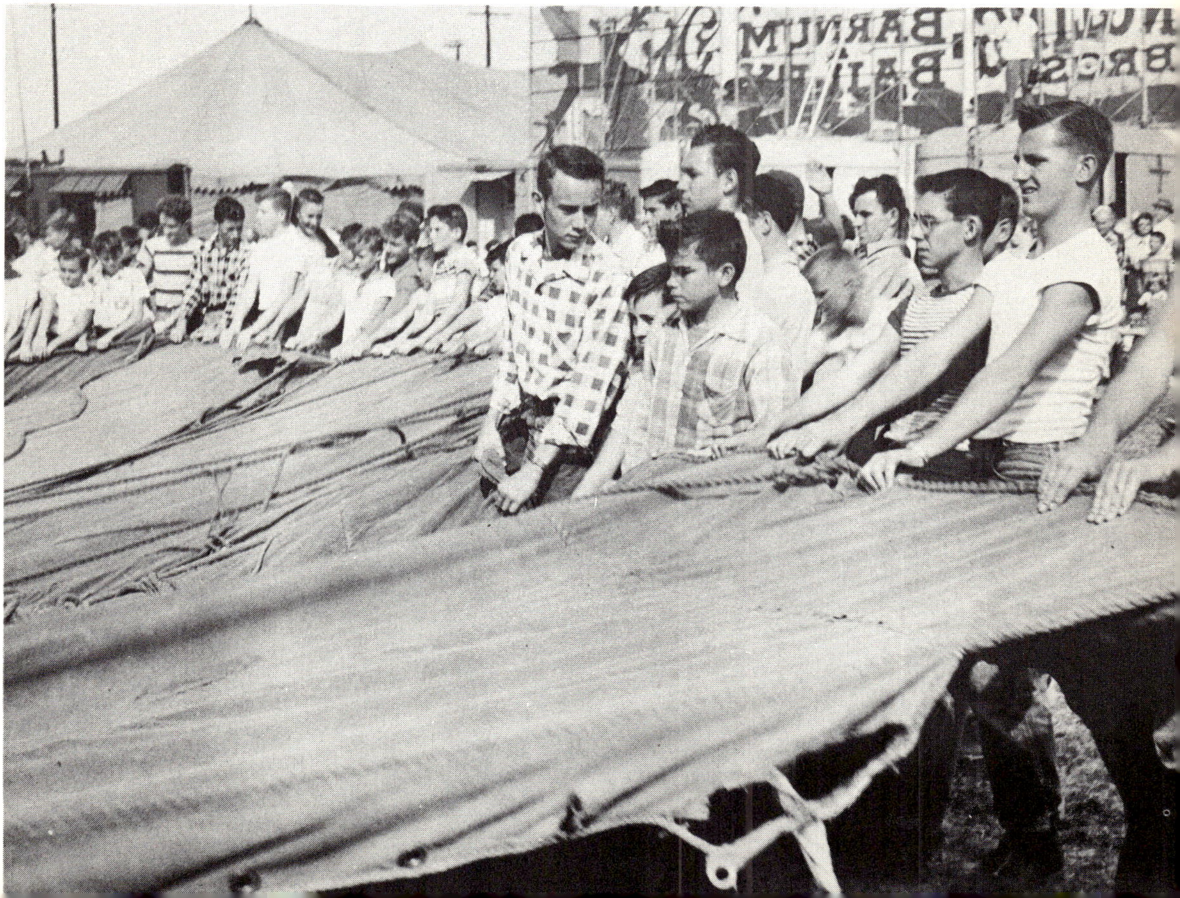

FIFTEEN-TON MONUMENT in the intersection of Five Points since 1928 is moved two blocks to the waterfront for rededication in 1954. The monument honored World War I servicemen, a gift from the American Legion Post 30. Removing the monument facilitated the flow of traffic at Five Points.

Facing page: ONE OF THE CITY'S great sports enthusiasts, Wilfrid Robarts, was curious enough about where Col. J. Hamilton Gillespie laid out his 110-acre golf course in 1905 to reimpose the nine holes over the property as it later developed. Here is the result, with the original clubhouse at bottom at Golf and Links Avenue, and the farthest hole, No. 5, out near Euclid Avenue.

NO. 5 GREEN
NO. 6 GREEN
NO. 4 GREEN
NO. 7 GREEN
RINGLING SHOPPING CENTER
NO. 3 GREEN
ACL STATION
NO. 2 GREEN
NO. 8 GREEN
NO. 1 GREEN
COURTHOUSE
MAAS BROS.
NO. 9 GREEN
TEE OFF
COL. GILLESPIE'S HOME
ORIGINAL CLUB HOUSE
ROBARTS FUNERAL HOME

EVERY AMERICAN MUSEUM, it is said, needs an auditorium, and the Ringling Museum acquired an eighteenth century Venetian theater that has no counterpart. It is the Asolo Theater, brought to this country in crates in 1951. Initially, it was installed in a lecture hall in the Museum, but not all of it could be assembled in the small space (only the ground floor boxes could be used). The need to make full use of the entire theater led to a new theater building adjoining the Museum. It was built with funds from the state in 1955-56. The grand opening on January 10, 1958, was a performance of Mozart's "Abduction from the Seraglio," an event that drew national news coverage.